'Why hasn't someone written this book before! Gemma Corradi Fiumara turns her considerable analytic and philosophical talents to look at not the Einsteins of this world, but to "ordinary geniuses:" those who, despite the toxins of modern society, pursue lives of creativity and growth. A wonderful, inspiring study.'

– Professor Janet Soskice, University of Cambridge

'With great "ingenuity" the author has broken the exclusivity of genius in exceptional man and relocates it in the common person. The approach is revolutionary, and yet tenable and obvious. I think she touched the tip of an iceberg, one which she will continue investigating.

This well thought-out book seems naturally to follow one of the author's recent contributions, *Spontaneity: A Psychoanalytic Inquiry*. Spontaneity now joins creativity and imagination as the creative core of our inherent ordinary genius; put another way, we ordinary selves possess the requisite quality and quantity of neuro-hardware and psychical-software to warrant genius rating.

This is an incredible work on a long overdue subject: the democratization of genius, and also its dependence on the imaginative creativity dormant within us. It is a fascinating book.'

– James Grotstein, American Psychoanalytic Association, Los Angeles

'In the author's perspective psychoanalysis is not only interested in distorted structures, but also in the incapacity to access the genius within. This is a "gifted" book which puts together discipline and a joyful outlook on human nature. A thought-provoking text for psychoanalysts, psychotherapists, philosophers, and for all in search of widening the domain of their attitudes and knowledge.'

– Antonino Ferro, Italian Psychoanalytic Society, Pavia

'This is an extraordinary book which readers will enjoy for its successful argument in recognizing "ordinary genius" in the daily lives of men and women. This is a scholarly book as well: the author supports her thesis by thoroughly integrating psychoanalytic insights with those from the fields of philosophy and literature.'

– Anna and Paul H. Ornstein, Harvard University Medical School

PSYCHOANALYSIS AND CREATIVITY IN EVERYDAY LIFE

Psychoanalysis and Creativity in Everyday Life: Ordinary Genius is an attempt to create a psychoanalytic space for the quest and questions of our everyday creativity. Official creativity is normally applauded to the point of obscuring all other types of creativity, with detrimental consequences for our psychic life. However, as **Gemma Corradi Fiumara** demonstrates, the creative force of ordinary subjects can be as vigorous as that of our acclaimed, official geniuses.

Corradi Fiumara focuses on the unsung creativity which emerges from relationships and the world at large. She explores how understanding the operation of creative impulses in an everyday setting can crucially inform psychoanalytic clinical work. There are three main themes:

– Donald Winnicott's psychoanalytic will
– Melanie Klein and the other side of genius
– Genius: ordinary and extraordinary.

Psychoanalysis and Creativity in Everyday Life advocates an inclusionary view of human genius, and demonstrates that creativity and genius can be manifested in everyday life with the ordinary as its focus of attention. It will be key reading for psychoanalysts, psychoanalytic psychotherapists, philosophers and scholars in social studies.

Gemma Corradi Fiumara is a training and supervising analyst with the Italian Psychoanalytic Society, and was formerly Professor of Philosophy at the Third University of Rome.

PSYCHOANALYSIS AND CREATIVITY IN EVERYDAY LIFE

Ordinary genius

Gemma Corradi Fiumara

LONDON AND NEW YORK

First published 2013
by Routledge
2 Park Square, Milton Park, Abingdon, Oxon OX14 4RN

Simultaneously published in the USA and Canada
by Routledge
711 Third Avenue, New York, NY 10017

Routledge is an imprint of the Taylor & Francis Group, an informa business

© 2013 G. Corradi Fiumara

The right of G. Corradi Fiumara to be identified as author of this work has been asserted by her in accordance with sections 77 and 78 of the Copyright, Designs and Patents Act 1988.

All rights reserved. No part of this book may be reprinted or reproduced or utilised in any form or by any electronic, mechanical, or other means, now known or hereafter invented, including photocopying and recording, or in any information storage or retrieval system, without permission in writing from the publishers.

Trademark notice: Product or corporate names may be trademarks or registered trademarks, and are used only for identification and explanation without intent to infringe.

British Library Cataloguing in Publication Data
A catalogue record for this book is available from the British Library

Library of Congress Cataloging in Publication Data
Corradi Fiumara, Gemma.
Psychoanalysis and creativity in everyday life: ordinary genius /
Gemma Corradi Fiumara.
pages cm
Includes bibliographical references and index.
1. Creative ability. 2. Self-perception. 3. Psychoanalysis. I. Title.
BF408.C6697 2013
153.3'5—dc23   2012046303

ISBN: 978-0-415-63727-5 (hbk)
ISBN: 978-0-415-63728-2 (pbk)
ISBN: 978-0-203-49862-0 (ebk)

Typeset in Garamond
by Cenveo Publisher Services

For Linda Fiumara, always at work with her aesthetic surgery,
and for Michele Fiumara, always at the heart of economics.

CONTENTS

1 Introductory remarks   1

    1. An epistemic space for ordinary genius 1
    2. An Aristotelian legacy 5
    3. Winnicott's psychoanalytic will 7
    4. Blinding by historic genius 11
    5. Opportunities for ordinary genius 16
    6. 'Blowing on the embers' versus jeux de massacre *19*

2 Unsung heroes   25

    1. Regardless of magnitude 25
    2. The question of relating 28
    3. The courage to surrender 32

3 Ego development and de-creation of our egos   37

    1. Ways to learn – and unlearning 37
    2. Ways to unthink and rethink 43

4 Genius: ordinary and extraordinary   47

    1. Introduction 47
    2. On the 'essential superiority' of acclaimed inventiveness 49
    3. Some contours of extraordinary genius 52
    4. Features of ordinary genius 54
    5. Melanie Klein and the other side of genius 57

CONTENTS

5 The connective function   65

   1. Creative connections and their defaults 65
   2. Creative connections and relational progress 70
   3. The capacity to include 74

6 The 'I' of the personality   79

   1. Preliminary remarks 79
   2. The embracing witness 82
   3. The insightful 'I' – beyond the ego 85

7 Creative service   89

   1. Am I my brother's keeper? 89
   2. Contact: risks and gains 93
   3. Caring: here and now 98

8 Minding our business   103

   1. The legitimacy of creativeness 103
   2. The affliction of parasitic projections 107
   3. Addictive thinking 110
   4. Escape from projections and ransom of the self 113

Notes   117
Bibliography   132
Index   143

1

INTRODUCTORY REMARKS

1. An epistemic space for ordinary genius

In the domain of the humanities, our psychoanalytic culture is both an addressive and an observational discipline – with therapeutic aims, moreover. In this area things primarily 'exist' if there is a cognitive/cultural space for them to develop. But then, when one happens to introduce an expression such as, for instance, '*ordinary* genius,' it may resonate in our minds and almost function as a magnet in the pursuit of our concerns. For, in fact, we cannot ask the question 'What is ordinary genius?' It only exists as a worthy focus of attention if we are interested in the quest and question of the everyday, inconspicuous, silent forms of genius. And although it cannot be approached as a matter of factual research, once our attention has captured the psychic intensity of the question, it will definitely enhance the quality of observation, reflection and interaction.

At this point in the itinerary of hominisation we could in fact create the epistemic spaces for the quest(ion) of our everyday creativeness. What is advocated here is an inclusionary rather than exclusionary view; that is, the appreciation of creative agency in more others, even though 'lesser' others. Their creative force, their poiesis, might be just as vigorous as that of their authorial authorities – of their official geniuses. The resistance to standard culture, and the enhancement of psychodiversity, can be fruitfully contrasted with the common enchantment/authority derived from historic geniuses. In our everyday creative endeavours there is no claim to become sources of authority – as if in a turnover of epistemic power. 'Theorists' of ordinary genius only insist – and insist they do with acumen and farsightedness – that minds can be very different and also that they have some creativity to contribute. We could note in passing that the applications of official inventiveness in the domain of social life can also become disastrous: just think, for instance, about the horrendous derivatives of the right-wing and left-wing Hegelian heritage.

INTRODUCTORY REMARKS

In order to create a stage for my thesis I should like to invoke a few remarks that are perhaps pertinent suggestions. Parsons, for one, suggests that a perception, or

> the expression of feeling in a turn of phrase – *all sorts of everyday things* – may suddenly ... show us ourselves and the world in a new light. These moments of illumination may be slight or epiphanic. Seeming to come from nowhere, they come from nowhere but within ourselves and ... give us the sense of a deep internal process...[1]

And of course renewed outlooks may bring about rapid changes. We begin by knowing little and believing much; sometimes ending up with an unsuspected hierarchisation of values. Whatever remains the same, we could tentatively say that the light is changing, and that we cannot find at noonday the pearly creative light of dawn.

Perhaps we could do well to reconnect the relative quiet of the analytic setting with the bustling world where our human creativeness – our ordinary genius – is persistently at work. In this way we could better differentiate what we call ordinary genius from the more official, exceptional forms of creativity. In fact, our common construal of (exceptional) genius is normally acclaimed to the point of rendering any other form of creativeness vulnerable to obscurity: eclipsed, foreclosed, ignored, silenced. Both 'kinds' of genius exist, of course, but ordinary genius seems usually neglected with undetectable, blinding consequences – as if we were immersed in a culture of forclusion or benumbment. And thus any discourse on creativity usually tilts towards forms of classical, historic, exceptional genius; this approach imbues our 'normal' world views – our current ontologies – to the point of excluding from our epistemic normality the ordinariness of our human creativity.

Interest in genius usually takes the form of an indirect exploration of the mind of the acclaimed geniuses, of enigmatic features that we strive to define. Almost as if genius was some fascinating, elusive entity or psychic character to be captured and revered. But we are not here interested in this question, because the creativity that we try to focus on does *not* pertain to scientific or artistic inventiveness. We would rather explore, for instance, that minimal, unsung creativeness surfacing from the immense variety of interpersonal relations with which we sustain the burden of life. And so, artistic or scientific genius is not our concern here. The aim is to appreciate, to take notice of, superior achievements or superlative quality in conducting obscure, ordinary, negligible affairs. Genius erupts into relationships and in the world in ways that require attention from our psychoanalytic domain. Beneath each and every creative nuance in our societal life lies an unacknowledged inventiveness that needs to be identified and appreciated. This is the creativity that we seek to explore and which we refer to as 'ordinary genius.' Of course it has always existed; and yet an effort to theorise the issue, to make it a focus of attention, may greatly enhance our capacities of insight.

By writing about the *Psychopathology of Everyday Life*[2] perhaps Freud meant to suggest that malady is not so exceptional or ineffable. Similarly, we could perhaps think that creativity is also no exception after all, and that it can be manifested in ordinary life. As Phillips and Taylor remark, by keeping the debate so exclusively about pathology the 'mind doctors of the twentieth century' have kept us and themselves in the dark about sanity, about our ordinary creativity.[3] He also seems to suggest that if there are madnesses, there should surely be sanities; and sanities that are not simply the unlived lives of the supposedly sick. Sanities (virtues, qualities, genius) could perhaps be elaborated in the way that diagnoses of pathology are: 'They should be contested like syndromes, debated as to their causes, and constitutions and outcomes, exactly as illnesses are.'[4] One of the shortcomings of our definitory tendencies is that we may even come to regard our intellectual heritage – our itinerary of hominisation – in terms of what official geniuses have been doing or proclaiming that others should be doing; and thus the majority of creatures appear as excluded from the creativeness of humankind. But if we conceive of our intellectual history as a story of struggle for psychic survival and quality of life, then we could have doubts about clearly defined boundaries. Psychic life in fact is not a 'given,' which we try to *name*. It has to be actually shared and lived. Even the so-called 'clinical material' is not a given as it exists only if it is personally absorbed and represented. Formulating definitions would be close to essentialising our human manifestations. And thus we should appreciate the creative pragmatism of those who encourage us to explore a topic of interest without the constraint of a preliminary definition.[5]

As humanness is now thought to belong to everyone, so too creativeness can be recognised in everyone. Grotstein's contributions seem to indirectly support this thesis. 'What is a genius?' he asks.

> In my eyes a genius is one who sees patterns, structures or gestalten in an incipient or incomplete form ... Put another way, a genius is one who sees through the camouflage of images and symbols and is in touch, so to speak, with the "thing-in-itself"... an experience that Bion terms a "transformation in O".[6]

But then individuals capable of these psychic transformations are not so rare after all; they are quite real and frequently appear in everyday life. Running in the present book is in fact an inclination towards the very small, infinitesimal, momentary events that shape our worlds of experience. These lived occurrences also constitute the often invisible key moments identifiable in therapies as well as in the nodal points in our profound relationships. The underlying assumption being that growth is rooted in creatively lived experience.

In a historic perspective, the genius to interact with things that are different – as contrasted with our natural sympathy for what is similar – could perhaps be illustrated by the creation of a written language by the Sumerians.[7] Even though pictograms already existed at the time, the most they could do was to enumerate objects or depict situations; they could not be used to communicate abstract thoughts or ambivalent affects. The written tradition was inaugurated when we became capable of achieving an unprecedented connection between distinct signs and distinct sounds, between two elements that do not resemble each other in the least. The gap that separates the use of pictograms from the use of writing is in fact so great that we can regard the 'simple' conjunction of graphic signs and specific sound vibrations as one of the major advances in the history of hominisation. And yet, it is not so easy to envisage a single individual genius inventing our written language. The inauguration of a written tradition is generally attributed to the Sumerians as a culture rather than to any particular individual who made the fateful connection. In fact the peaceful and agricultural Sumerians probably heeded the surrounding concert of nature and conversations so devotedly as to recognise the beauty and fascination of a variety of distinct sounds. The capacity to appreciate a sound so well that it can be sufficiently differentiated from others may be the precondition for linking it to a sign and thus disclose the immense perspective of a written tradition. From our capacity to communicate and record in writing we 'quickly' arrived to our globalised, on-line civilization.

Pristine authorship can thus be an illusion: innovative modes of thinking may well be at work even before an official genius proclaims them with sufficient clarity to determine paradigm changes. Even though a comprehensive logic capable of accounting for both affects and deductions has not been expressed in culture, it is possible (in principle, at least) that modes of relating that may generate a new rationality are already at work. It is not impossible that in Neanderthal times some members of the human community tended to 'think Greek,' that some of our contemporaries may incline to 'think Neanderthal,' and others still try to 'think future.'

As if in passing, we could note that one of our official, historic geniuses – Galileo Galilei – happens to write:

> Above all other stupendous inventions, what sublimity of mind must have been his who conceived how to communicate his most secret thoughts to any other person, though very far distant either in time or place, speaking with those who are in the Indies, speaking to those who are not yet born, nor shall be this thousand, or ten thousand years? And with no greater difficulty than the various collocation of twenty-four little characters upon paper?'[8]

Galilei says 'What sublimity of mind must be *his* ...,' but perhaps *theirs* would be even more appropriate. While Galilei applauds the invention of written language, perhaps he seems to still think in terms of a single individual's 'sublimity of mind,' rather than the mental sublimity of an entire community of ordinary people experimenting with signs and sounds.

This outlook may remind us of Marcus Aurelius' popular 'philosophy,' when he suggests that, 'If a thing is difficult to be accomplished by thyself, do not think that it is impossible for a man: but if anything is possible for a man and comfortable to his nature, think that this can be attained by thyself too.'[9] And this inclusionary remark may well resonate elsewhere, as even the 'sublime' Kant tends to look into the direction of ordinariness. In his *Anthropology* he suggests that,

> Purely natural minds (élèves de la nature, Autodidacti) can in many cases also count as geniuses, because, although indeed much of what they know could have been learned from others, they have thought it out for themselves, and in what is not itself a matter of genius, they are nevertheless geniuses.[10]

And here is a piece of testimony of an unknown ordinary genius confronting an aspiring historic genius in the thirteenth century. A simple chronicler, Salimbene de Adam of Parma (1228–1291) narrates that the great Frederick II of Sicily who, unlike the Sumerians, tended to do everything by himself, intended to discover which had been the first language ever spoken on earth, wondering whether it had been Hebrew, Greek or Latin. The enlightened monarch 'arranged' for a number of new-born babies to be kept in isolation, with the injunction that they be seen only for feeding and that no one should ever speak to them. The potential acclaimed genius had worked out that the language that the secluded infants would spontaneously begin to speak would be the first language that had ever existed on earth. But then the result of the experiment is unknown because none of the children survived it. And Salimbene remarks: 'How could they have survived without the cuddles, gestures, smiles and endearments of their nurses?'[11] Here the Winnicott-like creativity is in the obscure reporter, rather than in the famous, enlightened monarch-scholar.

2. An Aristotelian legacy

As is known, Aristotle was more inclined to natural history than Plato and perhaps more sensitive to the 'phenomenon' of human creativeness — wherever it can be observed. In fact, if we invoke the Greek origins of our western thought, perhaps we could already discern significant remarks advocating the relevance of genius in everyday life. Aristotle, for instance, seems to suggest that in order to effectively express our inner world and live our lives, we need to create our own metaphors, rather than simply borrow those of the official culture — even if nascent metaphors tend to violate the conditions governing standard ways of thinking. The celebrated Aristotelian definition says that 'Metaphor consists in giving the thing a name that belongs to something else.'[12] And he goes as far as to proclaim that 'The greatest thing by far, is to be a master of metaphor. It is the one thing that cannot be learnt; and it is also a sign of genius.'[13] Nothing less than that, in the philosopher's view. Indeed a sign of genius for creativity and survival.

It is even more relevant for us that Aristotle's view of our everyday use of metaphor can be significantly reconnected with aspects of his social/political philosophy; it is perhaps a philosophy tacitly aiming to safeguard some form of Platonic 'essential' genius, conducive to a distinction between geniuses and non-geniuses, wizards and muggles, citizens and slaves. In fact the philosopher seems to suggest, in a great variety of ways, that 'slaves' must speak 'plainly' before their masters and thus abstain from the genius of metaphor. He explicitly repeats that, 'It is not quite appropriate that fine language should be used by a slave.'[14] Their language should not include the beauty of our common metaphoric creativity. But why prohibit something that no one would be inclined to do? And so Aristotle must 'secretly' believe that *even* slaves are 'tempted' to commonly use metaphors, to actually manifest their genius in everyday life. If we could think of 'fine language' as an imaginative and metaphoric kind of language, then prohibiting it to slaves certainly indicates the suggestion of a social norm. But, for our purposes, what is even more enlightening is that slaves are implicitly recognised as capable of a fine language that includes the genius of metaphoricity. And thus, even trying to maintain servitude, he implicitly recognises that even slaves are capable of something that he explicitly regards as genius.

The creativeness of metaphoric language is potentially revolutionary in the sense that what is at stake is its capacity for profound turns of perspective. As is known, metaphors provide for the re-description of domains already seen through some standard, essentialist frame of reference allowing us to say, for instance, that a slave is in servitude because he *is* a slave; that some creatures are slaves simply because they *are* slaves. But then, as is known, re-descriptions can have major disruptive effects on previous ways of looking at situations. Again, in Aristotle's words, 'It is from metaphor that we can best get hold of something fresh.'[15] But the 'essential' slaves of course should not get hold of something fresh or innovative such as, for instance, an idea of freedom.

Imaginative linguistic links might indeed serve to influence a world view and, obviously, slaves are not supposed to question the world views of their masters. If we regard a 'slave' as an emblematic figure standing for whoever has insufficient contractual power in a paralysing situation, the injunction to avoid 'fine language' and to not engage in metaphors can be equated with the prohibition to even envisage changes of conceptual structures and everyday customs. To ensure that slaves remain constrained in such a stable way that the enforcement of their own servitude does not weigh on the masters but is conveniently placed upon the slaves themselves, it is an essential pre-emptive condition that they be persuaded to 'speak plainly,' to avoid creative language and everyday genius, to keep their minds confined within one standard vocabulary. Granting permission to address their masters metaphorically would be comparable to recognising the slave's capacity – or anybody's capacity – to migrate from one epistemic context to another, while their 'own' (imposed) vocabulary is geared to produce self-confirming prophecies supporting the social structure from which it emanates. No oil or electricity for the Greeks, and therefore 'slaves.'

3. Winnicott's psychoanalytic will

> You may cure your patient and not know what it is that makes him or her go on living. It is of first importance for us to acknowledge openly that absence of psychoneurotic illness may be health but it is not life. Psychotic patients who are all the time hovering between living and not living *force* us to look at this problem, one that really belongs *not to psychoneurotics but to all human beings*.[16]

If it is 'health' but not 'life,' what then is (psychic) life? I shall attempt to seriously accept the invitation and be *'forced'* to 'look at this problem,' – delving into it as honestly as possible. If it were true that 'patients hovering between living and not living' do actually *force* us to look at a problem that belongs not only to 'psychoneurotics' but to *all* human beings, perhaps the psychoanalytic community would have more assiduously explored the questions of our daily creativity, of our ordinary genius. But then, perhaps, we probably did not feel sufficiently compelled to do just that. The present work is an attempt to welcome the suggestion and explore it through the alternative routes suggested in the different chapters. If we could be theoretic and consequent enough, we would pursue Winnicott's exhortation to explore creative living; and thus, I would like to join the potential 'conversation' of the clinically committed and theoretic minds who are inspired by Winnicott's legacy – by his 'will' in fact.

The point here is that we can find in Winnicott's legacy a very clear and passionate encouragement to continuously explore the creativeness of our everyday lives. And perhaps a few of his remarks will suffice to highlight the top priority, which he seems to attribute to this concern. 'In order to look into the theory that analysts use in their work to see where creativeness has a place, it is necessary ... to separate the idea of creation from the works of art.'[17] He seems to suggest here that we allow for some distinction, although not a separation, between ordinary and extraordinary creativeness. 'Anything from a meal cooked at home' can be an instance of creativeness. And of course innumerable examples can easily come to our mind.

> The creativity that concerns me here is a universal. It belongs to being alive ... The creativity that we are studying belongs to the

approach of the individual to ... reality ... Everything that happens is creative except in so far as the individual is ill, or is hampered by ongoing environmental factors ... which stifle his creative processes.[18]

In the stunning light of official genius there is a steady directing away from personal creativity towards the paradigms of the reigning world view. A centrifugal sort of logic leading away from the core of the creative self can be gradually established. Through this we come to believe that one's incipient inventiveness should be regarded as unessential to projects of 'proper' self-formation. This imposed centrifugal power seems contrary to the fecundity so strongly advocated by Winnicott. It is the obscure, and thus unquestioned, equivalent of intimating that there is no creativity in the nascent individual, and that the 'real' creative thinking is only to be found in whatever dominant élite sustains a macro- or micro-culture – no matter how insane. Through constant deviation from what is personal to what is socially acclaimed, one is ultimately deprived of instruments for enhancing one's inner life. Restricting our ways of expression to elements borrowed from, or imposed by, the 'superiority' of educators, leaders, stars, the developing person will internalise 'gifts' that are ultimately intrusive and deadening.[19] Without the idea of some creativity in the process of internalisation, we would be left with an abstract, pro-formal exchange of positions. Without inner creativity only a reversal of respective positions of power would be possible – and no psychic growth. When the outer figures are not 'sufficiently good,' they are changed into intrusive, obnoxious figures; when they are perceived as exceptionally enlightening, or sublime, they can be transformed into equally crushing inner objects. There are of course conditions imposed on the developing individual, but there are also psychic adjustments that are creatively accomplished. Internalisation probably participates in both activity and passivity.[20] It is unfortunate, however, that the proactive, creative aspects of internalisation are often neglected, ignored.

The majority of humankind has never written a poem or invented a theory. The great majority of people may spend their lives as crop growers, cleaners, employees or whatever. Where is their creativity? One might say that there isn't any. My thesis is that creativeness is not in the job or in the product. The sort of creativity explored here can be unrecorded, unrecognised, inconspicuous – however real and intense. The most archaic interactions may prevail in a culture as a result of the confusion between power and force: there is *force* in our inconspicuous creativeness while there is mostly *power* in the admirable discourses of our official stars.[21] But we try to look in a different direction here, in the direction of those innumerable creatures who, for instance, are mostly intent upon common labour and services. It can be replied that their creativity is relegated into their private life. And this is probably a good reply – except that it is not good enough.

Regarding the historical, official creative achievements, Winnicott says that 'This creativity is valid and well understood, but a separate study is needed of creativity as a feature of life and total living.'[22] But then, who would be inclined towards cancelling relevant features of our life and thus choosing 'partial' living – whatever that may be? And he adds: 'It is in playing ... that the individual child or adult is able to be creative and to use the *whole personality*, and it is only in being creative that the individual discovers the self.' [23] We could ask in passing, 'Who discovers the self?' And also, 'Who or what is it that uses the whole personality?' For the sake of exploring this issue, we might refer to the 'I' of the personality as to this using and discovering agency. If we cannot use the personality and its egoic functions, then perhaps the ego/personality may engulf and absorb the 'I' so that we unwittingly homogenise with the personality/ego instead of using it in personal creative playing. But then, it is the ego that uses us; the personality that uses the 'I.' Winnicott also seems to suggest that unless the 'I' can use our egoic structures, the individual will not 'discover the self' and may come to blindly regard his ego/personality as if it were his true self. Of course the vocabulary that we use in trying to explore our inner world includes terms such as 'soul' (in Freud's German writing), 'psyche,' 'mind,' 'ego,' 'intellect,' 'self,' 'I,' 'reason,' 'heart,' 'mentality,' 'spirit,' 'consciousness,' 'personality,' etc. ... Resorting to a spatial metaphor we could try to understand Winnicott by tentatively trying to speak of the 'I' as a more central part of our psychic world and perhaps refer to 'egoic structures' in order to indicate the more 'peripheral' parts of the inner organisation. Bion, for instance, happens to judiciously remark that, according to Freud,

> It would be unrealistic for a psycho-analyst to compile a dictionary showing what various psychoanalytic symbols meant, because he foresaw changes; we, his successors, are not so open minded. It is unpsychoanalytic to adhere to some rigid system as a substitute for using our minds.[24]

This is especially relevant if we embrace Winnicott's definite shift of concern from extraordinary to ordinary creativeness.

According to Winnicott, when psychoanalysis has attempted to develop the issue of creativity it has largely lost sight of its main theme. In fact, 'The creative impulse is ... something that is present when *anyone* – baby, child, adolescent, adult, old man or woman – looks in a healthy way at anything or does anything deliberately.'[25] It is good to reiterate here that the sort of genius on which we intend to focus is not the celebrated creativity of art and science, but the lively creativeness of our psychic efforts aimed at survival, coexistence, empathy. Rosenfeld insistently highlighted the incomparable pleasure/joy of being able to function creatively, and the bitter sadness of defensive psychic rigidity.[26] If creativity is opted for, it usually becomes a principle of action within the self: it comes into being in the attitude of choosing and desiring it.

INTRODUCTORY REMARKS

A lack of creativeness indicates that the pressured behaviour derives from a condition in which the contingencies of the ego are detached from a central 'I.' 'The creative impulse,' Winnicott insists,

> is therefore something that can be looked at as a thing in itself ... It is present as such in the *moment-by-moment living of a backward child who is enjoying breathing* as it is in the *inspiration* of an architect who suddenly knows what it is that he wishes to construct.[27]

In both, indeed.

In Winnicott's view, those psychoanalysts who have rightly stressed the importance of instinctual experience and of reactions to frustration, have failed to explain with comparable clarity or conviction the 'tremendous intensity' of playful creativeness.

> Starting as we do from psychoneurotic illness and with ego defences related to the anxiety that arises out of instinctual life, we tend to think of health in terms of the state of ego defences. We say that it is healthy when these defences are not rigid, etc. But we seldom reach the point at which we can start to describe what life is like apart from illness or absence of illness.[28]

In fact, creativity enters into virtually every aspect of life. It is not a special 'faculty' but an aspect of our human intelligence in general; it is manifested in everyday abilities. So it is not confined to a minimal élite; every one of us is creative, to a degree. As Boden remarks, it is not an 'all-or-nothing affair. Rather than asking "Is that idea creative, yes or no?," we should ask "Just how creative is it, and in just which way(s)?"'[29] We are in fact exploring the extraordinary within the ordinary, in the language of Kristeva.[30] Genius is the inner attitude of ordinary people who do extraordinary, however subliminal, and negligible things; they are the people who do not simply comply.

According to Winnicott compliance carries with it a sense of futility and is associated with the idea that nothing matters and that life is not worth living. 'In a tantalising way many individuals have experienced just enough of creative living to recognise that for most of their time they have been living uncreatively... These two alternatives of living creatively or uncreatively can be very sharply contrasted.'[31] Paradoxically, in this perspective, instances of historic genius may give us a sense not of what we lack but of what we might do in our own role. And Winnicott insists:

> It is not of course that anyone will ever be able to explain the creative impulse, and it is unlikely that anyone would ever want to do so; but the link can be made, and usefully made, between creative living and living itself, and the reasons can be studied why it is that creative

living can be lost and why the individual's feeling that life is real or meaningful can disappear.³²

Of course it takes an effort to make new spaces for oneself in the inner and outer world; many of us do not even feel entitled to attempt to do so. We let ourselves be easily homogenised, soothed into conformity, even if that conformity takes away our creative dignity. Security, a sense of belonging, and a sense of being accepted are extremely important motivations that often keep us willing to be reduced to less than we are capable of. Our culture has difficulty with the antechambers of healing rather than with healing itself. It is on the level of disposition and desire that we need to help most, that we mostly need help. In fact, in order to use our idealisations for purposes of identification, we also need to re-conceive genius as a quality of the ordinary people who do extraordinary things in common and obscure vicissitudes.

In Symington's view we could perceive an interesting convergence between Winnicott's sense of creativity – when we are sufficiently free of illness – and the idea of inner freedom. In his effort to elaborate on creativity, Symington judiciously points to the difference between licence and freedom.

> Licence is acting in accordance with the obstacle. Freedom is emotional achievement; licence is emotional capitulation. To do that which I wish is a risk. What is the step that I wish to take but dare not? It is a step into a void, into nothingness, into a place of no guarantees, safety, or security.³³

In this step the human being *lives* his life; he lives rather than being lived. It is perhaps at this point that our classical instinct theories indicate the direction in which the person is bound to travel; but then, the problem with life is that it goes we know not where. Winnicott insists that there is a creative principle in each of us, and the exercise of this creativity engenders freedom. Its exercise expands the vistas of the self. It is for psychoanalysis to overcome our obstacles to freedom. And Symington concludes: 'The exercise of freedom is not to be equated with happiness. It is its own end.'³⁴ For a synoptic view, we could invoke Oliver's, suggestion that 'Psychic life depends on a sense of validation and legitimization of the possibility of creativity and greatness *for all of us.*'³⁵

4. Blinding by historic genius

The historic genius expressed by any culture tends to shape their respective ontologies and epistemologies. The derivative conceptual spaces tend to emphasise certain values of our culture as if they were necessarily, naturally valued because they are already there. But our dependence on perceived values may also induce a blindness for less imposing, but equally creative, forms of value. Ordinary geniuses are those who have not entirely fallen into enlightening/blinding world views. They are the resistors and can be found anywhere – among the literate and the illiterate. They can be our compassionate soldiers, combative midwives, hearty judges or proud servants. When we recognise the many collective follies of our human condition we must also admit that not all human beings participate in these perversions. Apart from innate human capacities that we cannot explore, the resistors must have developed some psychic ability not to be ensnared in mass forms of enlightened pathology. At this point, we should patiently develop, or at least allow for, epistemic spaces for the quest and question of our resistant, silent creativity.

Ferro suggests that a 'beam of darkness' is needed as an antidote to the tendency to impose meanings on what has no meaning; and we are so inclined because of our incapacity to wait for shreds of meaning to emerge. 'Like snails which produce slime, we are a species that continuously slimes meanings because we cannot bear the darkness of our not knowing.'[36] Pretending to know while we do not, cannot allow for authentic reflection and insight. Lear acutely notes that 'One has not radically evaluated one's life; one has simply evaluated it from the perspective of certain values.'[37] As derivatives of our official genius, dogmas – political and scientific – arise out of the erroneous belief that thought can encapsulate reality and truth. As is known, the products of the once historic geniuses can become our dogmas – our collective conceptual prisons. We are advocating a different perspective whereby ordinary genius is what primarily matters for humankind. The twentieth century, the apogee of our western genius, was, according to Phillips, a 'mass graveyard of idealistic, utopian projects for what was called in the eighteenth century the "perfectibility of man".'[38] And he adds: 'We are living now in the aftermath of the horrifying consequences of politically designed Good Lives; of the most militant and coercive blueprints of what people should be and want and do with their lives.'[39] In contrast, a life that is good is perhaps more often the outcome of ordinary, individual efforts.

The desire to belong to the sphere of official inventiveness in the realm of scientific discovery tends to somehow affect even the most brilliant minds. Far more acutely than most of his disciples, Freud was determined to give to psychoanalysis a biological foundation. His writings, his personal career and the conventions that he attempted to formulate for his followers, testify to an intense fear of becoming separated from the *enormous* prestige of the natural sciences. Almost until the end of his life, he hoped for tangible, experimentally verifiable confirmation of the theories he had put forth, even though he knew that his theories were developed on an introspective and clinical basis.[40]

An exploration of classical, historic genius is not incompatible with the exploration of ordinary creativeness. However, our use of historically acclaimed genius to disregard the many instances of ordinary creativeness is tantamount to using the idea of genius to restrict our perception of inner reality.

An exploration of everyday genius, moreover, is not in the least detrimental to the appreciation of the exceptional achievements of all the Mozarts, Shakespeares and Einsteins. Really, we have more to gain than to lose by resorting to an inclusionary reading of human capacities. In the sciences, of course, theoretical proposal or crucial experimentation is often inspired by individual talent. And yet there seems to be in scientific developments a communal, inertial motion towards discovery; perhaps had this person or that team not made the discovery, another scientist or team would have done so, possibly in that same stretch of time. The invention of calculus, of 'natural selection' or of DNA are famous cases in point. And even in artistic productions there are elements of contingency. In every case they could not have been. 'The work of art, of poetics, carries within it, as it were, the scandal of its hazard, the perception of its ontological caprice,'[41] in the words of Steiner. In this general outlook, ordinary creativeness 'also' appears humble and willed, as if a secret labour of love; its origin is in humility and in the willingness to let some meaning flourish in life.

It is sometimes asked, 'How can we tolerate being rich, while others are poor?' The problem, moreover, is not so much that there are the poor, but that we do not really see them. But then, we have the same problem in the psychic domain. How can the 'geniuses' tolerate their condition while the others are 'obtuse' and 'uncreative'? We seem inclined to blindness when we fail to perceive the struggle for creativeness in the innumerable people whom we perceive just being there, in space and time, 'just' carrying on with the burden of life. This is our common superficial thinking. We need deep, personal roots to save ourselves from the invasion of such surface images. The blindness induced by historic genius can turn into a malady of the soul. Ordinary geniuses are those who do not easily fall ill – victims to the common blindness of the soul. By not being petrified by phantasmal ideals, ordinary creative people make it possible for others to detect some personal, dispositional differences; they can thus be 'used' as persons who are relatively free of a blinding affliction that is considered simply natural – because it is exceedingly widespread. Only those who do not fall victim to blinding lights can be of help to others. They are geniuses without knowing it, and we all need their contribution.

In the alumni/alumnae class notes of prestigious institutions there is a kaleidoscopic display of daring projects, awards, honours, challenging positions – almost an endless sequence of fireworks. And the most regarded of institutions develop and advertise imaginative curricula, as if promising that everything will be done to enhance visible creativity and even induce success. Our higher educational systems seem to be focused of course on the development of those skills associated with greater contractual power in a logocentric, logocratic world and are thus inconspicuously intent on ignoring the values of our 'lesser' inventiveness.[42]

According to Bollas, the quest for spontaneity is the process of allowing the uniquely personal features – the cipher, the 'I' – to emerge in the personality.[43]

And this is a challenge that confronts all of us and that may have always been present. This quest may now become a priority as personal creativeness is silently and ubiquitously under attack by the homogenising effect of mass culture; we are imbued of external élitist messages and affected by the contagion of indifference. Not only is the issue clinically essential but it is becoming culturally urgent.[44] If we think of intellectual history in terms of what the official geniuses have been doing, then the majority of creatures appear as excluded from it and thus culturally irrelevant. But if we conceive of our intellectual heritage more as a story of personal struggles for psychic survival, relations and values, then we could have doubts about clearly defined roles and boundaries in human efforts. If we separate the travail of creatively dealing with inner suffering from the elitist rendition of these efforts, we are in a better position to ask about what the vast majority of people have been doing. This is an alternative to simply investigating what any cultural élite – our official geniuses – says that the majority of people are doing or ought to be doing. The way we live when we are enchanted with our official inspirers can keep us adrift on the surface of ourselves and unable to reach deeper levels of searching. This happens within individuals, but it is also a cultural unfreedom, a shared desolation. As psychoanalysts may appreciate, our culture has difficulty with the antechambers of healing rather than with healing itself. It is on the level of disposition and desire that we need help most, that we mostly need help.

To previous generations it was unthinkable that a population at large should be entitled to some basic literacy or sufficient food. The question is now whether or not individuals should be entitled to the recognition of their own creativity, as the anonymous, unsung heroes of their secret daily lives. Perhaps the idea that defines the boundary between modern times and the past is the opening of knowledge and mastery of risks to all of us; it is the shared notion that the future is not determined by unbreakable cultural circumstance or by capricious divinities. Only the very good literature occasionally explores the secret genius of each one of us. This creative dimension is not sufficiently recognised in daily interactions and is thus not theorised; no logical space is allowed in our communal thinking for the appreciation of creativity in our daily struggles. And so we might unwittingly collude in obscuring these human expressions in perpetuating a caste system in which the right to creativity is only reserved for the licensed geniuses. If secret, daily ingenuity is not conceived of in our ontologies, it would be like having immense resources that we tend to waste on account of a perverse caste system that prevents us from truly seeing. We can look but we cannot see. Our scholarly groups are generally obsessed with breaking into the top layers in order to escape from the alleged uncreativeness of the lower layers. Both macro- and micro-cultures can be dominated by relatively persistent motivational paradigms that are so accurately contextualised and rendered so appealing, that they appear as totally enlightening and ultimately superior. These hierarchisations, moreover, can be as powerful as they are elusive and evanescent. Our everyday geniuses are the resistors to these enchantments. Especially in totalitarian regimes, ordinary geniuses see the world going psychotic but are not pulled into the vortex of madness. They endure even the most prolonged of crises and wait for a pause.

Perhaps we should protect ourselves from the enlightenment of great minds, from its excess of intrusion. There is a high payment exacted when there is an occupation of inner life by external irradiation. Modell reminds us that in some character pathologies there seems to be an unexplainable vindictive rage, as if the self had been totally usurped, or as if it were irremediably besieged[45]; in this sense, psychopathology simply illuminates by exaggeration that which is present in all of us. I believe that there is in fact a tension of separateness that cannot, or should not, be resolved. In Scheman's view we need to be aware of the terrifying extent to which any culture, person or part of the self has been reduced to the dreams and theories of any official genius or of the coalition that supports such genius;[46] and yet, any marginalised micro-culture, person or part of the self can hold on to its deeply felt, though perhaps unaccountable, untheorisable conviction that it is something *other* than the product of such dreams and theories. The epistemology of our current classicities comes to appear as an outlook of brilliance that anyone should acquire even at the cost of insulating one's personal creative self. And the inclination to accept these seductions ultimately comes to appear as a virtuous attitude. This is a nameless, inconspicuous propensity that could perhaps be called 'co-optosis,' in the sense that as long as one can aspire to be co-opted into whatever higher ranks, one can sacrifice one's authentic, creative life.

In the attempt to gain a synoptic view we can perhaps resort to the overarching insights of Giambattista Vico:

> It is another property of the human mind that whenever men can form no idea of distant and unknown things, they judge them by what is familiar and at hand. This axiom points to the inexhaustible source of all the errors about the principles of humanity that have been adopted by entire nations and by all the scholars. For when the former began to take notice of them and the latter to investigate them, *it was on the basis of their own enlightened, cultivated and magnificent times that they judged the origins of humanity*, which must nevertheless by the nature of things have been small, crude and quite obscure. Under this head come two types of conceit, one of the nations and the other of scholars.[47]

In fact in our academic culture the official stars tend to dismiss whatever might threaten their sense of power. The authorial/authoritative agents of knowledge tend to theorise their subjectivity as unitary and coherent. But then, although hierarchised as more rational and free of confusion, the cohesive selfhood of official scholars (that differentiate themselves from the uncreative subjects), can be shown to be anything but strong. They primarily have power, not force. In fact it is the sort of collective selfhood that succumbs most easily when confronted with the slightest pressure from the vestiges of the reptilian brain that operates alongside cognitive structures in human beings. Even the central theatres of western brilliance and rationality – the stages for Vico's scholars – are periodically shaken by horribly destructive festivals that unfold with total indifference towards the enlightened authors: the strong, superior minds incapable of resisting the archaic mechanisms of our embodied condition. 'Superior' minds who, nevertheless, resume their normal expression of scholarly brilliance as soon as the period of terror has come to an end.[48] If we do not understand this and learn to be wary of the dangers of allowing our egoic structures to be directed by our ancient brain/mind passions, we can be in a delusion: as if allowing biologically immemorial, territorial mechanisms to utilise and rule on our more recent competences. Our old feelings are automatic and effortless whereas our new brain/mind is slower and reflective. Our ancient passions can hijack our mental capabilities, and then we can only produce brilliant satisfactory reasons for complying with their dictates. But not everyone homogenises with this inclination: some secretly creative, lively creatures may even conceal themselves as mildly insane.

One of the secret reasons why we so assiduously attend (psychoanalytic) congresses is perhaps fuelled by the desire to capture some of the 'stars' innovative, revolutionary solutions for the labours of our daily practice; something that can transform, for the better, our operational logic. Perhaps we secretly seek some enlightening formula. As if we tried to find a super mind that could bestow a new force to our theories and favour a transition into a superior form of psychoanalysis. And so we converge to the presentations of the great ones, seeking to capture something to internalise for subsequent dramatic results. The ordinary genius of the common individual may thus tend to be stunned, and we risk being confined in a stable comfortable immaturity. 'It is so convenient to be immature!,' exclaims Kant,

> Thus it is difficult for the individual to work his way out of the immaturity which has become almost second nature to him. He has even grown fond of ... formulas; those mechanical instruments for rational use (or rather misuse) of his natural endowments, are the ball and chain of his permanent immaturity.[49]

5. Opportunities for ordinary genius

As is known, the *Psychopathology of Everyday Life* is focused on common mistakes that often go unnoticed: forgetting names, errors in reading, mislaying things and so on. These 'banal' errors appear to be random but, according to Freud, they are products of unconscious/subconscious desires. And even if one decided to put aside Freud's own explanation, we could certainly applaud his effort to seek significance in occurrences that are usually overlooked as haphazard and purposeless — ultimately negligible. Just as Freud saw psychopathological significance in certain everyday actions, we could also seek creative significance in minimal everyday doings. Freud sought indications of conflictive factors, but perhaps we could also seek out the expressions of human creativeness. We could thus become the seekers of the person's creativity. In fact an analyst does not have anything to teach in the conventional sense of the word or does not have anything to bestow on the analysand such as new information, beliefs or rules of conduct. The primary function is perhaps to help remove that which separates the person from the creative self he already silently is or could be. There is also an added sense of urgency here: this transformation of consciousness no longer appears as a private luxury available only to an infinitesimal percentage of humans; it is rather a general developmental project, a common conversation from which we can draw psychic healing. Lear remarks that often philosophers suggest that humans are distinctively able to raise the question of how they intend to live their lives *as a whole* — just as Winnicott pointed out and advocated the use of *the whole* personality. Lear insists that unless we can answer the basic question of how our lives are to be lived, we may not be able to answer the more immediate practical questions such as, 'What shall I do next?'; for I may not have any idea what to do next if I do not understand how that next action fits into life as a whole, as a creative itinerary. Our immediate practical concerns thus open onto a more radical reflection. According to Lear, perhaps psychoanalysis and philosophy meet in the idea of a radical evaluation of life as a whole.[50] In the face of these problems we do not usually consult professional psychoanalysts, philosophers, counsellors. More often we seek secret ordinary geniuses among our fellow human beings; they are often capable of bringing us back to the roots of our creativeness. They may not be trained formally, but they can be very discerning.

We often think of creativity in terms of unique achievements in the domain of art and science. And yet, an equally relevant expression of creativeness probably transpires in our human capacity for insight in relationships; this involves a talent for generating unforeseeable developments. We could reiterate Winnicott's conviction that the creativity that concerns us here 'is a universal and belongs to being alive.'[51] It is in fact the extraordinary within the ordinary. It is the inner attitude to do extraordinary — however small — things for oneself and the other. This is often achieved in spite of scarce training or bad training. And, more relevantly, it is achieved in spite of wrong theories, bad formulas, insufficient knowledge. For the sake of example, think of the pilots and physicians of the past. Pilots used to navigate using wrong astronomic theories such as the Ptolemaic view of our physical world: our earth at the centre of it and the sun revolving around us. In spite of wrong theories conjoined with mythical beliefs, some of the navigators were known as safe and reliable. The same is true with regard to physicians and midwives. Their knowledge too was most defective and none of their theories correct; and yet some of them were most highly regarded and gratitude was expressed – while others were often known as charlatans. They certainly had the genius for acting creatively in spite of the most adverse of cognitive circumstances. We too may be frequently trying to work at our best in spite of wrong beliefs.

But then, paradoxically, the result is not what really matters in the perspective which we are trying to pursue. The capacity to secretly dare, or strive, or struggle is in fact the essential feature of the creative potential that we try to approach. This could perhaps be expressed in the incisive language of George Eliot where she remarks that 'Here and then is born a Saint Theresa, foundress of nothing, whose loving heartbeats and sobs after an unattained goodness tremble off and are dispersed among hindrances, instead of centring in some long-recognisable deed.'[52] In a very different but converging perspective, Berlin suggests that 'We ought to seek the knowledge that is involved when a piece of work is described *not* as correct or incorrect, skilful or inept, a success or a failure, but as profound or shallow ... perceptive or stupid, alive or "dead".[53] Compliance, imitation and adhesiveness to standard views carry with them a sense of futility and are associated with the conviction that nothing matters and that perhaps psychic life is not worth living. Most people live without experiencing their inner richness while being confined within routines and roles. Most often they have to keep themselves down, put themselves away, hold their breath until later. For many people there is not much of a 'later' either – and their inner selves become silent and almost disappear. They wonder if inside there is anything to them. As Winnicott suggests, 'In a tantalising way we may have experienced just enough of creative living to sadly recognise that for most of the time we have been living uncreatively ... These two alternatives of living creatively or uncreatively can be very sharply contrasted.'[54] And human relations are perhaps the arena for our creative living. It takes in fact a genius to speak with an infant – literally, a non-speaker – or to talk with a dying person who is abandoning all discourse. Not to mention the creative involvement with the very special language of sexual intimacy. It would be difficult – and disheartening – to imagine what life would be like if our *personal* experiences of being born, reproducing and dying were not sustained by our continuous ordinary creativity.

If behaviour, both creative and pathological, were so heavily determined, it would not make sense to speak of strategising attitudes, options, efforts and aspirations. After all, hope would be meaningless in a wholly deterministic order or in one of arbitrary absurdist ethics. We are often inclined to think that narcissists are subjects who have been traumatised at an early age, and that this is sufficient to causally explain their condition. Of course the way we respond to determinants is also considered, but we primarily tend to talk in causal terms. However, it is not so much the cumulative trauma but the individual's *passive* response to it that constitutes the basis for a narcissistic attitude to life. Any creature is somehow responding to life events, and it is this responsive creativeness that we tend to underestimate, ignore – to the detriment of clinical acumen. This area of responsiveness is the space for ordinary inventiveness. We might be therapeutically more effective if we could think in this perspective. The idea of ordinary creativeness – of creative actions rather than mere reactions – can be a guideline in our search for more spaces of expression. In our search for psychic spaces in which creativity can be manifested, we should concede that causal explanations alone do not reveal much meaning. We could say that a determinist theory primarily operates at the level of explanation while a theory of interpersonal relations encompasses the area of meaning, purpose, intention. Creativeness basically refers to what we do at the intentional level. The determinist view and the intentional attitude are both necessary of course. But the one with which we are more concerned here is the intentional one. The two, moreover, can only be separated logically, for purposes of discussion, for in fact they are inseparable in our human species.

6. 'Blowing on the embers' versus *jeux de massacre*

The idea of 'resilience,' a wonderful human capacity for psychic survival, increasingly attracts attention. The point, however, is not laud of this psychic potential, but to appreciate the innumerable imaginative ways in which our fellow beings are resilient; ventures are regularly pursued by the unsung geniuses of any era. We are trying to focus on the superb and very human talent for 'blowing on the embers,' in the language of Cyrulnik.[55] There is constant talk going on in our lives and most of it is not just selfish business; a good share of it is perhaps devoted to the quest for self-healing or to the restoration of resilience in others. Humans seem in fact to always grope around for therapeutic others.

We should point out that toxic projections, deadening remarks, psychic suffocation are not performed with the excitement and glorified rhetoric of proper war. No, our *jeux de massacre* are often carried out as boring pastimes, as barely pleasing ways of managing relations, 'for everybody's own good' – in our blindness. It takes no devilish intelligence to thrive on this sort of devastation, for anyone can do that. As possible alternatives to our very common *jeux de massacre* – with which we are never satisfied, of course – we could explore a proactive way of playing at resuscitation; that is, engaging in reviving games, in 'blowing on the embers.'

If we grant that most of us are ill to some extent, that we are 'psychic survivors,' in the language of McDougall, we could also wonder how most of us try to obtain some cure.[56] Many of the 'therapies' that we seek are just temporary compensations, but we also seek and find authentic maturational experiences – even out of the area of the accredited healing practices. Of course psychoanalysis is one of them – perhaps the most highly regarded. And yet, untrained human beings can often be of help. Not all those who are plagued with inner suffering necessarily degrade into madness. In our human community of billions of creatures, only an infinitesimal part is exposed to 'proper' therapies. As patients come for treatment at a certain age, we should also wonder how they managed previously to cure themselves in order to go on. Major literature in fact often shows in detail the intricate ways of healing unfolding inside the vicissitudes of friendship, solidarity, survival.[57]

We do in fact have ordinary healing geniuses in everyday life: those who help us carry on with the burden of living, who do not claim to 'cure' us or influence our moods. They do not insist on making the other feel more hopeful for they know it may be of no use and might even be felt as an oppositional insult. More frequently in their kindly inventiveness they just present us with *their* compassionate, insightful view of *our* way of viewing things. They are capable of holding up to us our own mentality without any judgemental attachments; and we can see it too, when we can perceive our inner world as besieged with vindictiveness, negative self-pity inclining to abjection; just by having it clearly shown we can perhaps take a position. If we are clearly shown our terrible inner images, we can more easily stand up against them or simply take a distance from them. When the ordinary geniuses manage to show us with clarity some terrible inner pictures we can perhaps proceed to discard them. The step towards reviving always begins with some sort of knowledge of course, which is perhaps why it is so often avoided. The grandiose side of the self may well enter the scene at such moments of beneficial shared knowledge. It points out with exaggeration the inner awful condition and accuses the subject of the disaster. This can make us even more negative and self-destructive. But the peaceful geniuses simply do not adhere to the perverse game. They are only interested in some soul warming game, in 'blowing on the embers.'

We cannot speak of resilience unless we think of a trauma followed by the resumption of some sort of development. And it is not a question of normal or defective adaptation, as traumas extend from the lethal to the more bearable ones. Since the trauma is somehow inscribed in memory, it becomes part of a person's history, almost a ghost that accompanies the individual. Gifted life companions help us not only to survive but even to live with ghosts. The filters with which we can defend ourselves from our unacceptable ghosts and their toxic emissions are among the most creative functions that can be developed through interaction with our life companions. How do we filter poisonous nourishment? And once it has imploded in us, how can we deliver the self from it, or metabolise it into something else? We have to count on choices and interactions that could even become paralysed by not being used. Ordinary healing geniuses blow on the embers of potential revisions. If the child or the adult is given an opportunity to form a representation of what has happened, some sort of story, we can set in motion a process of resilience by reviewing or re-interpreting events. As if, for instance, saying, 'Dear Robin Hood, you are not a thief, you are a helper and a libertarian!' If the exchange takes place within a bond of solidarity we can probably witness transformations. When a child is verbally abused – and terrorised – by a furious parent, it is surprising to notice the beneficial effect of simply pointing out, for instance, that 'Today, mum is in a rage.' The very young child may react to subsequent episodes more calmly and remark that, indeed, 'Mum is in a rage again' – as if observing a storm that does not blow him away. As Cyrulnik points out, we can think of trauma only if the overwhelming experience floods the person and carries him into a torrent, in a direction he would have not wanted to go. 'At the moment when the event tears his protective bubble, disorganizes his world, and sometimes throws him into confusion, the person who is not fully aware of what is happening to him is at a loss ... and suffers blows.'[58] It is essential to confer some simple meaning to the sudden disaster; whoever happens to do so as soon as possible, helps the creature out of a state of confusion in which he cannot make any decision because he does not understand anything. In fact, trauma can be seen as a near-death psychic experience – a mortifying event. All we have left are a few sparks of life on which others might gently blow. Our companions may help us outline some story, however sad, that confers some visibility to the terrifying event and help us look at it with some distance so that we do not homogenise and drown in it.

It is often reiterated that mental health seems to come about through the internalisation of empathic self-objects, of sufficiently good parents. In general not much place is allowed for the individual's *internal* determinants. In Symington's view 'The predicate is that a person's psychopathology is due to unattuned self-objects, so that all the bad is out there, and we have a theory with a paranoid base.'[59] But then, as Houser et al. eloquently demonstrate, there are many clinicians who are not drawn into such a paranoid outlook; they have had the experience of treating adult patients who as children and adolescents suffered psychic hardships and traumas, and yet as adults functioned surprisingly well.[60] These patients' eventual success is indeed a puzzle, which Houser et al.'s book attempts to tackle in a new way, free of 'paranoid' premises. In fact we are usually content to 'explain' the pathology that we confront on the basis of interactive traumas that individuals have suffered from others. We rarely ask why even worse interactive circumstances have *not* determined the same degree of psychic devastation. What is the nature of this capacity, of this genius? Has anyone sustained it?

Although the findings of Houser et al. only begin to address the question, their discussion of the narratives throughout their book is seen as most enlightening – in the review of Susan Bers.[61] In her view the authors maintain that it is likely that narrative coherence, 'the capacity to develop a "good story" in which circumstances and personal experience are meaningfully integrated' ultimately reflects adaptation. In addition, they hold that most aspects of a narrative actually *influence* and *shape* adaptation. And also, they claim that there are numerous illustrations of the way 'changes in stories trigger new perspectives and new perspectives influence later choices.'[62] But then, at this point we cannot help remarking that, in fact, narratives are only possible if there are listeners. We should perhaps radically reverse our logic and come to think that narration only exists if there prevails a listening atmosphere. In developmental terms we could say that it is not true that we listen to children because they speak; children will only speak if we seriously listen to them. Houser's thesis is that certain individuals develop surprisingly well (in spite of persecutory objects external to themselves), on account of sufficient opportunities to create their personal stories. Here again it seems that maturity is achieved through the ordinary geniuses who are capable of listening to the narratives that we tentatively try to develop. The extraordinary geniuses, by converse, are primarily remarkable for their capacity to speak out and express their cogitations. And thus our listening genius is the basis of psychic growth. In the interviews of the adult study participants, a few of the authors expressed astonishment that some subjects had been former psychiatric patients. Of the former patients the 'surprising' ones enjoyed their lives and talked about them openly in a lively manner, engaged in satisfying work, had lasting relations, and also expressed enthusiasm about becoming parents. The authors found that narratives can be a 'gold mine ... a key ... a new window on many of the aspects of resilience we do not understand yet.'[63] Once again, passionate listening by ordinary geniuses is the key to enter the 'gold mine' of the narratives.

Perhaps we should reiterate that it is incongruent to simply uphold the common view that when a child is mistreated at an early age, he learns that violence is a normal way of life and will therefore necessarily repeat the abuses that he suffered. Such a view can easily be used in a dogmatic, blinding way. Of course it is true that offensive caretakers can be seriously detrimental to psychic development. And yet we cannot use the abundant clinical evidence to this effect, in order to obscure the function of whatever constitutive agency is spared, unaffected, resilient, and, most importantly, to ignore the function of possible supportive agents. This is a compatible perspective that tends to be neglected in our incessant quest for causal determinants of pathology. The idea is that the coexistence of the two perspectives can enormously enhance the quality of clinical acumen in such a way that we can read, re-read and read again our therapeutic vicissitudes. In fact, what impresses Cyrulnik are the children who, in spite of the blows of fate, manage to hold on and even to escape: 'These are the children who need to be studied if we are to understand what happened inside them *and* in their environment, so that we can better help those who find it hard to construct themselves.'[64] In a similar way many who escaped the lethal ideologies of the past century have assiduously pursued the innumerable paths of resilience. Unbelievably disheartened and sometimes psychically prostituted, they worked to repair their lives.

Cyrulnik maintains that, 'Verbally abused children are the humiliated ones whose self-esteem has been crushed. Yet it is in this group that we find the most imaginative, mythic, or heroic forms of resilience.'[65] He also says that when we study this problem we should assemble separate forms of abuse: physical abuse, verbal abuse and neglect. But in our human condition such distinctions are rarely clear since it is not unusual to find a creature who is insulted while being battered and segregated away. And yet, whatever external interventions might highlight embers of resilience – the poiesis of the child's responses. A young one may still be deadened from abuse when someone comes over and consoles him with simple words. On such an occasion he may discover the pleasure of interpersonal warmth, the price he is willing to pay to get some of it, and the importance of his own emotions. And yet, sometimes we can even resent the support for it does not prove to be the perfect ideal that we had imagined in our despair. Phillips and Taylor judiciously remark that if hatred is as innate as love, as Freud gradually came to believe, then hatred seems to be the stronger of the two. 'Love never seems to deliver what we want it to do. Love never works as magic, but it can work as kindness'[66] – which we do not sufficiently appreciate. They also suggest that we can be more violent and destructive than we want to be; but also less destructive and violent than we are inclined to be.[67] We can only survive by inhibiting aggressiveness; but inhibiting it can make us ill. In fact inhibited aggression, like inhibited love, can feel like self-betrayal. But the expressions of kindness could be the alternative games to be theorised as possible exciting options, in the way of pleasurable, resuscitating games. Geniuses are those who manage to not fall ill, who resist the pull towards psychic degrade. And Phillips and Taylor conclude by suggesting that only by taking hatred and love seriously 'one can begin to take kindness seriously (that is without sentimentalizing it).'[68]

And yet, some people are frightened of kindness and even resistant to the idea; they see its derivatives as potentially unsettling. If they consent to self-kindness, it might ignite feelings of grief as they would then recognise how neglected they have felt for so long. If memories are of abuse and *un*kindness, the feeling of such experiences can re-emerge. And this is of course the difficult pass in the attempt to develop a liking for healing games. Re-warming a frozen soul is not easy, even though it can be an enjoyable way of playing. Moreover, those who have been repeatedly assaulted may find it harder to respond to support and interpretation, and thus decrease the chances of help. And yet, there are always minimal embers of resilience for talented players to blow on. Cyrulnik in fact believes that it is hard to deprive a child of affection entirely and also he wonders why 'in the case of serious deprivation only 75 percent of the children are affected. Why not 100 percent?'[69] Of course there are genetic conditions. But still, they probably survive because around the deficient, assaultive parent, there can be an institution or person that offers some underpinning of resilience. In a convergent perspective, Fromm suggests that to see some truth and to escape confusion is not primarily a matter of intelligence but a matter of character. Our interpersonal vicissitudes sustain our character; perhaps our most fatal decisions in life depend on the choice of friends, when possible.[70] They may help to salvage the most precious capacity, the courage to say 'no,' to disobey the intimations of power and of terrible events, to cease being asleep in a stupor of helplessness and futility. But the capacity to say 'no' meaningfully, implies the capacity to say 'yes' forcefully. It is much more than 'freedom from:' it is 'freedom to.'

2

UNSUNG HEROES

1. Regardless of magnitude

Encouraged by Winnicott's (provocative?) remark that there can be creativeness in a 'backward child who enjoys his breathing,'[1] *Regardless of magnitude* could perhaps be the appropriate head-line (caption) for an exploration of our unofficial, unhistoric, unexceptional ways of inventiveness.

What we often hear from the young is that in our times it is impossible to be oneself; that superficiality is the rule and mediocrity is everywhere; that expression of anything that goes beyond the banality of routine, and of pastimes sounds just too strange and may even involve expulsion from peer groups; that it is easier to settle for the way things are. And yet, there can be ulterior ways of looking at things, of uncovering fresh opportunities and occasions for wonder; within easy reach of anyone there can be undetected signs of authentic, creative living. As George Eliot suggests, silent creatures have been born who find for themselves no epic life or the unfolding of far-resonant action. They only seem to display a life of 'mistakes:'

> Perhaps a tragic failure which found no sacred poet and sank unwept into oblivion. With dim lights and tangled circumstances they tried to shape their thought and deed in noble agreement; but after all, to common eyes their struggles seemed mere inconsistency and formlessness.[2]

In fact, culture prescribes very narrow roles for certain creatures and little room to stretch beyond them without risking disapproval, or worse. But they can have a sort of inner serendipity, an attitude that enables one to take advantage of anything that may fall across one's path. But how do these creatures avoid feelings of resentment or regret about missed opportunities? Perhaps they are just too busy coping with the routine; with 'banality' moreover; culture does not encourage self-questioning or any form of 'examined life.' There are just not enough opportunities out there for them to use or not to use. But then, when we find out what the sources of their inspirations are, their stories suddenly become intriguing and somewhat heroic. The genius of their everyday life becomes evident. Still, the notion is troublesome, and we thirst for the literature that plays out, exhibits and explores these barely visible, heroic struggles.

It is commonly believed that the narcissistic route may be taken on the basis of one's response to trauma. Of course narcissistic disorders often emerge from a traumatic scenario, but it is probably the quality of the response to it that ultimately tips the scale towards narcissistic default. And still, even the devastated patients forever condemning the inadequacy or viciousness of their primordial partners are often persons who do not give up (analysis) and struggle in their pursuits — wilful creatures indeed. They seem to pursue some healing experience of truth, contact and creativity — what Bion indicates as 'O.' As Ferro suggests, 'O' is the goal of analysis as a whole; getting close to 'O' is perhaps the goal of each single session. An 'O,' of course, that far from being impersonal would then become subjective and specific.[3] But can we say that only those who can afford and endure analysis can approach 'O,' this healing experience of creativity? Not quite. Perhaps our ordinary, unsung geniuses are those who embark upon the itinerary by themselves, without a professional guide, or else with the judicious use of whatever companions they may find on their way. In fact they may develop with very little help. Both the help they use to develop and the genius that they display can be truly minimal. In fact, sanity, 'O,' creativeness are barely visible. By converse, madness often tends to be conspicuous and verges on the theatrical. Sanity tends the other way. According to Phillips, sanity has no drama like the 'good' characters in literature; the sane do not have memorable lives. 'They don't seem quite so real to us. Insofar as we can imagine them at all, they are featureless, bland, unremarkable,'[4] — there is no appreciable magnitude. The obscure everyday condition is their psychic habitat. We spend most of our lives in un-dramatic, negligible situations. But this world of minimal choices is where our lives are tried and tested most.[5] Great literature has perhaps dared to depict the ravages of ordinary life, and at the same time its hidden heroism. Within the smallest details of each day we shape who we are, and un-dramatic heart-learning can take place. And yet, there seems to be a tendency to despise the smallness of the ordinary and to only value the magnitude of the special.

Winnicott once again: 'It is in playing and only in playing that the individual child or adult is able to be creative and use the whole personality.'[6] Since Winnicott speaks about using 'the whole personality,' we should also ask how this psychic 'whole' is coordinated and which is the 'agency' that actually uses this whole space; in this sense we can perhaps conceive of an 'I' of the personality.[7] Even though we may persistently pose questions that standard epistemology has ruled illicit or unanswerable, we keep playing life by asking such questions and insist on using our *personality as a whole*. Steiner remarks that exultation and sorrow, love and hatred will continue to demand shaped expression;[8] they will continue to press on language which under that pressure may become literature, or may also become the capacity to talk to those who do not yet speak, to the dying who wish to speak no more, to make reproduction a creative *human* experience. And though condemned to ultimate circularity, perhaps our persistence in the use of our whole personality is 'thought made urgent' – in the words of Steiner.[9] Splitting and diffusing our minds are the antagonists of living life with our whole personality. These assaultive attitudes may remain hidden and occult while being definitely crippling and deadening. In his monumental works Eissler states, as if in passing, that

> It is one of the hallmarks of the works of genius that they are the outcome or the reverberation of the *total personality*. I have elsewhere called such states "unifunctional"; they are characteristic of genius not only in the field of the arts, but also in that of science. The talented person can work with only one part of his energy ... In the genius the whole personality conjoins toward the creative act.[10]

But then, at least this one characteristic is also true in the smallest, minimal daily vicissitudes. If we are interested in appreciating instances of creativeness, we need to study people's lives, their entire personalities and not only their minds. Hofstadter suggests that what happens in the minds of (ordinary) geniuses is of course highly relevant as a source of evidence about what they are doing; but what they are doing is perhaps barely visible to a trained observer, 'as the activities of plants and mountain streams'.[11]

If we are incapable of being devoted to the minor, minimal, subliminal inventiveness of 'psychodiversity,' we can easily succumb to 'co-optosis'; as if we were saying, 'Why not join the biggest players?,' 'it is mandatory to do just that.' Neologisms such as 'psychodiversity' and 'co-optosis' are used to indicate the risk that our rich variety of psychic modes of survival – our ordinary genius – may be inconspicuously absorbed into major homogeneous types, or even that indifference to our inner resources may induce us to always seek admission to the courts of dominant geniuses – co-optosis.[12] Aspiring to high-ranking modes of expression could in time become a mental narcotic that damages psychodiversity – if unexpected interrogation or crises did not occasionally expose its futility. It is almost as if we could be deceived not only by falsity but also by truth and value, in the sense that any de-contextualised truth or value can be crippling and misleading in an inconspicuous way. This is a nameless and denuding inclination; as long as one primarily aspires to be co-opted into the top ranks, one does ultimately sacrifice individual resources or the gifts of what we might call psychodiversity. And, moreover, if the compulsion to win and excel provides us with essential meaning, it would become suffocating if we simply could not win or if our winning talent should come to an end. Success in whatever field may thus become perverted in the delusion that it is primarily meaningful because the others, millions of others, do not quite reach it. Of course this does not mean that we should not try to succeed. It probably means that we should link success to psychic growth, to the 'whole personality' so that a deeper meaning follows in whatever form of 'success.' When success is not possible we may clamour for the need of a revolutionary social change; only *after* that we could be free enough to be creative. In this (limited) respect we could tranquilly say that, indeed, 'revolution' is the opium of the people.

Psychoanalytic work often induces us to realise that the expression of genius may really lie more in the search than in the attainment, more in the creative process than in the tangible end result. The idealisations by which we value the end result more than the appreciation of the silent process, lead us unrealistically to expect some fulfilment that is completely free from inhibition, ambivalence, limit or fragility. Almost as if 'genius' were some essential, immutable Platonic 'form.' But then, the idealisations and denials conducive to the putative state of absolute creativity are sustained by our own projections of narcissistic fantasies or grandiose images. This sort of idealisation may so devalue the creative process itself and its innumerable ramifications, that they become purely 'instrumental,' something to be marginalised and regarded valueless with respect to the 'acclaimed' end result. In this sense, idealisations may conspire to degrade any creative itinerary, as if one were compelled to always act in view of some postponed success. But then, by converse, our ordinary creativeness seems to never procrastinate – no matter what the circumstances may allow.

2. The question of relating

By way of paradox, Winnicott says that

> One could suppose that before a certain era, say a thousand years ago, only a very few people lived creatively ... To explain this, one would have to say that before a certain date it is possible that there was only very exceptionally a man or a woman who achieved unit status in personal development.[13]

But then, along with Winnicott, we are interested here in the barely visible creativeness that does not manifest itself in any extraordinary 'unit status' through which one could 'live creatively.' In fact our focus is 'simply' on the question of our infinitely varied ways of relating – what we inevitably do throughout the life cycle. We try here to re-orient our gaze so that we can read, re-read and read again the daily vicissitudes of our coexistential condition. The significance of this way of viewing human relations might be eloquently expressed resorting to the poetic prose of George Eliot. In the description of one of the characters we read:

> Her full nature ... spent itself in channels which had no great name on the earth. But the effect of her being on those around her was incalculably diffusive: for the growing good of the earth is partly dependent on un-historic acts; and that things are not so ill with you and me as they might have been, is half owing to the number who lived faithfully a hidden life, and rest in unvisited tombs.[14]

In Winnicott's view, however, there can also be an uncreative fixity, or stereotypy, that belongs to inheritance and to environmental factors.[15] By contrast, he suggests that the area available for manoeuvre in terms of creative playing is extremely variable. This is because creative living 'is a product of the experiences of the individual person (baby, child, adolescent, adult) in the environment that obtains.'[16] The ability to know our minds as well as to sense the inner world of the *others* – 'the environment that obtains' – may be the singular human talent, the key to nurturing healthy minds and hearts.

Winnicott again:

> One can think of the "electricity" that seems to generate in meaningful or intimate contact, that is a feature, for instance, when two people are in love. These phenomena of the play area have infinite variability, contrasting with the relative stereotypy of phenomena that relate either to personal body functioning or to environmental actuality.[17]

But then, that invisible creative energy, which he describes through the metaphor of 'electricity,' cannot of course be limited to the occurrence of 'two people in love'; in fact he judiciously says that it is generated in 'meaningful or intimate contact;' that is, in whatever interaction we manage to transform into a significant personal experience. And also, in our inter-subjective vicissitudes we do not simply wish to receive love, because the final step that could be missing in the process of simply receiving love, is the desired *awareness* of being lovable; Janet Soskice insists that we ultimately want to become 'lovely.'[18] It is not so much what we receive that counts, but the recognition that the other enjoys giving love to us *because* we are essentially lovable and lovely; love, or being in love, perhaps does not really function until we come to feel lovely. At this point, however, we should remark that there is nothing idyllic or sentimental in creative healthy relations because it is often a question of enduring negotiations. Like all other living creatures we must draw nutrients from sources other than ourselves; whether these sources are sufficiently or insufficiently good, we must cope with 'otherness' just as we originally learn to accept physical reality. And also it takes maturity to detect the nuances of these relational vicissitudes. Stern, for example, reiterates that his observation of parents and infants has made him familiar with the process of constant derailing and repairing in dyadic interactions;[19] interactions in which people try to become lovable and lovely for each other. Stern suggests that

> There are many "missteps" every minute in the best of interactions, and the majority of them are quickly repaired by one or both partners. For certain stretches of interaction, rupture and repair constitute the main activity ... The manner of negotiating repairs, and correcting slippages, is one of the more important ways-of-being-with-the-other.[20]

It amounts to learning to be lovable in our imperfect human ventures – highly creative ventures indeed.

The negotiations of reciprocity are often based on our unpretentious capacity to be kind, in the sense that processes of repair can only function in an atmosphere of sufficient kindness – indeed an essential catalyst for interpersonal arrangements. Devastating conflicts often follow preliminary negotiations; in fact failure is often due to the absence of a metabolite – 'kindness.' Apparently negligible, it ultimately proves indispensable. Phillips and Taylor suggest that 'Indeed the modern obsession with child rearing may be no more and no less than an obsession about the possibility of kindness in a society that makes it harder and harder to believe in kindness.'[21] And they add: 'Compassion and altruism have never found their place as significant terms in modern psychologies. And the apparent realism of all the self-interest stories ... has made the kindness stories sound soppy and wishful.'[22] As the Qoelet goes, there is a time for joy and a time of sorrow. When sorrow is unbearable it damages the self and inclines us to mental illness; the secret geniuses are those who help in the times of sorrow with 'just' some kindness. It is perhaps no metaphor to say that severe pain does break the heart, that it devastates our inner world. The 'mere' kindness of everyday geniuses is what often makes it endurable, and ultimately gets us across the fire. It is not true that those secret geniuses do not exist because in fact they are frequently at work – and get us across. The humble geniuses are those who can resist devastation and are not pulled into perverse logics. They are not superior minds who think that they can face any confrontations in the conviction that they can avoid contagion, and defeat any perverse logic with their own superior logic. These common heroes are anonymous and unregistered; but it is folly to say that they do not exist. Sometimes they keep families from becoming impossible, they keep relations from irreversible deterioration. They can also be the auxiliary forces that are essential in restoring the processes of constant repair described by Stern.

Relating is of course based on experience – as long as it is *personal* experience. In Kant's anthropology we read that

> The most important revolution from within the human being is his exit from his self-incurred immaturity. Before this revolution he let others think for him and merely ... allowed them to guide him by leading-strings. Now he ventures to advance, though still shakily, with his own feet on the ground of experience.[23]

This is *personal* experience, of course. Geniuses are those who can easily read others, who enjoy the gift of discernment and who can carefully notice what goes on behind appearances – ultimately they facilitate *personal* experience.[24] The 'insufficiently good' parents often expect their children to do the job for them. They want their children to catalyse their escape from immaturity – and get *them* across. Psychoanalysis or therapy offers daily opportunities to be personally creative, at least in small, minimal ways. But what does 'small' mean after all? What is 'small' in coping with life? In Kahn's view, 'Because each patient is unique with idiosyncratic emotional ... constellations, each psychoanalyst ... has the opportunity to decipher these unique ... symptoms and thus creatively construct original meanings.'[25] But what can 'original' possibly mean? These 'original meanings' probably refer to our inconspicuous, profound psychic resources, our potentials for coping with ever changing, uncertain circumstances. But then the point here is that whatever is vulnerable to obscurity can hardly be theorised and cultivated; it is perhaps too 'original' to thrive in our cultures and become appreciated.

All that one can know about our unconscious sources is, by definition, apprehended exclusively by inference. Consequently, the honesty used in making such inferences is of critical relevance. In fact, a century after Freud, little of the familiar foundations of psychoanalysis remains unchallenged; most of the conceptual and clinical premises that guided our founders are being called into question. And still, we go on and on. Similarly, if we hear the significant voices in the social sciences they seem to suggest that in our times of endemic uncertainty we 'simply' have to go on and on, developing into ordinary, original geniuses. Nothing less than that. Bauman, for instance, claims that the transition from 'solid' to 'liquid' modernity has determined an unprecedented setting of challenges for each one of us.[26] There are no forms and institutions that can serve as frames of reference for long-term plans; they would only function as the Kantian 'leading-strings.' Creatures must now combine a sequence of minimal, short-term, original efforts – which do not necessarily add up to an idea of progress. Such an uncertain world requires us to be flexible and adaptable in our nearly invisible moves; it requires us to be constantly ready and willing to pursue opportunities according to their current, unpredictable availability. In 'liquid' times the individual must act, plan actions and calculate the likely gains and losses in acting, or failing to act, under conditions of endemic uncertainty. Bauman seems to simply 'require' that we develop a talent for cultural survival. But of course answers on the specific ways in which to relate in view of this goal are not given: 'They would be peremptory, premature and potentially misleading' – says Bauman.[27]

We hear, for instance, that some countries are more responsible than others for pollution and environmental degradation; similarly in any micro- or macro-community some individuals are psychically more polluting than others in the sense of igniting perverse ways of relating. So we need a profound revision of our concepts of interpersonal equity and balance: only certain levels of intoxication are tolerable and a certain level of pathogenic emissions cannot be exceeded. And yet, some individuals are more intoxicating than others; the very creative persons have more efficient capacities for *processing* toxic elements into maturational experiences. Perhaps we need a renovated view of inter-subjective relations. Do we individually or as a group exceed in our quota of toxic emissions? But of course there are always geniuses who secretly do the detoxifying processes on behalf of others. In Oliver's view, in fact, the idea of genius is equated to an antidote for the degrading stereotypes that pollute psychic spaces and impede the movement of drives towards signification – that is, psychic life and humanisation.[28] Genius provides the inspiration that allows ordinary people to even speak *through* the intoxicating clichés of a culture. Of course there are expressions of healing ventures that are documented in our cultural heritage; and yet, there can be innumerable acts of detoxification that are not in the least recognised or recorded. They are the expression of our 'genius for relating,' which often only speaks to the singularity of another individual.

3. The courage to surrender

As is known, we can only apprehend our unconscious and its conflicts by means of inferences. There is no direct route. There is nothing we can learn by just fighting our unconscious conflicts; and thus the creative, maturational approach to the unconscious is through acceptance, acknowledgement, consent – paradoxically a surrender to our conflictive vicissitudes. In a psychoanalytic perspective, we could say that it is not the perceptivity or the acumen of the interpretation that really counts, but rather the creation of a symbolic domain for the expression of instinctual vicissitudes. Paradoxically, there can also be an addiction to the 'excitement' of instinctual conflicts, even in the disguise of drama and pain. But a preliminary sort of neutrality is created in the analytic setting; a sort of accepting forgiveness without a forgiving agent, and thus an innovative opportunity for transformational experiences. The opportunities that are concealed in every crisis are not appreciable until they are acknowledged, rather than used as a pastime: they must be accepted in a preliminary outlook of surrender and forgiveness. With the acknowledgement and acceptance of our psychic currents also comes a measure of freedom from them. When a symbolic milieu is created for knowing that we are in distress, this knowing allows for a still space that surrounds the conflict in an accepting way – a 'talking cure' that replaces the combative approach. It may then transmute our thick, conflictive tangles; what interpretations can primarily do is to create a space for transformation to happen. And so whenever our (transference) relationships bring out our madness, we can 'gladly' accept it so that we can symbolise it in ulterior ways of knowledge; this knowledge may function like a psychic embrace. We thus become encouraged to hold on to the knowing of our inner state.

It requires an inner effort to come to know our negation as well as our refusal to surrender to what is in us. And this may perhaps sound like an impossible call to accept abuse and frustration; but it is not. It is 'merely' the acceptance of an opportunity to actually see more of the situation before acting, to accept inner reality rather than be pulled into the vortex of reactions. What we are witness to in the Oedipus story is a mind in the grip of malign negations. The seminal and well-known Oedipus myth could perhaps be used to also illustrate our fragile talent for acceptance, acknowledgement, consent. As Symington suggests, when Oedipus murders Laius, he believes that he will be free from his conflicts.

> He is deceived into thinking that an external act will deliver him. An act is needed, but it is an internal act. There is something that he has to slay, but it is a mental power within, not king Laius riding out on his chariot. He has reason enough to hate Laius, but slaying him did not free him of the inner childhood wound ... He needs to exercise power, great power, but an internal power.[29]

And so Oedipus is deceived because his reactions look like genuine, lively attitudes while they are false and misleading; they are so misleading that we cannot quite bear them, they have to be surmounted at any cost – if the malign delusion of negation were not so deep seated. Things are not so simple; in fact it is not a matter of total attack or unconditional acceptance. It is incumbent upon the self to exercise its wits to discern what it is that we should surrender to and what it is that we should fight – and when, how and to what degree. Of course, there is no acceptance without risk. But the attitude of acceptance is not often tried and found creative. It is found difficult and is often left untried. There is an action required of Oedipus if he is to break free from the power of negation, and it is not an act of bravery that will be recorded in the memory of the community; it is a small, quiet action of acceptance, the outcomes of which are enormous. It is an internal act that goes unnoticed, the work of an ordinary genius. 'It is not an action that will have any attraction for those who want fame, no lure for those who long for power.'[30] It is an inner question of surrendering to what is, which is the privilege of ordinary geniuses. It is the action that gradually, with undoubted forwardness, contrasts the power of negation that has such a grip on all of us.

Negation and unwillingness to accept what is the case might be a devious derivative of envy. There may in fact be an insidious envy of what parental figures are and of what they can do; there could even be a perverse envy of those who are in power in a context of social oppression, or of any shade of racism. We can truly be devoured by the sort of envy that is not preceded by a degree of surrender to interpersonal conditions. And yet, our denial of envy seems a quasi-universal attitude. 'When one reads of individuals dominated at home' – says Winnicott – 'or under lifelong persecution because of a cruel political regime, one first of all feels that it is only a few of the victims who remain creative.'[31] But why? Many of the victims could even come to envy those who can dominate and persecute others. The few of the victims who remain creative are perhaps those who begin by accepting what is – and start from there. Epstein in fact suggests that envy may be the most deadening of the 'seven deadly sins.' It insidiously affects the other six 'minor' sins. Epstein specifies that

> Greed may begin with envy; it certainly figures in lust and gluttony (one does not really like to see others fornicating or eating too well, does one?); it is a division of anger, of the hidden, smoldering kind; and pride and envy are inextricable, with the wounding of one's pride leading onto envy as surely as spite follows defeat.

And he adds: 'Of the essence of envy is its clandestinity, its surreptitiousness.'[32] It only thrives on negation.

Perhaps we should remember that our egos need problems, conflict and 'enemies' to strengthen and confirm their psychic roles as managers of reality. Sometimes our ego feels like a thick tangle of currents demanding feedback – and not getting enough of it; as if the need for argument, drama and conflict were not being met. Acceptance of what is, that is a preliminary acceptance of outer and inner reality – Winnicott's 'environment that obtains' – is contrary to the attitude of our egos as the superb supervisors of events. If we cannot actually accept an envied parental figure, then we could perhaps try to perform the silent, *inner* action of acceptance. All the disasters that followed in Oedipus' story could have perhaps been avoided if he had taken the laborious path of surrender and of laboriously migrating from childhood to adulthood, and perhaps finding an ordinary girl to marry – not really a queen.[33] In fact the key to perceive what is damaging is to look at what has not been done. Of course it is not easy to describe what is not done, to approach an absence. And yet it is often in the vacuum, in the void that we must look for the source of human distress. 'It looks as if Oedipus was an adult,' remarks Symington, 'yet he was but a baby with Mummy. We must conclude from this that adulthood is not conferred by acts of heroism that draw the applause of the crowd ... not even by holding the post of king. Positions of high status do not confer adulthood.'[34] And so a conclusion seems to emerge: adulthood is not based on any external actions, however impressive or magnificent, but only on creative internal actions. Of course internal moves may have external consequences, but it is ultimately the internal act that generates adulthood. No less well known than the Oedipus myth, the story of Adam portrays our primordial father not taking the laborious route in trying to surpass his *limited* human condition. He did not use personal, gradual, inner efforts, but opted instead for a shortcut, a magic trick, that would solve all his problems in one stroke, by just eating a piece of fruit; only once, and he would reach the star system.

Phillips claims that despite the fact that the relationship between being stricken and being damaged is indeterminate, many shocking events only make a relative difference. The idea of trauma in fact reassures us that we can locate a causal sequence, and that there is an external beginning worth finding; that some causes are worth taking seriously.[35] But then, unlike pathology, the creativity of health does not derive from a putative tangible cause but rather from our accepting recognition of whatever traumatic situations. This unnoticed, unnoticeable inner attitude enhances fruitful outcomes. Let us not forget that Oedipus somehow 'knew' that his father wanted to eliminate him at a time when he simply had no means of defence or retaliation. What would have happened if Oedipus had had a steady good friend? Acknowledgement of a murderous reality and acceptance of our inner hatred of such a hostile reality could perhaps be the way out of a perverse vicious circle. If not recognised and accepted, this inner hatred is bound to attack everything in our human surroundings. And thus a destiny almost seems defined by our quota of destructiveness. And yet, in every milieu, obscure geniuses often mitigate our destructiveness and even bring us to tolerate an awareness of our inner hatred. In Phillips' words,

> Insanity is the hatred that for some reason – and the reason is difficult to discern – hates life. For this model to be tenable there have to be people who are able to speak on behalf of life, who can tell the difference between a destructive and a creative inner act.[36]

They are ordinary persons. We all need to be rescued from the madness we are heirs to. And our secret geniuses have every reason to be concerned as they try to avoid adding to the sum of the world's natural insanity.

People are always in situations, and to some extent they can influence the situations that they are in; but there are some situations that carry inevitability and that bring us to the edge of our existence. In these situations all answers and explanations seem to fail. We simply do not 'know.' Paradoxically, surrender means giving up trying to understand and being at peace with our lack of perspicacity. And yet, Winnicott insists that 'One has to allow for the possibility that there cannot be a complete destruction of a human individual's capacity for creative living and that, even in the most extreme cases ... there exists a *secret* life that is ... being creative.'[37] But in which attitude is this '*secret* life' revealed? Perhaps whenever the individual comes to completely accept what is, he/she is being creative; and, at the extreme, there can be creativeness in surrendering to the inner fact that we cannot surrender. This '*secret* life' is probably vulnerable to obscurity; minimal, unnoticed and yet it is the virtue of our finite condition.

If we, for example, think of ancient deities, we could recognise that the immortal gods are quite similar to human beings except for their 'privilege' of not being subject to death. These myths also indicate that our finitude is not only our limit but also our strength – indeed our genius. Of course our mortality can break us and induce unexplainable sorrow. But it can also be the source of our yearning for life, of our deep compassion and of our understanding of tragedy. This is perhaps Winnicott's *secret* creativity. With immortality we might perhaps resemble our ancient divinities – so often arrogant, vindictive, frivolous; they are like those of us who omnipotently ignore finitude – those who are glossed and styled in our advertising world. Our western primordial hero, Ulysses, refuses the 'gift' of immortality: perhaps he had the profound intuition that ordinary genius would be impossible apart from a condition of finitude. And so, in the words of Steiner, 'The wrestling match with the dark angel ... has been archetypal of human creativity despite, because of, its foreordained outcome. The loser is annihilated but prevails.'[38]

3

EGO DEVELOPMENT AND DE-CREATION OF OUR EGOS

1. Ways to learn – and unlearning

The widening horizons that we dreamed of finding in our analytic culture sometimes seem replaced by ante-rooms and winding passages that apparently lead nowhere. Similarly, the analysand who is trying to be born again is not led into static self-knowledge but into the meanders of transformation. Ferro and Grotstein suggest that we are the 'victims' of an excess of light continuously produced by a successful egoic knowledge, a sort of pseudo-knowledge that pollutes our minds and prevents us from truly developing. 'Let us switch off the lights and wait for something to emerge, even if it is only shady shreds.'[1] To the extent that it is a knowledge that does not derive from our *whole* personality, it cannot be authentic, and thus we become faced with the problem of unlearning it.[2] If successful, this venture will allow for a reconnection of ourselves to the 'I' of the personality and for surpassing the illusory identification with our managerial egos. We could thus try to 'weave shreds of meaning with the parts of ourselves which were kept disconnected or which were denied ... and open our minds as wide as our current degree of evolution will allow.'[3] In fact, the need sometimes arises to step outside of our rational schemas and risk a leap into the void, in order to escape the fixity of the egoic structures that constrain us almost as strictly as the signals of our instinctual nature. Paradoxically, the hereditary load of programmes that in part determine our responses to life seems to assume a lesser position in the face of a dominant egoic structure so 'well formed' and 'successful' that it finally tends to respond to nothing but itself, perpetuating some false self. We can readily appreciate the merits of someone who develops into a successful person, strenuously maintaining the contours of her psychic and professional accomplishment. We could, for instance, think of some individuals who excel – as clinicians, theorists or whatever – and who reach a stellar position in a micro- or macro-community. It is possible that those individuals would greatly benefit from a process of self-decreation as an alternative to becoming fixed or constrained in their interlocking personal and professional structures. At the extreme, they become caricatures of themselves.

It usually makes good sense to try to hold on to our own successful egoic construction. Sometimes the very 'functional' people may encounter analysts who 'propose' a better prospect, while the analysands have no good reason to believe in it. We could, for instance, invoke the case of a patient who lives in the conviction that she can only obtain the love of others by enchanting them with her superior argumentative skills; she knows of no other way of surviving in spite of her difficulties in securing just the love she craves. Thus she can only dialectically insist on 'capturing' the analyst and sees no reason to abandon this 'superior' capacity. And yet, while the analysand may gradually come to relinquish her egoic powers for the sake of a more rewarding adaptation, so must the analyst strive to let go of his own patiently acquired view of things for the sake of some new insight into the analytic confrontation. In other words, the two of them – and not just the patient – must be(come) capable of unlearning. It takes a genius to refrain from using one's very clever ego, and it is impossible to make any changes when we are totally identified with it. People are often so identified with the thoughts that make up their worldview that their thoughts solidify into mental positions infused with a sense of self. Once this has happened, we defend our convictions – our 'identity;' we feel and act as if we were defending our entire personality and psychic life.

Because we have learned enough of the right things – which are now incorporated into our self – and because we identify with it for psychic survival, there seems to be a compulsion to prove others wrong; indeed a common human attitude. Once our egos are fortified by our successful learning, we just cannot unlearn lest our egos be weakened. And thus we often assume that others should think in the same way we have learned to think – at great expense and effort. If they do not, we will be entitled to 'correct' and 'retrain' them, provided we pre-emptively manage to demonstrate that we are right and the others wrong.

The attitude of entitlement provided by our high-quality learning is often expressed in a language that is lucidly coercive: arguments are best when they compel others into agreement – and are not so good when less cogent. There seems to be a constant attempt to get the other to believe something, whether he wants to believe it or not. Conversely, it is sometimes unthinkable that we might begin to unlearn. If our learning sustains our ego, then our successful 'teaching' should be based on arguments that coerce others. The ideal discourse would be the one that leaves no possible answers to the interlocutor, reducing him to impotent silence. In the language of Nozick, 'We need arguments so powerful that they set up reverberations in the brain: if the person refuses to accept the conclusion, he *dies*. How is that for a powerful argument?'[4] But then, approval of our learning is of course never quite sufficient and thus we seek to secure ever more external supporters and more compelling means for recruiting them. According to Symington, our egos can be erotised through stimulating their surfaces by oneself or by getting others to do so. We want the others to unlearn, and to erotically adhere to the learning of our egos; almost like an autoerotic activity that has to be constantly elicited and renewed – even in psychoanalytic contexts.[5] To always be in the right can even produce stories in the form of complaints. These are unconsciously designed to enhance our deficient egos through being right and making something or someone unbearably wrong. Being right places us in a position of imagined superiority and so strengthens our false sense of self. This attitude also carries as a by-product some kind of inimical reality as if the ego needed enemies to define its boundary – and, even the weather could serve some sort of 'inimical' function. Sometimes tribes, nations and parties derive a strengthened sense of collective identity from having enemies who are definitely 'wrong.'

In this outlook the identity of the ego comes to depend on comparisons and gorges on more and more of the same; it will use anything to this end. If all else fails one can sustain this fictitious identity by perceiving oneself as *the most* unfairly treated by life, or certainly suffering more than the others. The problem with unlearning and of more accepting forms of interaction is that they are definitely rendered inconspicuous in our culture because they deviate from an immemorial, territorial way of reasoning – constantly concerned to prove others wrong. Unlearning can hardly be theorised. On the other hand, alternative ways of argument are far more creative, complex and profound, even though less exhilarating than the consequences of 'being right.' And although we may succeed in defeating our interlocutors by proving them wrong, they often do not change their convictions – or begin to unlearn. This may be an indication that they pursue some different inner project that is just not captured by our 'superior' learning. By combating another's conviction we may persistently miss the point that determines the conviction. A polemic attention to 'segments' of others means that we ignore claims which hardly ever exist in isolation, and that they are aspects of a complex (integrated) form of life. But to the extent that we identify with our egos, we must constantly strive to be right and 'teach' others. The inner action of detachment from our learning is apparently a non-action, for it is certainly not an external, visible move; and thus it requires an invisible sort of inner creative propensity. The ego of an acclaimed genius has difficulties in thinking of this procedure, while an ordinary genius is perhaps more intent on transforming a debate into a 'dance,' for instance – rather than on simply being a winner.

In the story of the sorcerer's apprentice the young, innocent pupil is portrayed using a magic trick to make a broom carry buckets of water from the well; but he is not able to stop the broom performing the service because he does not know the counter-jinx. The master sorcerer, of course, does know it, and arrives just in time to avoid flooding. Well, of course, the apprentice should have asked and learned both the spell and the counter-spell. All this is probably meant to judiciously illustrate the potential damages of a limited knowledge. But then, a further implication could be seen: while the apprentice simply does not *know* how to stop a very successful process, a master sorcerer might not really *want* to do that. Our master sorcerers – in fact our 'wizards' in science, technology and management – may not be capable of putting a stop to their sublime tricks. Our technological and managerial geniuses are often so enthusiastic with their talents that they will simply not interfere with them. If wonderful packaged goods come out of one exit while carbon emissions flow out of another, our geniuses may become so enchanted with the entire venture that they indefinitely carry on. Why not split more atoms, put more satellites in our orbit or produce more wonderful goods? If one has a talent for making money, why stop? If one is a strategic genius – say, like Napoleon – why not brave the Russian winter? Invisible inner actions for redirecting outer actions would probably require an ordinary creative person to advise an extraordinary creative genius. And, of course, the official genius and the ordinary one can also be regarded as emblematic figures standing for aspects of our own personality. And if we entirely identify with our egoic wizardry we cannot give it up for fear of psychic collapse.

That we are not entirely satisfied with the power of our admirable capacities may be revealed by the secret, inexpressible admiration we experience for those who contend in a playful way, who transform a battle into an encounter, or who do not seem to take any arguments too seriously; but this does not prevent us from constantly praising the winners – *Vae victis!* after all (be careful, losers!). That we can be victims of our strategic wizardry can be shown by conflicts between the poorest of our human communities that fight to the end – to extinction. Of course, basic destructive drives can easily make use of our clever egos. And even though we may know how and why a controversy is initiated, we definitely do not know how to stop, or how to transform it into some different, possibly creative, interaction. The everyday geniuses, with their inner actions, may be capable of doing just that. We may of course perceive the sterility of an endless conflict and wish for an inversion of the adversarial trend – before it naturally exhausts its cycle. The belated conclusion of a conflict may indeed be the result of our identification with a combative ego, ultimately seeking to perpetuate itself by outsmarting others.

The fashionable games of our subcultures lead us to avoid vital issues by litigating over marginal ones. A compulsion to abide by the offensive/defensive roles may thus, unnoticed, impoverish our approach to inquiries. This detrimental use of our ego, as if it were our whole personality, may even induce us to subdivide into ever smaller groups, which are characterised by a decreasing understanding of each other's concerns. But this is neither a necessary feature of inquiry nor of course an advantage to it. Such an involution of our natural love of knowledge – our human epistemophily[6] – may ultimately be due to a lack of interest in psychic life itself. It is not a matter of giving up something 'false' or useless, but of partially renouncing something that has previously been quite useful – and this is the distressing aspect of the process. Secret geniuses are capable of allowing for such a turn. The point is that to achieve a continuation of development – as distinct from a repetition of 'successful' moves – we probably have to sacrifice the way in which we have conceived of things up to a point. Our previous ego does not of course become 'false'; rather it becomes insufficient for ulterior different creative purposes. It is not to be discarded, but its limited function must be recognised for the sake of different levels of creativeness. It is reported that certain monkeys are so ingenious as to insert an arm into the thin neck of an amphora in order to catch the food perceived at the bottom of it. Very clever indeed. But then they will not give up on this very good move, even though unable to pull out their arm with a closed hand full of food. Under these circumstances they can be apprehended by their smarter companions – the humans. But then, are we really smarter when it concerns our own affairs? Perhaps we the wizards cannot give up performing our best tricks, our most successful games – even our *jeux de massacre*.

When considering our young ones, we think that the sooner they achieve mature ego functions the better it is for their psychic lives. The thesis here is a comparable one: if we invoke some hypothetic point in our life cycle, a time of accomplished self-formation, then the process of self-decreation should immediately be initiated – and not delayed. A delay in de-creation would be as serious as a problem of delay in the development of our selves. Our well-formed egos may be regarded as the admirable result of our struggle for survival. And yet, once the masterpiece of a strong functional ego has been accomplished, this may go on functioning indefinitely by enforcing the same relational policies even to the point when they can be detrimental to our whole personality. But then, the question is whether it is possible to let go of the ego, or of parts of it. It would seem insane to dismantle a 'successful' apparatus for managing drives and reality. In fact it may take a genius, our secret ordinary genius, to creatively envisage just that option.

Our memories and our whole story are invested with a sense of self until they actually become who we perceive ourselves to be. In the long run this identity can become an illusion that monopolises our whole personality. We hold on to our old emotions because they indefinitely strengthen a comfortable identity. But what is the price of identity? It could be excessive. In fact, once the ego solidifies into an identity, it does not want to let go; it would feel like psychically dying. In some cases the subject even clings to a psychic illness to the extent that it has become the most important part of whom he perceives himself to be. An openness to deconstruction is not to be confused with denial. Our thoughts, emotions and reactions are of course acknowledged and in the inner action of recognition *some* dis-identification seems to take place. We become not only conscious of our survival vicissitudes, but also we become aware of a conscious 'I' of the personality that can possibly witness those vicissitudes.[7] This is not a *doing* but a psychic *seeing*, an insight – an inner action. In this sense it is true that there is nothing we can *do* to surpass our ego; but when some *perceptive* shift happens, the 'I' of the personality, or the entire self, becomes more operative. When we are able to catch ourselves playing any of the roles determined by our egoic story, then we are able to create an inner space, a gap, between the self and the role; a liberating inner move. To the extent that we are identified with a specific psychological role, we confuse our defensive management of reality with who we truly are. Our famous object relations become problematic when we are locked into a 'role'; even if it is the universal role of the knowing 'adult,' which we all tend to play very seriously.

It seems that Freud never relented in his attempt to win formal approval from scientific milieus – that is, the confirmation that psychoanalysis is a *science*. Perhaps Winnicott, Bion and Matte Blanco can be said to have taken a different route. In their view the science that is appropriate for the psyche is a science of emotions and affects that are infinite sets – complex and un-linear in nature. This could be an opening, an opportunity for psychoanalysis to seize upon the idea of a 'complexity theory,' a discipline inclined to non-linear phenomena.[8] In this specific respect, Freud was not so good at unlearning. Ultimately, unlearning could be seen as a preliminary for the evolution of our human learning. But Freud was not one to evade seeing implications such as, for instance, the profound significance of the First World War. He realised that a sort of motivation was involved there, that his theories could not account for. Science, in its strict sense, seemed not quite enough to face this challenge. But then, if we gaze at our social life in the perspective of death instincts, it is the occurrence of Eros, and indeed of life itself, that is intriguing. We could wonder, in passing, what Freud might have said if he *also* had known that the ideological follies of the *entire* twentieth century amounted to over one hundred million casualties. Even before that, with his usual courage, he turned his attention to the breadth and depth of human destructiveness, and tried to think of people as responsible agents and instigators, not just as victims. He recognised in *Civilization and Its Discontents*[9] that he could no longer understand how we could have overlooked the universality of non-erotic destructiveness being rationally sustained and serviced by our best forms of thinking – the development of our ideologies. And thus he was also sufficiently good at unlearning. He actually sacrificed the belief he had thought necessary for his rationale, namely the belief that people can only act for their own advantage and pleasure. And so we might be acutely in need of something virtually impossible: the collective unthinking of ideologies. In the most disparate ways, our ordinary geniuses are perhaps the daily resistors to these ideologies.

The virtue of being open to novelty is that whatever comes in through the openness of unlearning is in a sense out of control. At the extreme, we may find ourselves forced into unlearning what we know. It is only from the

EGO DEVELOPMENT AND DE-CREATION OF OUR EGOS

unforeseen, the unexpected, that we can begin to learn again. For instance, we may not really like others. But when we have become sufficiently adept at unlearning, at perceiving even our own destructive inclinations, we 'naturally' become capable of accepting the irritating fragilities of others. We may not *like* people, but the further we unlearn, the more we are capable of accepting their perplexing behaviour, whether erotic or destructive. In a synoptic view suggested by Steiner, we could say that the utopian 'futures' presumed by our western heritage – from Plato to Marx – may no longer be available to our syntax: 'We now look back at them. They are monuments for remembrance ... We now remember the futures that they were.'[10]

2. Ways to unthink and rethink

A glance at the phases of human creative ventures seems to indicate a reciprocal dependence of antithetic human propensities: construction and deconstruction. There seems to be a paradoxical connection between our capacity to both use and relinquish our paradigms of thought. At some point in the creative trajectory, the ability to set aside the use of certain successful cognitive functions becomes downright indispensable, almost as if accepting the risk of not knowing, or of losing control, was a necessary component of creativity. We may now ask: Why does therapy not succeed more often?; Why does it sometimes fail to make a real difference in people's lives?; When it does not succeed, what is it that those patients and analysts do? In fact, what the successful patients do in their therapy hours may be different from others. What could this crucial difference be? The difference probably lies in what the successful patients do inside themselves, namely unthink and rethink with their whole selves. By converse, when one encounters the shifts and breakdowns that could motivate us to try to unlearn, one may find it easier to begin to 'complain' about whatever the case may be, and to export the innermost crisis onto peripheral, marginal crises; almost a default in creativeness. Patients sometimes experience an inner state of discontent, almost a rage, which could be described as a sort of diffuse resentment. Under this affective state there can be certain firmly held convictions, or enduring thoughts.

In our everyday life we may engage in thinking our customary thoughts in the same way that we generate dreams at night. The individual does not truly know that her ego is constantly thinking its repertory of thoughts, just as the dreamer is not really aware that she is dreaming. The subject has reason enough to treasure her current thoughts, so ingenuously developed to cope with reality. But then, in time, in our vicissitudes of growth, perhaps the ego thrives on resentment of reality, of whatever the case may be. A domineering, quasi-adversarial attitude to reality is perhaps one of the main features of the ego. Why? Our egos have a successful history of mediating between drives and reality; a story of being clever managers in this developmental process. It is even possible that our own well-developed, powerful egos might determine the negativity that they must control, and thus the 'unhappiness' that they thrive on. Complaining is, in fact, one of our favourite strategies for illusorily relieving ourselves through projective identification. Our complaints could be ego-produced narratives that we come to entirely believe. Whether we openly complain aloud, or only in the secrecy of our minds, makes little difference. The ego perhaps 'loves' the assaultive inadequacies of others. Instead of overlooking them, we make them into the others' identity and strive to 'correct' them. The laborious working through of transference is certainly one of the ways to unthink many of the ego's artefacts. Of course the ego surmounts difficulties but we may become slaves of this function. When we can live in acceptance of what is, there is no 'good' or 'bad' for us to fight or applaud; there are only better options in the sense of an increasing capacity to tolerate frustration. We can be stricken but not deadened. Also, we are allowing people, 'others,' to be as they are. This capacity to permit others to exist as they are may take us beyond the ego, beyond those controlling strategies that determine positive–negative polarities; it is like unthinking them and creating an opening for ulterior creativeness. In this connection we could point out that the successful, brilliant individuals are certainly not the 'easy' patients. The struggling ones can be more amenable to creative renovation. We are not talking here of opening our way to 'happiness' of course. We often cannot just be happy about what happens. But we certainly *can* be creative. We do all we can while also accepting what the case may be. We almost seem to unthink the mental products of our egos.

The story of Oedipus is a well-known myth that can function in the history of a group; but of course it can also function for the individual within the group. In this sense, King Laius may represent an inner object, an inner psychic reality. Symington suggests that we try to imagine an alternative scenario: the seer Tyresias removes the curse of the oracle and Oedipus settles down at his princely tasks; and of course it is a long time before he can become king. He must struggle into adulthood and find himself a bride. 'By killing his father and jumping into bed with his mother, he bypasses all that. He grabs his father's power, yet he remains a child ... Although it looks otherwise, he is, in sorry fact, a child still with his Mummy.'[11] And moreover, the father is just not there; he is absent. 'What is absent, then? What is the inner reality that is absent, that has been murdered?'[12] The answer is the internal act of creative knowledge – of thinking in a different way, of unthinking and rethinking. To dis-identify from the more comfortable ways of thinking is to be the silent observer of thoughts and behaviour, especially of the repetitive cunning patterns produced in the way of shortcuts to the goal. In fact analysis does not generate happiness but maturity, at best. One may have entered proformal adulthood in the proficiency of well-practised roles. Patients may learn to unthink the gains that they had originally expected from their roles and begin to rethink the development of their entire inner world – Winnicott's 'whole personality.' An effective therapeutic work enables us to pass from being possessed by our insanity, to the ability of coping with it; which can be an awesome transformation because, of course, we tend to conceal our madness from ourselves. But then, in this laborious transformation we can also become aware of our strengths and creativity. Once an individual realises her assets she cannot remain the same. One relinquishes the more comfortable (even though damaging) psychic habits and embarks on the projects that are suitable to one's assets. And when new forces spring to life we can start all over again.

In psychoanalytic cultures we are familiar with the discipleships of one analyst towards another. It is thus especially challenging to unthink and rethink when we have absorbed the thoughts of a quasi-divine master and snatched a superb identity. Symington insists that,

> The rage towards the erstwhile mentor is the hatred of the submissive act. It is the submissive projected act that is hated, but it becomes projected and hypostatized in the outer object ... The attempted liberation became perverted. True liberation requires realization that the enslaving principle is the inner submissive act, and that total liberation requires an understanding that the enslaving principle is one element in the narcissistic structure.[13]

Our ordinary geniuses are those capable of enough pragmatism, simplicity and sense of humour to resist such forms of enslavement to deities.

It is equally enslaving to find an identity in being a heroic victim. Of course the whole personal story is very well researched and thought out by the individual – the brighter, the better. But if we cannot unthink it, we cannot possibly rethink it. Sometimes the realisation that one is 'different' may force us to dis-identify from customary patterns of behaviour; although it can be painful it may also give an advantage as far as rethinking is concerned. On the other hand, if we develop a sense of identity based on our unfortunate difference we may avoid a trap only to be ensnared by another. Having endured situations of neglect or abuse, subjects may become imprisoned in an outlook of entitlement that is contrary to all creativity. Freud perceived this quite clearly. In 'The Exceptions' he remarks that whenever analysts invite patients to make a provisional renunciation for the sake of a better, more creative prospect, or

> to submit to a necessity which applies to everyone, one comes upon individuals who resist such an appeal on a special ground. They say that they have renounced enough and suffered enough and have a claim to be spared any further demands; they will submit no longer to any disagreeable necessity, for they are *exceptions* and, moreover, intend to remain so.[14]

And so, identification with a hero/victim identity may prevent the individual from effectively dealing with an inner, thick tangle of pain – almost a tangible one.

They say that after all the harm that they have suffered from others, they are fully entitled to a victim identity and willing to use it as a capital, as an 'inexhaustible' asset. But they also keep themselves imprisoned in this identity, which recurrently fails them. If one is still holding on to anger, resentment or condemnation one is firmly holding on to the inner tangle of painful threads; almost an inescapable tangle that keeps in bondage to the past, and blocks the way to creativity. But this tangle of painful memories cannot be defeated by fighting it. It seems to have a consistency, a life of its own; that is, constantly fighting to survive and expand: the exceptions intend to remain so[15] – Freud warns us. It almost functions like an entity that pretends to be the whole personality; the sick tangle claims to be you. It is not easy at first to be there as a witnessing presence especially when the suffering tangle is somehow activated; it uses the person and situations to get what it wants – easy gains, or even more pain – and even when it succeeds it is never satisfied for long. This seems the arch-enemy of creativity, and only clear awareness may contribute to dissolve it.

As is known, when we use our egoic brilliance and practised roles we usually succeed. But success does not coincide with creativity. There are cycles of success and cycles of failure. When failure comes we have to let it unfold in order to make room for new ventures to arise, or transformation to happen. If we cling and resist, at that point we are refusing to go with the flow of psychic life, with the whole personality. It is not true that the up cycle is good and the down cycle is bad, except in a very limited, partial judgement. Growth, for instance, is usually considered positive, but not everything can grow forever; if it were to go on and on it would eventually become unliveable. Creativity requires activity and passivity. Dissolution is needed for new growth to happen.

Eissler reminds us that humankind would not have evolved had there not been *'the few'* who were able to unthink the world as it was and to 'think a new world, to recreate one that is more gratifying or more illuminating than the one they found.'[16] But there are many more, and not so few, who can at least facilitate the attempts to 'think a new world.' Some ordinary geniuses are the catalysts that favour creative transformations. According to Steiner, the history of the psyche is one of incessant change:

> Within the flux, there are episodes of mutation, of revolution or, as current mathematical models have it, of "catastrophe" ... but they can also manifest energies of acceleration, of metamorphoses so vehement, so far-reaching as to make our ... explanatory theories homeless or, at best, conjectural.[17]

4

GENIUS: ORDINARY AND EXTRAORDINARY

1. Introduction

This is an attempt to differentiate the praise of extraordinary, 'official' works of genius from an appreciation of the innumerable expressions of 'unofficial' everyday creativity – which are usually vulnerable to obscurity. In one sense genius is historical, public and acclaimed, while in another, it is personal, private, psychological. In writings about creativeness we recognise these two different senses of 'creativity.' And even though the context often supports one or the other, they are at times used interchangeably. And yet, there are constant oscillations and contradictions even in those outlooks that are in favour of a sharp, essentialist difference between ordinary and extraordinary creativity.

The ordinary and personal sense of creativity concerns attitudes that are surprising and seminal with respect to the individual mind and its daily relations; the historical sense applies instead to novelties in art and science that are relevant for the entire human community.[1] In the majority of cases, in fact, when speaking about 'genius,' people refer to the exceptional, acclaimed figures of human history; and even though this is the more celebrated notion, personal, unnoticed creativity is the more important one for our purposes here. Perhaps we should note in passing that sometimes even new achievements, in the historical sense, actually develop through some kind of serendipity, in apparently unprincipled, idiosyncratic ways.

Of course one may fulfil the expectation to use a term – for instance, 'genius' – in a classical, canonic way, just the way in which the majority of people are using the term in a given period of scholastic hegemony. Regarding the use of a term we could here invoke Bion, saying that

> If I disappoint the expectation (aroused by the penumbra of associations of which I do not divest it), I may reasonably be said to mis-use a term. It is then open to me, if I agree with the criticism, either explicitly to divest the term of its penumbra of associations or, to accept the conventions of use implied by the associations.[2]

That is, going along with the customary use. And so here we opt for a more inclusionary – however disappointing – idea of genius, which comprises our ordinary, personal and inconspicuous manifestations.

In Oliver's view, Kristeva and Howe describe *the* genius as a subject who lives at a cultural intersection and that crystallises its possibilities; but they also maintain that genius belongs to all of us as a 'therapeutic invention' by which we create and live.[3] It is the capacity to imagine the extraordinary within our ordinary lives. We might perhaps fear that the *quality* of genius will be affected, or made banal, if we remove the aura of mystery surrounding it – that penumbra of associations. In a naturalised outlook perhaps our geniuses 'simply' show us what humankind is capable of. And according to Howe 'It is only when we acknowledge that geniuses are not totally unlike other people that our minds open up to all that we can learn from them.'[4] In this sense the attribution of genius can be directed to artistic or scientific achievements as well as to the common doings of ordinary people. As Kant significantly remarks, a human being's genius is 'the exemplary originality of his talent ... But we also call a mind that has the predisposition to this "a genius"; then this word is to denote not merely a person's natural gift, but also the person himself.'[5] Indeed a struggling, surviving creature – whatever his gifts.

If we now refer to the monumental contributions of Eissler on the question of acclaimed artistic creativity, one can sense that he often favours an essentialist difference, an impassable gap between extraordinary and ordinary creativity. We read that, 'Mankind would still be living in caves ... had there not been the *very few* who were able to "unthink" the world as it was and to "think" a new world – that is, to recreate one that is more gratifying, or more illuminating then the one they found.'[6] And yet, at this point, we should also ask whether inventiveness only regards the very few who can think a new world, or else if it could also regard a communal, interactive venture. As we have seen in chapter 1, this has been the case with the fateful invention of a written language. There are official geniuses in our cultural heritage although there were probably pristine creators who originated the sort of products, subsequently associated with a celebrated official figure. Indeed some of our human creativity, of our poiesis, has been nameless. The cave painters of Lescaux, the architects of the pyramids, the composers of ancient music transmitted throughout centuries remain anonymous.

In a distinctively cognitive perspective, Boden remarks that what the inborn factors of genius are, assuming that they exist at all, is not known. 'But whatever they are, they are not supernatural. And almost certainly, they are more efficient versions of mechanisms we all share – not something profoundly different.'[7] And here 'profoundly' probably means essentially. By converse, Eissler seems to display a propensity for an essentialist view of genius and thus reiterates:

> I am properly convinced that the structure of the genius personality ...
> is in essential respects different from that of other human beings.
> Freud was most careful ... not to draw any inferences regarding the
> specific character of Leonardo's genius from analogies with his everyday
> clinical observations.

But then, paradoxically, he somehow contradicts himself in an enlightening way and he adds: 'In a question that concerns the contents of human life, we regularly observe that the genius wrestles with contents that are *identical with those that the rest of mankind must cope with.*'[8]

2. On the 'essential superiority' of acclaimed inventiveness

The question often arises as to whether acclaimed genius is the outcome of some very special, numinous, supernatural destiny. And this interlocks with the question of an essential, qualitative difference between genius and other minor forms of creativity. In the contributions of Eissler[9] one can perceive an oscillation between the view of genius as absolutely superior, 'transcendent,' and an understanding of it as a more earthly, human enterprise. Here we only attempt to show these fluctuations from the extreme, supernatural, view of creativity to our more silent, ordinary ways of being creative. At this point we should also look into a subjacent mentality that allows for the notions of 'destiny,' 'unicity' and 'numinosity;' an outlook that encompasses antiquity and endorses a view of genius as a unique, 'superhuman' form of expression. We shall attempt to briefly look into a view of genius as of an exceptional, mysterious phenomenon, sometimes preceded by equally exceptional and mysterious signs – omens, almost; such a genesis sets it entirely apart from our concern with everyday, unexceptional creativeness. With no claim to documental competence or textual accuracy, we would like to point out that there are in fact variations in the perception of absolute creativity and that the idea of genius as some kind of Platonic 'essence,' so to speak, is not unitary, and even questioned by its proponents. One of the preoccupations of psychoanalysis has been the effort to delve into the psychological 'mystery' of human creativity. As is known, Freud's humble, daring, many faceted approach to this question already began in his correspondence with Fliess, and included the study of a genius *par excellence*, Leonardo da Vinci.[10] The subsequent contributions of Eissler contain cogent formulations of the psychology of genius – as well as occasional ambivalences.

Leonardo jotted down on the verso of a page of text devoted to observations on the flight of kites – which led to the invention of our 'flying machines' – this childhood memory, or perhaps this recollection of his childhood:

> To write thus clearly of the kite would seem to be my destiny, because
> in the earliest recollections of my infancy it seemed to me that when

> I was in the cradle a kite came and opened my mouth with its tail, and struck me within upon the lips with its tail many times.[11]

According to Freud, this scene with the kite was probably not a memory of Leonardo but 'a phantasy, which he formed at a later date and transposed to his childhood.'[12] In Eissler's view in fact 'Freud drew the conclusion that his recollection must refer to the infant's early oral phase and that the bird's tail was a substitute for the mother's nipple.'[13] But then this recollection, or fantasy, is subject to further, different interpretations. Shapiro reminds us that the recording of episodes of the kind that Leonardo reported regarding his own infancy is an 'established literary pattern,' perhaps a 'genre,' which often occurs in mythology. He cites Cicero's text on divination and

> traces the source from which Leonardo might easily have known about typical incidents that in antiquity and later were attributed to the infancy of heroes and outstanding personages as omens of future greatness. Some of these incidents refer to both animals and to the infant's mouth, and are actually of the structure of the childhood recollection reported by Leonardo.

Whether this story was a simple recollection or, as Freud suggests, the impulse to *form* the asserted 'childhood memory,' it stemmed from Leonardo's ambition, or from his conviction that he was a genius. In Eissler's words:

> He would have wanted to make sure or was sure that he would hold a place of greatness in history, and therefore claimed to have had in his own infancy an experience which by tradition was a propitious sign in the lives of those who later ascended to great fame.[14]

Of course Freud was fascinated with the question of outstanding creativity and especially with Leonardo, perhaps an emblematic figure of genius – both artistic and scientific. But the immediate stimulus to writing his essay on Leonardo appears to have come in the autumn of 1909 from one of his patients who seemed to have the same constitution as Leonardo without his genius; and thus, here, Freud's clinical acumen seems to spare him from embracing the idea of some constitutional, innate view of genius. The links with extraordinary experiences and identifications is not uncommon, and even resonates with Kant's anthropology; 'For *invisibility* (of the cause of an effect) is an accessory concept of *spirit* (a *genius* which is already assigned to the gifted man at his birth), whose inspiration he only follows, so to speak.'[15]

In an oscillation between a natural, embodied domain on the one side, and the domain of inspirational, revealed books on the other, Freud clearly says: 'My deep engrossment in the Bible story (almost as soon as I learnt the art of reading) had, as I recognized much later, an enduring effect upon the direction of my interest.'[16] Eissler in fact claims that Freud identified with the Biblical Joseph to such an extent that his identification almost acquired a sense of reality along the lines of feeling just like the Biblical Joseph, 'destined to be a famous dream interpreter and to come to high honours.' Identification with heroes with whom children become familiar by hearsay or reading, is a frequent cultural phenomenon.[17]

In his oscillations Eissler often seems to champion the idea of a qualitative superiority of genius, with respect to mere talent. For instance, he notes that it was a step ahead when the qualitative richness of colours was converted into a variation of wavelength. But he regrets that, as a by-product, there emerged a way of thinking that tends to dissolve all differences into quantitative ones:

> Whether this principle of converting differences of quality into quantitative differences can be extended into the human world appears questionable ... Likewise, the view that the difference between talent and genius is solely a quantitative one appears to me to be misleading.[18]

By converse, Freud, in spite of *his* Biblical Joseph, often inclines for a more natural account of sublime creativity that also involves the everyday travails of sublimation. He writes:

> Observation of men's *daily lives* shows us that *most people* succeed in directing very considerable portions of their sexual instinctual forces to their professional activity. The sexual instinct is particularly well fitted to make contributions of this kind since it is endowed with a capacity for sublimation: that is, it has the power to replace its immediate aim by other aims which may be valued more highly and which are not sexual.[19]

Whether or not it is a 'mere' question of sublimation is of no concern for our purposes. What is relevant, instead, is that Freud emphasises that it is an observation of *'daily lives'* and that it regards *'most people,'* that is, the life of those ordinary creatures who struggle to make the burden of life more bearable and even desirable.

In still other paragraphs of his extensive contributions Eissler inclines for a more conditional, humbled view of creativity, often dependent upon circumstances; still another fluctuation. He remarks that 'It is not probable that the genius capacity is so profoundly rooted in an innate constitution that, once given, its penetrance would conquer any environment, no matter how unfavourable.'[20] And also, when investigating the external reality in which an overpowering mind developed, the psychoanalyst expects or, perhaps, would even like to discover some unique features. But then Eissler, paradoxically, also expresses an unconditional view of creativity as if the *talented people* and *geniuses* were essentially different:

> The psychologist is all too inclined to confuse *talent* with *genius*. While the talented person does rid himself from disease by way of his creative productions, the latter is strong enough to face the complications of human existence without having to escape into illness. His psychopathology is characteristic of the creative process and in that regard essentially different from illness. In creating he does not rid himself of anything; it is only the talented person who does these things, utilizing creativity for therapeutic ends.[21]

In his outlook, therefore, if an obsessive symptom were observed, and if it turned out that the symptom was necessary for inventiveness, then 'there would be no sense in calling it a neurotic symptom;'[22] whatever the nature of neurosis may be, the concept of illness only makes sense when it is correlated with a deficit, not with productivity, as if 'geniushood' were so powerful as to dissipate illness and to transmute everything into itself. But Freud's view does not entirely favour such an essentialist, impassable gap, and in his work on Leonardo we read: 'We no longer think that health and illness, normal and neurotic people, are to be sharply distinguished from each other, and that neurotic traits must necessarily be taken as proofs of general inferiority.'[23]

3. Some contours of extraordinary genius

We may think of genius as of an innate gift, as a natural light, even though we often realise that it is the end result of strenuous negotiations. It is almost as if geniuses know very well that one is not the genius that he deserves to be because in fact one is the sort of genius that he has negotiated or achieved. As we do not think of genius as a supernatural occurrence or absolute mystery, we could attempt to 'describe' some of the discernible features of whomever we regard as an acclaimed genius. But also in the approximation to the 'maximum' in the end result, it is a question of degrees. With regard to literary creativity, for instance, Koestler remarks that 'The history of science has its Pantheon of celebrated revolutionaries – and its catacombs, where the unsuccessful rebels lie, anonymous and forgotten.'[24]

In Boden's view, consistently acclaimed individuals have a better sense of domain-relevance than the rest of us. 'Their mental structures are presumably more wide-ranging, more many-levelled, and more richly detailed than ours.'[25] Such exceptional creatures can locate 'and transform high-level spaces much larger and more complex than those explored by other people ... Where we can do nothing, or at best mentally toss a coin, they are guided by powerful domain-relevant principles onto promising pathways.'[26] Thomas Edison is often quoted as saying that creativity is one per cent inspiration and ninety-nine per cent 'perspiration.' In Steiner's view the top level is for the very few; below them congregate the talented, industrious, ambitious creatures of the second class. And he insists:

> There are the elect and the almost chosen ... The actual divide may be formally or numerically trivial – a fractional point on an examination score, one hundredth of a second on the giant slalom, one black ball in the club committee or board room – but the gap yawns. It is non-negotiable.[27]

The attainment of official success seems merciless. This can induce a perverse view and a hierarchical mentality that we may hope will become obsolete. Testimonies to these torments are surprisingly rare as if the theme were almost a taboo. Perhaps we just mentally need some Olympic, stellar locus for 'superior' minds just as we make use of stars in every domain and, even worse, make use of charismatic leaders to give sense to our lives. In his *Unwritten Books*, Steiner paradoxically suggests that we may inflict both joy and desolation on ourselves by studying the works of official geniuses, by enhancing their celebrity, by pointing to the winners' success. 'We make ourselves the condemned shadows of these stronger lights.'[28] We voice support and try to disseminate the products of our leading stars; Montessori calls them *condottieri* (leaders). In some parasitic guise we appoint ourselves agents of their ascent and eminence. In the words of Steiner, 'Greatness has had its groupies since Pythagoras, its ancillary minstrels since Homer.'[29]

Goethe said quite openly that if he had not been 'condemned' to his talent, it would have been foolish of him to burden himself with the torment and the toil that are inherent in creativity.[30] There can of course be such a torment and toil if one is definitely inclined – 'condemned' – to an intense admiration for one's own creative capacities. The official genius must be able to be enchanted with his work, to be enthusiastic about it, and to ultimately be overcome by emotion. Referring to Leonardo, Freud acutely remarks:

> When, at the climax of a discovery, he could survey a large portion of the whole nexus, he was overcome by emotion, and in ecstatic language praised the splendour of the part of creation that he had studied ... This process of transformation in Leonardo has been rightly understood by Solmi.[31]

And he quotes from him: 'Such a transformation of natural science into a sort of religious emotion is one of the characteristic features of Leonardo's manuscripts and therefore there are hundreds and hundreds of examples of it.'[32] In other words, acclaimed creative minds must be enchanted with their own performances. But then, we could speculate that someone who is, or aims to become, an official creative individual and also adheres to the romantic idea that geniuses are somehow the 'chosen ones,' set apart from the rest of us, might not be inclined to an awareness of these torments, of his enchantment with oneself, in the pursuit of a stellar position – a place in the Olympus. And what one does not want to find, one does not so assiduously seek.[33] The strenuous compulsion to succeed may surreptitiously turn into an unassailable condescension and lack of appreciation, even disrespect, of others. To become an historically acclaimed figure cannot be easy either on the creator or on his immediate environment. We owe to Gardner a stimulating contribution on the 'exemplary personality' of highly creative renowned figures. Drawing on detailed personal memories of Freud, Stravinsky, Martha Graham, T.S. Eliot, Einstein, Gandhi and Picasso, he describes such people as single-minded, driven, ruthless and selfish.[34] And this is not surprising because if one is to transform a culturally significant space, this personality profile will be of great help.[35]

4. Features of ordinary genius

The thesis here is that creativity does not only refer to the end-products of the successful super minds; it largely regards the quality of what humans do in their obscure, ordinary trials. We could think of the creative approach as of the attitude of dealing with whatever reality in a creative way. We could contrast canonic creativity with our variegated, creative efforts to surpass compliance and seek ulterior dimensions in common life. The attitude is not quite that of genius proper, and can be expressed in Winnicott's incisive language:

> It is creative apperception more than anything else that makes the individual feel that life is worth living. Contrasted to this is a relationship to external reality which is one of compliance, the world and its details being recognized but only as something to be fitted in with, or demanding adaptation. Compliance carries with it a sense of futility for the individual and is associated with the idea that nothing matters and that life is not worth living. In a tantalizing way many individuals have experienced just enough of creative living to recognize that for most of their time they are living uncreatively, *as if caught up in the creativity of someone else*, or of a machine.[36]

The creative self, the 'I' of the personality, cannot be found in what we do out of compliance, however successful we may be at it. In fact, even in the absence of 'masterpieces,' of 'finished creations,' we can perceive expressions of our ordinary genius. If an artist in whatever field is primarily looking for success, then, in Winnicott's view, we can say that there is already some failure for that artist in the general domain of creative living. There are, however, paradoxical convergences between extraordinary and ordinary forms of creativity. Freud remarks, for instance, that even at the highest levels of creative expression there can be limits and failures. In fact the ordinary genius pursuing intersubjective ventures has often the feeling of not having accomplished much, and also feels that whatever he attempts may remain incomplete. We read in Freud's essay on Leonardo that after the most exhausting efforts to bring to expression in the work of art 'everything which was connected with it in his thoughts, he was forced to abandon it in an unfinished state and to declare that it was incomplete.'[37] It is also worthy of note that our mind's creative life presents paradoxical aspects because it is at once dependent upon others while considering itself autonomous in generating knowledge. In fact, reigning world views appear to both rely upon *and* disavow the role of 'the others' in their epistemic schemes. There would be no enclaves of 'pure creativity' or 'official genius' if they were not sustained by the connective forces of ignored ordinary geniuses. Moreover, our 'minor' geniuses seem to meet the challenges of life so efficiently as to relieve the production of historical genius from these burdens. Such 'lesser' functions of our mind and culture almost protect the expression of the 'higher' levels of creativity by steadily coping with relational vicissitudes on their behalf.

Official 'geniushood' is often idealised in a perverse, occult way, while ordinary creativity is more immune to these forms of idealisation. We may use acclaimed inventiveness as a way of remaining for ever passive spectators, devotees of acclaimed stars. What is worse is that once we have resigned from our own ordinary creativeness we tend to spend our life energies to attain tangible 'success' – something that will presumably compensate for our impossible creativity. And yet, we cannot argue against idealisation – without which human existence would be unendurable and which is the prerequisite for every access to the other, whether identificatory or erotic. Silverman criticises the smooth, automatic meshing of idealisation with culturally defined norms derived from the extraordinary minds. The cultural versions of our idealisations not only restrict value to certain objects smoothly declared as essentially valuable, but also render *other* objects unworthy of admiration.[38] The more we get to value ordinary creativeness the more we learn to idealise oppositionally and provisionally. The more we learn to idealise oppositionally and provisionally the more we accede into an outlook of plurality and uncertainty. And thus we need not fear what might appear as 'chaos.' Forthcoming is only a 'chaos' of plurality, plurivocity and differences that resist the reductivism of universality and univocity. Only to individuals constrained in a rigid conception of orthodoxy could multiplicity be interpreted as 'chaotic' in a derogatory sense. Not being sufficiently free for personal thinking and for creativity can be a major crippling conflict, aggravated by a latent sense of guilt about refusing to homogenise with the official sources of value, or about resisting the seductions of some idealised contributions.

When individuals recognise that this homogenisation can be detrimental to contacts with one's own deep subjectivity – perhaps the 'I' of the personality – they may be freer to overcome some perverse sense of guilt about the effort to be a spontaneous and separate person; indeed a sense of separateness which cannot, or should not, be resolved.

Perhaps at this point we should admit that there is no agreed language to try to approach the topic of unrecognised creativity; we must then use language in a slanted way: to twist terms somehow to try to capture what could otherwise escape, to extend terms so that they may include what a stricter vocabulary must leave out as indigestible elements. Alternatively, the terms must be slightly forced so that they may be open to more variation. Either we use language with a slight emphasis, or else we must be silent on what we most cherish. But if the twisting is done with moderation and discretion for the sake of enhancing the appreciation of our human complexity, it is likely that it will be tolerated. Starting from basic questions implies not jumping too early into compliance with an elegant and comforting jargon; it feels so good when any proper discourse is presented in a limpid, classical language, as when we are fluent in Freudian, Jungian, Lacanish, Bionish, etc. The sufficiently cultured interlocutors easily understand what we mean. It almost feels as if a choice of jargon is mandatory.

Kahn and Piorkowski reiterate that 'Fortunately creativity is possible ... in any field of endeavour.'[39] And we could add that it is also possible in trying to make some sense of our vicissitudes, in persistently trying to attain 'creative living.' Apart from what is due to our genetic inheritance – which might be minimal or maximal – it takes a genius to profit from sufficiently good nurture and to manage a reasonably good level of mental health. It takes a genius to be healthy and conscious enough to avoid being unduly damaged by others' toxic emissions or false self. We might say, 'Oh look, he is mentally healthy! How very fortunate!' But maybe it is not a question of luck but rather of inner creativeness. By refusing to be fixed in a fictional character derived by passively internalised world views, we can also monitor the dangers of mimetic subjection to whoever is most admired. At times, individuals may even be inclined to mute their passion for their profound identity in order to create a spurious harmony with the theorising that they most admire. The damaging attempt to be like-minded with the authorial authorities of a culture almost requires breaking the affective links that we have with our own creativeness. Doing this, however, impedes proper contact with one's constitutional self – and with one's potential for creativity. We may, thus, sadly abandon our sources of psychic growth in order to adhere to the constraining power – not 'force,' just 'power' – of whatever coalition of 'authors' comes to appear as the enlightenment of the moment.

Consensus on a definition of 'genius' is not presently possible, but we can agree with Eissler's statement that those designated as geniuses 'were persons who were capable of re-creating the human cosmos, or part of it, in a way that was significant and not comparable to any previous re-creation.'⁴⁰ But then, our ordinary geniuses do often re-create our inter-subjective cosmos; and 'cosmos' means beauty in a way that is essential to the persons involved, and certainly not comparable to any previous re-creation. Any analyst can easily testify to the stunning uniqueness of 'cases,' however comparable the pathologic expression. The ordinary genius creates micro-worlds for daily psychic survival. Just think that humans seem to constantly talk. The latent function of our incessant talking is perhaps a constant search for both therapy and creativeness. The ordinary geniuses who can creatively deal with an infant, with a moribund, with acute suffering in the vicissitudes of life, have not been specifically trained or instructed; they are indeed autodidactive, self-training beings who do not care much to imitate. As Kant acutely remarks, 'The proper field of genius is that of the power of imagination, because this is creative and, being less under the constraint of rules than other faculties, it is thus all the more capable of originality.' And the philosopher goes on: 'It is true that the mechanism of instruction is indeed disadvantageous to the budding of a genius as far as his originality is concerned, because instruction always requires the student to imitate.'⁴¹

5. Melanie Klein and the other side of genius

By way of illustration of what may happen when we are exposed to the work of an acclaimed genius of the calibre of Bion, Winnicott or Jung, we may look through a paper written by Melanie Klein – a most eminent contributor to our psychoanalytic culture. The paper is entitled 'The Family Romance in *Statu Nascendi*.' But then, in sorry fact, more than a 'romance' it may definitely come out as a disheartening story or drama. The title of the original work is 'Der Familienroman in *Statu Nascendi*,' first published in 1920 in the *Internationale Zeitschrift für Psychoanalyse*, and the child that the author talks about is her son Eric Klein. A subsequent paper, entitled 'The Development of a Child,' published in 1921, used parts of the previous paper. There perhaps in order to comply with objections to using clinical material regarding one's own child, the name of the little boy/patient was changed to 'Fritz.'⁴²

And so, even at that time there was presumably some perplexity regarding the possibility of presenting clinical material derived from experiences with one's own child. This may not be due to any consideration of children's rights; since parents 'love' them, why bother about rights? In fact, the reason may be of a different nature: if one's own child cannot be regarded as a 'proper' patient, then the clinical narrative cannot be regarded as proper 'scientific' material, and is therefore not legitimately utilisable for a psychoanalytic publication. Perhaps we could note in passing that 'children,' as subjects of right, only appeared in the twentieth century – just yesterday – and one never hears of them in the written heritage of centuries past. But I think of course that there have been innumerable unrecorded exceptions: our unsung ordinary geniuses, in fact. The problem with the paper, therefore, is that the contents might not be regarded as sufficiently 'scientific.' If that is the real difficulty, then the possibility that one's published clinical report could later on cause embarrassment to the grown up Eric, is not even remotely considered. The implication here is that there is no problem with divulging the inner torments of an identifiable little boy: Eric Klein. In Klein's 'diagnostic' report we read that 'in practical things and in his sense of reality he was very much behind other children of the same age.'[43] Not very flattering, especially if a friend or a spouse were to read that later. But here we only try to suggest that even though Klein was an acclaimed genius, she probably was not an *ordinary* genius.

The third paragraph of the paper consists of a block of 19 lines in which the laborious vicissitudes of Eric's cognitive development are described. To divulge the travails of a patient one usually encounters the disapproval of colleagues, whereas if one exposes the difficulties of one's own offspring there seems to be no problem, especially if it concerns a very young child – the youngest one. As we disregard the nakedness of a baby in distress we might also ignore the psychic nudity of a young child. It is thus possible that for the pursuit of one's scientific concerns, one may sacrifice the privacy of one's own children. While, in fact, the privacy of her older children and of her industrious housekeeper, Mrs S., are carefully protected, there is no ambivalence in the narrative about the privacy of a child who is described as 'retarded,' and also shown desperate, sobbing, defeated. But then, in the text it is also specified that Mrs S. in fact 'decided on matters regarding fruit and garden and in the household had a leading position in the management of things.'[44] She is perceived as an important person to deal with and as someone whose privacy must not be violated – not just as a 'little' one.

The most perplexing aspect of the whole story is that the translation into Italian of 'Der Familienroman in *Statu Nascendi*' elicited no comment whatsoever from the psychoanalytic community. But perhaps it would have been the same in any other country. In fact even a psychoanalytic milieu can be so prone to the admiration of genius that they may become psychically blind. And my subsequent article criticising this perplexing situation had no responses, of course.[45] From a psychoanalytic point of view the absence of any comments of Klein's paper is the most significant aspect of the whole event: our minds almost stop functioning when confronting accredited talent. Likewise, in reading this paper we may have a glimpse of the insidious danger of entirely identifying with one's own acclaimed capacities. Even the most brilliant of creatures can be afflicted by some kind of passivity that asphyxiates ordinary creativeness. The temptation to succumb to one's own acclaimed identity, to some inner phantasmal power, can be so intense that most of us are vulnerable to it. It could thus be instructive to ponder over the case presented by the celebrated Melanie Klein. We are often so dazzled by the brilliance of others, and even of ourselves, that we may incline to disregard the diverse and ulterior dimensions of a contribution; one is so intent upon capturing the enlightening contents that one can ignore the significance of the complex situation. It may thus happen that when we are exposed to an authoritative enchanting voice, one may not even think of listening to a less eloquent little voice. But let us try listening to it.

Probably in the intent of developing her son's insufficient sense of reality – 'well behind others' – Klein sees fit to give peremptory negative replies to questions regarding Easter rabbits bringing eggs, storks bringing babies, angels and devils. The style of the replies admits no rebuttals. For instance: 'When he asked whether the Easter rabbit existed or not, and when I clearly denied its existence, he accepted this piece of reality with visible disappointment.'[46] The author does not pause on the 'visible disappointment' of the child, as if it were entirely irrelevant with respect to the goal of proclaiming a piece of objective truth. But the little one does not give up defending his right to have his own (however unaccountable) inner world of beliefs derived from the housekeeper's children; and thus he strengthens his alliance with the children of Mrs S. – a more supportive and sharing relationship as compared to dealing with well-learned and authoritative persons. When Eric insists that the children of Mrs S. own a real Easter rabbit, Klein retorts that those children only own a normal rabbit, and not a magic one that brings Easter eggs; this last being fictional, false, inexistent. And then Klein adds: 'More or less at the same time Eric told me about the devil.'[47] Not only in the same period of time but also in the same paragraph, Klein includes the devil and the Easter rabbit, perhaps in order to be more effective in restoring the child's inadequate sense of reality. After all, intellectually, she is certainly not on the same level as her housekeeper. In the next paragraph there is an ulterior cognitive correction of little Eric. There seems to be no reason why a parent should put up with the unverifiable stories of children while she exactly knows which are the things that exist and those which do not exist. And so Klein shows to Eric that the 'brown devil' that he had seen in a nearby field was just a foal. And moreover she says that, 'It was then *easy* to prove to him, through his own eyes, that the big brown devil was just a foal!'[48] In the text there is of course an exclamation mark as if to emphasise the final triumph of objective truth. The question of whether or not it is beneficial to show to someone, 'with his own eyes', what we want him to see or not to see is entirely bypassed. There could be an implication here that not only now he would begin to see the world through her eyes, but also that he must realise that her eyes are his functional eyes and that without her eyes he could only be blind or delusional – and naughty.

On the same page as she narrates these episodes aimed to impart a notion of reality constructed by the knowing managers of culture, the proverbial 'children of the servant' are mentioned again: Eric strengthens his bonds with them and gradually decides to move to their place and live with them. Perhaps Eric was trying to exercise some right to cognitive autonomy and to develop by himself his view of reality – at his own pace. Perhaps he did not quite feel like immediately embracing the dictates of the knowledgeable adults. And Klein goes on about her intervention: 'He was only half convinced for it was not easy at all for him to relinquish this conviction.'[49] On the basis of her suggestions in fact, one after the other he should have abandoned all the 'wrong' beliefs of his inner imaginary world. Perhaps she wanted a dutiful disciple rather than a son. In fact there is an injunction to annul one's inner contents, so to speak, inasmuch as this is required by the knowing parent, the only emissary of reality. It seems moreover that the visible inner pain of the child should be ignored while also denying the negation. Indeed a sequence of attacks to his affective and imaginary world. In this way a child can feel guilty and insane at the same time.

We then read that a little later Eric asks: 'When I was not yet in this world, where was I?'[50] Obviously the very adult mother says that 'before coming into this world you were in my belly;' it seems here that all of the 'before' is circumscribed to his intrauterine life. But the brilliant child insists and says: 'But if I was within you, then I was in this world as well.' If less intimidated, the child might have continued in this way: I actually want to know where I was before existing inside you. And thus the gist of the answer to the question 'When I was not yet in this world, where was I?' could be that before inhabiting her belly he did not exist at all; fair enough. The narration goes on to say that in that same period the brave child refuses to return home from the garden and quit his little friends because he was determined to go and live with the children of the housekeeper.[51] But Klein is well in touch with reality: 'As I objected that the grass was wet and that he would catch cold, he replied that they had their little home there (a little covered lean-to room) and that they would be sleeping there together.'[52] Of course Eric is more concerned with psychic health than with physical health, and actively seeks some sort of sanctuary where to organise a more liveable inner life. Perhaps no child would be content with physiological health at the cost of sacrificing aspects of one's inner life. And we read: 'Some times he proclaimed himself a brother of the S. children.'[53]

Subsequently Eric also asks her: 'Mother, how does one make a child?'; 'I gave him a very detailed and exhaustive explanation; I told him that there are forty little oŏcytes (ovules) inside a mother and that from one oŏcyte an embryo develops, etc.'[54] In the 'very detailed and exhaustive explanation' there is no mention of sperms or of any male contribution, as if in an outlook of parthenogenesis; perhaps also implying that there would be no reproductive force in a little *boy*. Another perplexing passage in the narrative is where Eric proclaims himself the little brother of the S. children, and the son of Mrs S.: 'He already gave himself the name of Eric S.'[55] She then asks him whom *she* would have as a child. In a benevolent and fatherly manner, Eric answers: 'You already have J. and R. (his own brothers).'[56] She then objects that his brothers are older and says: 'I absolutely want a *small* child, and I could then get myself in your place as a small child your little friend Grete.'[57] *Questa o quella per me pari sono!* goes the aria of Don Juan (This one or that one are just the same for me!). And perhaps, assessing the interchangeability of persons is an incisive form of devaluation. It is tantamount to saying that I absolutely need a little one to cuddle whomever he/she may be and you are completely replaceable. But the very resilient little Eric insists and asks if she would continue to love him after having been replaced by Grete. (What would have happened if Grete – the little daughter of Mrs S. – had refused to leave her housekeeper-mother? The question does not even occur to no less a person as Melanie Klein.)

> My answer – that I would have of course loved Grete *instead* of him, visibly wounded him, but he controlled himself and became silent; and this was all the more surprising because the simple threat (*sic*) of becoming less loved had a profound impact on this extraordinarily vulnerable and affectionate little boy.[58]

After some hesitation he accepted the tough deal. But Klein persists and objects: 'What will happen if I will not permit that, and I will not let you go?' He replied in a decisive way, 'I will go just the same.' Indeed, a resilient boy.

> I nevertheless reminded him that he should first ask Mrs S. whether or not she wanted to have him in her home. After lunch he declared "Now I will go and ask Mrs S." I then made one last attempt: "Are you not sorry to leave us? Who will love you as much as your mother?" But he objected "Mrs S. will love me much more than you do!". In the afternoon he said "I have had her consent and I already live with them!"

The paper goes on, saying:

> I was able to realize the seriousness with which he conducted his new family relationship when he refused obedience to me ... He spoke of me as the mother of J. and R. He finally said "I do not want to speak to people such as you." It was a very uncharacteristic way for him to speak.

But then, just when Eric had hoped of experimenting with a more liveable psychic home, he found instead an accurately organised expulsion plot. Right after that, we read in the paper: 'We let the thing to its own course, but we suggested to Mrs S. to tell him that she was unable to accept him in her household, because something like that was really out of place.'[59] The Italian translation says '*fuori luogo*,' (out of place), something that should not enter the theatre scene – *ob-scaenam*, ('obscene'), unheard of. In the text Klein writes that 'We let the thing to its own course ...'; there is a *we* here rather than the usual *I*. There is perhaps an indirect reference to an unmentioned husband (only oöcytes for her) who would in any case approve her enlightened strategies; (but it could even be reminiscent of a *pluralis maiestatis*). Klein writes that she had in fact made direct arrangements with her housekeeper so as to annul Eric's project. It is usually considered inappropriate to speak about people behind their back; but of course with young children the question does not even arise. One could of course imagine that Mrs S. might have suggested something like this: 'Let him stay at my place for a while, and then we shall see what happens....' But of course Mrs S. did not even think of suggesting this possibility. In fact we read at the beginning of the paper that Eric posed questions regarding childbirth to his nanny 'who, contrary to the instructions received, had kept saying that the storks bring children and who *was therefore shortly after sacked.*'[60] And probably Mrs S., however 'important in the management of things,' must have been aware of the episode and unwilling to take risks.

And the sad story goes on in this way:

> At dinner time he was again in the children's room. I pretended I was very surprised and asked him why he was dining here and not at Mrs S.'s place. "I only want to live here" he mumbled. "But did they say anything to you at Mrs S.'s place?"; "The children said that it was only a joke," he added. But I did not want to make things that easy for him and I remarked with an indifferent tone "I want to personally speak to Mrs S. and find out whether or not she will keep you." His eyes filled with tears, and while sobbing he said "But even if she permits it, I do not want to live with her." "Why?" I asked him. "Because I love you so much, mother!"[61]

There is here no awareness of the possibility of inducing a paranoiac outlook by destroying one's solidarity and trust in friendship among peers. Also, it is reported that victims of abuse sometime express pleasure and gratitude in order to avoid even worse developments. We could note in passing that if the sobbing child says that he loves his mother so much, it cannot be untrue in Klein's view because it is in fact the child who proclaims that. It is not even speculated that perhaps the stifling of any inner voices is so accurate, and authentic listening so remote, that the child can only see and feel through the parent's mind. The text goes on saying that Eric told a nanny: 'Mother has been most sweet. You haven't seen us, but we gave each other many kisses and we are reconciled.'[62] He certainly paid a high price for reconciliation and peace. And yet, the implied conclusion seems to be that all is well on the western front. In fact this adhesive fusion with his beloved mother is perhaps the only possible way to attempt some coexistence; it is therefore an easy victory to extort a declaration of love in such a coercive situation.

GENIUS: ORDINARY AND EXTRAORDINARY

In the development of the family romance the genius extraordinary says:

> The situation was apparently resolved for him. He never spoke about it again and when – in spite of the instructions given to everybody not to ask him any questions on this topic – his brother had made an attempt to resume the matter with him, the little one declined.[63]

Traces must be carefully erased and solidarity discouraged. The text says that 'instructions were given to everybody not to mention the episode again.' Something reminiscent of the isolation methods used in certain political regimes. In this way Eric would not be able to share and metabolise his very difficult experience. We could note in passing that in illegal groups of any kind the most important unwritten rule is not to talk to anybody; those who speak rarely survive. In a psychoanalytic jargon, we could say that forclusion had become the rule in the family romance.

In the last pages of the paper some interpretations are expressed regarding Eric's desire to move into Mrs S.'s home with her children and especially with her little daughter Grete:

> I had the impression that my little boy – who has a sweet love for one of Mrs S.'s girls, has acted as so many young men do (without apparently confessing that); namely, together with the bride he also chooses new parents, as we frequently observe in the custom whereby a bride brings the new husband in her own family.[64]

The second explanatory thesis – which Klein concerted with Ferenczi – is as follows:

> With regard to the impulse to seek a different and better family – as the housekeeper's family must have necessarily appeared to him – it must have been stimulated by the unconscious desire to find persons who could rank higher in his evaluation, that is people who, in his conviction, were not born in such a banal way.[65]

That is, not just stemming from lonely ovules. But perhaps, more simply, there could have been some awareness that psychic survival would be easier with the *peasant* couple of Corinth rather than with the *royal* couple of Thebes. Both interpretations offered by Klein could be regarded as tentative and debatable. But what is remarkable is a clinical, interpretative attitude directed towards her own child. As if she had simply absorbed, rather than debated, the more controversial aspects of the psychoanalytic culture at that time; a culture that even allowed taking into analysis one's own offspring. Reference is of course to Freud's analysis of his daughter Anna; and, as is known, Freud admits that there would have been more difficulties with his son. Of course we could forever explore the blind side of any of our acclaimed geniuses just as we could always find psychic blindness in the simplest of persons. The point we try to make is that perhaps all creatures are constantly vulnerable to the asphyxiation of ordinary creativeness. Here we could perhaps invoke a simple remark by Marcus Aurelius: 'I have learned to observe that ... generally those among us who are called "patricians" are rather deficient in paternal affection.'[66]

5

THE CONNECTIVE FUNCTION

1. Creative connections and their defaults

We could tentatively think of psychic health as of a sufficiently well connected inner world, and we could also think of Winnicott's notion of 'living creatively' in terms of a capacity to combine, adjoin and integrate personal experiences.[1] We do not of course adhere to a Cartesian myth of the mind as a bounded, united centre of awareness; we cannot lose sight of our ineliminable conscious and unconscious components that we struggle to reconnect with our whole personality. Transactions between people's official selves and their 'shadows' – those aspects of the personality that are sometimes exceedingly difficult to include and that we even tend to reject – do not receive much attention from standard culture and thus remain disconnected. By contrast, they are sometimes cleverly treated by imaginative writers.

Freud at times insists that 'You can analyse the elements inside a person but the actual job of *bringing them together and making something*, that is nothing to do with the analyst.'[2] The creative activity of the analysand is the effort to connect parts and make them into a whole; a process comparable to joining together disparate colours and notes in a work of art. By contrast, the condition of living uncreatively, of being incapable of inventing connections and of being dispersed in external identifications – our celebrated 'alienation' – cannot simply be accounted for as the psychic residue of a problematic society. This condition remains a very personal problem, indeed a default in connective creativity. Freud thus suggests that the psychoanalyst analyses, but the synthetic function, that is the process whereby parts become integrated, 'is provided by the patient.' This is the analysand's own response: elements are not expelled but are repossessed and put together. Through analysis, 'The great unity which we call the ego fits into itself all the instinctual impulses which before had been split off and held apart from it' – remarks Freud, rather hopefully.[3] And also, 'The psycho-synthesis is thus achieved during analytic treatment without our intervention, automatically and inevitably,'[4] he adds, even more hopefully. He must have had in mind the most creative of patients. These remarks by Freud are primarily invoked to highlight the relevance of our connective capacities, of our ordinary genius constantly at work.

In her life cycle the ordinary genius soon begins to connect and metabolise whatever is received from others in order to give birth to her inner life; it is just not a matter of having been born at a certain time but of subsequently being born in a constant creative itinerary. Not simply 'I was born,' but rather 'I am being born,' 'I am giving birth to myself.' From this enduring experience derives the Eros, pathos and logos that shape our destinies: and perhaps there are fleeting moments, blinks of experience when these may converge into awareness. And it is for us to *cultivate* just these attitudes so as to make of nature some sort of garden, some inclusive composition: a more liveable place. But then, not even in a garden can we find peace; there is always a hissing presence promising shortcuts to integration and maturity – to be obtained by means of little tricks. Just eat a particular piece of fruit and that will remedy the disproportion, the distance between heavens and earth. At this point, whatever labour to include and cope with is no longer necessary. We just succeed with a little trick bringing permanent results – a delusion. There is nothing idyllic or romantic in our human creativeness because we are ambivalent and contradictory creatures; creativeness of course does not truly reign in our lives, but it would be a pity if it were unduly smothered. We oscillate between carbon and diamond, between comedy and tragedy, trying to weave a personal story. When we deal with human creativeness we must resort to a circuitry of metaphors pointing to something that does not admit to being described. And yet it is something quite real that helps us mediate, medicate and meditate. It is a topic that should be approached from several different perspectives so that it may become psychically 'tangible' and perhaps even theorisable.

Our ordinary genius consists of doing and seeing something ulterior, something interpretable beyond what is seen, done or perceived. It is the necessity of reconnecting the empirical approach with a hermeneutic approach. It is an interpretive understanding that cannot be severed from any doing. As Cyrulnik reiterates, resilience calls for repairing the real blow, *followed* by a repair of the representation of that blow. A master in coping with extreme situations, Cyrulnik writes that,

> A child who has been washed and fed and bandaged will do better in the here and now, and clearly one has to do these things. But if the bandaging is not *felt, imbued with meaning and direction*, the child will return to the street. Everything will have to be done over again from the beginning, only this time the child is secretly blamed, – After all we have done for you![5]

In a Kleinian perspective, we could say that we do things in phantasy and thus we might be tempted to contrast phantasy and reality, and thereby come to believe that when something is done in phantasy it is not really done at all. And yet in Klein's view, phantasy with a 'ph' refers to a specific domain of action: the psychic and affective reality. In fact, in our inner world we can do things that are real and unbearably ambivalent – thus, disconnected. By converse, our search for an equally real struggle for connection and integration can be regarded as a proper work of genius. Symington provides a synoptic view of the issue when he dares to ask the crucial question, 'How does the mind fashion unawareness, unconsciousness, of what it does? The answer is, I believe, startlingly simple: it is that consciousness is the product of parts in harmony, and unconsciousness is the product of parts in antagonism.'[6] Creativeness is the art of increasing connections rather than the sloth to let splitting indefinitely reproduce. The development of such mediating, connective forces is perhaps the expression of our daily itinerary to living creatively. In Symington's words:

> It is, of course, very uncomfortable – unpleasurable, if you like – for me to realize that I am damaging my own mind and that of others. It is the knowledge of what I do that produces the unpleasure ... We cannot do evil; we cannot do what is damaging to our mind and to that of others – and know it.[7]

After all, even in our physiological life the appropriate connection of elements is health while disconnection is illness. Self-awareness arises through a relation between parts. The labour of the creative act lies in being confronted with those parts of ourselves that we tend to disown. Symington insists that 'Psychoanalysis examines in fine grain ... those forces that prevent freedom, that rob us of our human birthright.'[8] But not quite: it is a birth-'right' only to the extent that we succeed in activating our connective function. An excessive detachment from our inner sources of curiosity for the sake of a lucid and coherent intellectual discipline becomes close to a schizoid attitude insofar as it denies the profoundly affective fabric of all of our culture. In Eissler's view, we should in fact marvel at the degree of harmony that surrounds the achievement of genius insofar as the end-product is a synthesis of the infantile and adults worlds; of repressed contents and contents that are approved by a demanding self-critical ego; of the rational and the irrational.[9]

A synoptic view of contemporary philosophical works on the popular topic of emotion seems to ultimately present the 'modern affects' as docile creatures that are only prone to cause 'minor' perturbations such as righteous indignation at hunger in the world, or temporary embarrassment over being corrected. It must be said that grief and joy, terror and fascination are also sometimes listed, and nicely described. Writers of literature, on the other hand, can touch the more horrendous topics with the pre-emptive stipulation that their work is, of course, 'fiction.' Apart from the attention from the psychoanalytic domain, the awesome qualities, disquieting details and unthinkable combination of affects are largely ignored. Paradoxically, they are often left in the hands of our ordinary mediating, medicating, meditating geniuses wherever they can be found. The affects that destroy or constrain inner life are left in charge to whoever is around, to those who are entrusted with, or who cannot escape from, harbouring them: they become the bearers of devastating affects, even though they are alone and unprepared. We could note in passing that according to Gilligan, women tend to form decisions based upon the imperative to maintain relationships, to enhance connectivity, while men tend to be guided more by principles based on appeals to autonomy and individual rights.[10] As if there were basically two ways of wrong doing: against oneself and against the other. And hence the two interlocked questions: on the one hand, 'Why not let the capacity for care spring to life?'; and 'Why hinder the development of self-affirmation?' on the other. Both can be included.

To better grasp the relevance of connectiveness and the consequences of its insufficient development, we could take a closer look at inner disconnections. Splitting could be seen as an *innocuous* trick, while it ultimately amounts to damaging one's own self. According to Symington, 'An action whereby I smash up my own mind is the archetypal evil, and this action of its nature fashions unconsciousness.'[11] And unconsciousness is attained in order not to know the self-damaging evil that we do. By way of 'clinical' example we could here refer to the not-so-strange case of Doctor Jekyll and Mr Hyde.[12]

As is known, Doctor Jekyll recognises early in life that his medical ambitions are in conflict with his inclination to dissolute behaviour. He thus manages to separate the two inclinations so that each can pursue its interests without the interference of the other.[13] According to Midgley, he seems to embrace the view that man is not truly one but actually two, ultimately to be known 'for a mere polity of multifarious, incongruous and independent denizens.'[14] But of course Dr Jekyll the respected physician did not think of this as a dangerous venture requiring a drastic disconnection, but rather as an equal distribution of power to the two parts, perhaps functioning on a time-sharing basis.[15] The 'clever' Dr Jekyll simply regards this stratagem (expedient) as a sign of brilliance that will allow the pristine Jekyll the pleasures of dissipation while safeguarding his own social image. A very smart trick, functioning on the hypothesis that it 'does not matter what you do with your shadow;' in fact, a misleading hypothesis based on the wrong understanding of inner splitting. At first obsequious, the segregated part may rapidly grow increasingly intrusive and reduce the pristine inventor of splitting tricks to the role of its servant. When resisted it may even kill. Dr Jekyll illusorily believes that he can shift from integration to fragmentation in order to maintain his medical reputation. The main point here is that vanity – a cult for our social image – is not the worst of the vices; the problem is instead that it makes all the other 'deadly sins' appear unacceptable, truly unbearable in view of one's reputation. And so vanity necessarily leads to projective, splitting policies. According to Midgley, 'The acknowledged shadow may be terrible enough. But it is the unacknowledged one which is the real killer.'[16] In fact Dr Jekyll has not so much become 'two persons,' as ceased to be anybody. The specificity of our talent for healing is to invent linking strategies instead of falling to the more vacuous and damaging projective inclinations – because of course we can only project what we have previously split.

When we seek motivational factors of ordinary creativity we find individuals who can provide some sort of explanation. By contrast, in the case of destructive plans, the motivations provided by perpetrators are not so clear. Midgley's acumen points out that when we look for someone who conceived a self-damaging plot, we often cannot find him at all. Why? Because when we seem to have found one, we often find a number of 'parts of the self' with no clear connection with one another.[17] And that 'person' appears sincere – while lying all the time. The segregated parts always lie when speaking for the individual, whole person – forever innocent and wicked. In such cases, we might give up for causes rooted in human motivations, and must fall back on other sorts of explanations in the theoretic domain of death wishes and repetition compulsion. If we could think of illness and death as of a living system falling apart, then divisive plots could perhaps be better perceived. And so the creativeness involved in our connective processes no longer appears as a benign, sentimental psychic luxury – the celebrated desire for creativity – but rather as a means of survival. This is congruent with the general idea that it is the 'essential' creative nature of the mind's life that is sane when it governs the events, and is ill when it fails to do so. We cannot ignore agency (as contrasted to passivity) and so even in early life we are active in our connectiveness. But then the question remains whether something that is mechanically split may subsequently become autonomous and even rule us from within, turning into a secret Mr Hyde.

We could thus answer Winnicott's radical question of why we should seek and enhance 'living creatively' with a rather simple reply: in order to survive. In fact the belief that we 'cannot understand' a destructive conduct is probably misleading because it leads us to treat evil unrealistically, as something entirely alien; and so we misunderstand it and ignore our own contribution to it. Perhaps what we acutely need is to recognise that the problem of evil is a real one, rather than accepting the 'benevolent' assurance that culture tends to offer: that everything is basically all right.[18] Sheer credulity about such an 'assurance' is often an important part of our difficulties. And moreover, an essential aspect of being a person is the creative combination of good and bad components; an individual who primarily splits and therefore obliterates the 'wickedness' in himself is doomed to be largely a 'non person': 'The worse the savagery' – says Symington – 'the better hidden it must be. In order to hide the savagery, it is frequently necessary to hide the whole person.'[19] The individual is thus tempted to homogenise himself with whatever collective identifications offer usable ideals of a meliorist, progressive, idealised humanity, and thus disowns fearsome inner currents into surrounding groups. This we have seen with our own eyes in recent history.

2. Creative connections and relational progress

If we cannot increase our connective capacity we may have to decrease the elements that we can accept – to the detriment of whatever relation. In an intra-psychic perspective, the connective function could be seen as an inner capacity for communication and processing. In an enlightening synoptic view, Grotstein remarks that this is ultimately communication between the 'dreamer who dreams the dream' and the 'dreamer who understands the dream' – that is, the 'ineffable subject of the unconscious' and the 'phenomenal subject of consciousness,' respectively.[20] These experiences of creative connections could also be appreciated in terms of 'present moments,' in the sense and scope developed by Stern.[21] In his view, our vicissitudes of creativeness 'are so obvious that they usually go unnoticed. They are hidden in full view'[22] – paradoxically. In a psychoanalytic setting the talent for connections unfolds in an interwoven progression of intra-psychic and inter-subjective experiences. These connective ventures are well described by Stern who remarks that relational progressions basically trace a pattern of change; the therapist and the patient have to construe what is happening to the relationship as it unfolds, taking into account somehow where it has just come from and where it seems to be going. And he writes:

> One single present moment is clearly not sufficient for this task ... We need a subjective process unit that is intermediary in size, larger than a single present moment and shorter than a whole session. Several occur within a session. I call these sequences "relational progressions" because they carry a sense of movement toward relational end-points or resting places within a session.[23]

The question is when interpretations should be made, or held off, in order to remain inside the co-created dyadic process; we could thus 'kindly' wait until it has run a fuller course. This question probably indicates that 'The emphasis *shifts* temporarily from intra-psychic content to inter-subjective regulation'[24] and the basic rule in these circumstances is probably an attitude of sincere 'kindness.' However one chooses to define the shift, as psychoanalysts we know that in the course of a session we frequently shift. As we assiduously listen, imagery, ideation and our own feeling states alternate with 'theoretical' evaluations. As is known, in a transferal relationship primary unconscious processes and secondary conscious evaluations operate hand in hand. This requires flexibility and courage, even a bit of rebelliousness, to resist the pressures to conform to generally accepted theories. Kahn writes that 'These pressures stultify and rigidify thought and inhibit the formulation of new transformations.'[25] In fact it takes courage to spend one's life as an ordinary creative therapist.

If we now opt for an extra-analytic perspective, for our common coexistential world, we could say that our friendships are time/space conditions where our capacity for life is nourished by others by means of presence and fidelity through changes. If we discover new wavelengths of presence, then we can find our essential and detoxifying nourishments: a friend is one who can see our shadows and then be a mirror for so much *more* than our shadows. It means embracing the 'saint' and the 'demon' in the other person. But a 'kindness' that embraces the shadows requires a slow blossoming over years; this is the real measure of our adventures with one another. As it happens with some patients, when the rage and the fury have been at least partially metabolised, a different perspective begins to emerge.

Gardner reports Poincaré stating that anyone can make new connections between mathematical expressions, but

> to *create* consists precisely in not making *useless* combinations and in making those that are *useful*, and which are only a small minority: invention is discernment, choice ... Among chosen combinations the most *fertile* will often be those formed by elements drawn from domains which are far apart.[26]

There seems to be a resonance of our human talent for relating, actually for getting in *touch* in a creative way, even in the formal domain of mathematics; the process depends in fact upon our imaginative capacity to link and make 'good' connections between 'domains which are far apart' or at a great qualitative distance from one another. It probably takes more creativity to establish cultural exchanges with 'savages' or fearsome extra-terrestrials than to enjoy comfortable interactions with neighbouring states. If the term 'connection' seems too abstract, we could think in terms of 'touching' and say that when these occurrences of 'touch' become real, they seem so natural, so obvious that, paradoxically, they may even go unnoticed as if they were hidden in full view.

Perhaps we could think of a 'catalyst' as an element that favours chemical or, for our purposes, 'alchemical,' reactions generating precious novelties. In Phillips' and Taylor's view, our ordinary 'kindness' is a component, or a facilitating environment, for connective relations at all levels of intensity.[27] And also, we could juxtapose this talent for *inner* integration to the most disparate ways of interpersonal kindness with very different people; but of course we refer to the 'strong' kindness of empathy rather than to the 'weak' kindness of sympathy. As we know, while sympathy is a natural inclination, empathy is a creative venture. Paradoxically it is a way of knowing and being known that almost exceeds our capacities. Sympathy is the inclination for very 'short' psychic moves that may not go beyond our narcissistic sphere; empathy is a capacity for more extensive moves that reach the difference-bearing features of others.[28] Whenever the expression of our inner world is articulated by our official geniuses, and deprived of our personal touch, we lose the creative insight for coping with unpredictable consequences in the vicissitudes of hope and dread, attachments and separations. Such a surrender of one's creative propensities to the stellar managers of culture could be seen as inducing the atrophy of one's kindly creativeness. The authorial authorities, the articulate geniuses, may in fact express views that are not at all essential to one's personal creativity.

According to Phillips and Taylor, it is all too easily assumed that people are basically selfish, and that fellow feeling is either a weakness, a luxury or perhaps a more sophisticated form of selfishness.[29] In this outlook, kindness becomes something we are sentimental about, a longing for something that we fear may not really exist. In this connection we could recall Schwartz-Salant suggesting that 'gold-making,' or the generation of value, was not the major concern of 'alchemy' but rather was part of the alchemical metaphor for personality transformation. She writes that 'Alchemy was a system of transformation, and its genius lay in the assumption that change was part of an interaction between subject and object in which both were transformed.'[30] And no gold-seeking was involved.

To put it as simply as possible, it seems that after Freud people are no longer suffering from 'sexual frustration;' they seem to be labouring with loneliness and isolation. Phillips and Taylor insist that

> Either modern people were suffering because they were having the wrong kind of sex, or sexuality should be regarded as a kind of privileged – and perhaps over-privileged – metaphor for what goes on between people. Either there were secrets we needed to know about sexuality in order to get it right, or our sexuality was part of the larger exchange called relationship.[31]

In fact, we are now most concerned with individuals who cannot exchange anything with us. And psychoanalysis tells us that the capacity to exchange, of becoming subjects who can see themselves as part of an exchange, is a developmental achievement – definitely a creative advance. In Phillips' and Taylor's view, sincere kindness is an exchange entailing unpredictable developments: 'It is a risk precisely because it *mingles* our needs and desires with the needs and desires of others, in a way that so-called self-interest never can.'[32] In Janet Soskice's gaze, kindness is a way of being transformed and of being known beyond our understanding of it: 'Love to the loveless shown, that they might lovely be.'[33] We are kind whenever we involve ourselves with 'strangers' coming from different stages in the life cycle, from faraway places, from different illnesses. In Phillips' and Taylor's view, 'Kindness is potentially far more promiscuous than sexuality.. People have long known this, and long forgotten it. The history of kindness.. tells the story of this knowing, and forgetting, and re-knowing, as central to western ideas about the good life.'

And that the ethics of kindness has not made much progress 'is the truly sinister symptom of modern life.'[34]

In describing the counter-position of the unconscious constantly interacting with consciousness, Jung makes several references to the (creative?) *rhythm* between consciousness and unconsciousness. We could note in passing that, viewed more dynamically, what emerges is a pattern of oscillations between two polarised or disparate psychic states. And Jung invokes Goethe's analogy of the rhythmic breathing of a heart: 'Goethe's idea of a systole and a diastole seems to have hit the mark intuitively. It may well be a question of a vital rhythm, of fluctuations of vital forces.'[35] Miller suggests that we tend to describe psychological phenomena and structures in static terms, possibly as a defence against the overwhelming feeling that might be caused were we to acknowledge how fluid, changing and even unstable we are. And Miller insists that 'geniushood' seeks connections in seemingly unconnected things, indeed in all things. It sees all dualities as neither one or the other but rather as being related in some way. Unlike science, which focuses on the ways in which things are structured, creativeness concerns itself with the relationships and fluctuations in any system.[36] Perspicacity is the embodiment of the process in which opposites or differences are held, where the choice between either one or the other is suspended so that the relationship between them becomes the focus.

Perhaps our judicious kindness facilitates complex processes of connection by contributing to the *ground work* for development. Stern in fact asks why or how relational progressions are concluded or come to a rest, making a temporary unit.[37] This is a key clinical point. The awareness of a relational progression comes into consciousness as an emergent property. And of course there are different types of relational progressions, each describing a differently felt story. These differences are elaborated out of awareness, until the relational progression is 'ready' to emerge into consciousness. At this point, according to Stern, the progressive pattern is assembled and surfaces in a fresh 'present moment' in which it is grasped. And he significantly concludes that this is possible because 'Most of the *ground work* has already been done'[38] – probably the ground work of kindness. In a broader perspective, the idea that psychic attitudes possess a certain interdependence is an intuitively plausible thesis. This interdependence derives from relations with other attitudes. As a consequence of this hypothesis, any change in the relations that constitute a system will result in a qualitative change in the system overall. The interdependence of attitudes also seems to imply the absence of any independent ground from which a generic cognitive gaze may proceed. We try, in fact, to privilege the question of the enhancement – or inhibition – of those intersubjective connections that are the sources of our creative thinking. From this perspective, the desire for life-enhancing connections acquires visibility as one of the essential ways of human creativity. According to Miller, genius mediates between opposites and prompts the emergence of a new, third attitude that transcends the two.[39]

Although not belonging to language proper, common bodily behaviour is a way of expressing things that cannot (yet) be articulated. And the transition from behavioural expression to symbolic articulation might also be regarded as the initial capacity to link seemingly alien domains. It is our specific genius for developing connections between biological life and mental life that ultimately enhances the development of our creativity. And, needless to say, this progression requires an atmosphere of kindness. Gesturing philosophers engaged in friendly conversation are portrayed in Raphael's painting known as *The School of Athens*: Plato pointing his index finger in the direction of the heavenly spheres, and Aristotle moving down his hand towards the earthly grounding of things. Although centuries apart between them – but inside the same picture – these philosophical gestures are suggestive of which would be the main trajectories of our nascent western philosophy – roughly, idealism and empiricism. And yet, these bodily, ageless, expressions are not only an ostensive indication of our main cultural orientations: they can also be seen as a gesturing conversation, as the everyday movements that concur to shape creative *relational* connections. The two philosophers moreover appear as involved in a leisurely walk, not in a sharp debate requiring a 'moderator.' Our connective genius may consist in the disposition to forge links between the primal expressions of our living condition and ulterior levels of expression, thus inducing a circulation of interdependencies, a virtuous circle; an enterprise that is both very serious and very playful as is our ordinary, daily creativeness.

3. The capacity to include

There are perhaps a number of psychic elements that are essentially primitive, fragmented or simply so dangerous that they are not easily usable for mental integration. And thus, in *all* of our interactions we are constantly confronting the choice between, on the one hand, restricting whatever it is that we have to face within our limits; and on the other hand, opting for the creative challenge of developing and perfecting our inner capacities for containment and processing. As Ferro suggests, we have to either diminish contents or else increase the container; this is the challenge of psychic growth.[40] Paradoxically we could say that most people, including therapists, face choices comparable to those of the mentally ill person. Grotstein tries to summarise this predicament in a hypothetic collective statement, as if an emissary of the more severely damaged people were saying:

> The truth of the matter is that I cannot face truth because I know the truth all too well, having not been sufficiently shielded from it, and I know the limitations of my inner resources (my alpha function) to deal with it – and that's the truth.[41]

A provocative and enlightening assessment of our very frail and very precious capacity to include, and connect, and grow.

Phillips quotes Winnicott, suggesting that through creative expressions we can hope

> to keep in touch with our primitive selves whence the most intense feelings and even fearfully acute sensations derive. We are poor indeed if we are only sane ... We grow up to protect ourselves from these feelings; and then, as adults, we call this defence "sanity."[42]

Phillips believes that 'For Winnicott the question was not what can we do to enable children to be sane, but what can we do, if anything, to enable adults to sustain the sane madness of their young minds.'[43] Nothing less than that. Of course there are no rules for this critical inclusionary venture. And perhaps a basic attitude of kindness is the prerequisite (Stern's *'ground work'*) for the whole enterprise. In other words, kindness somehow opens us up to the world of other people in ways that we long for and dread. How can people, from childhood onwards, feel confident enough to take such risks? We often say that a certain person is 'very kind.' Why? In what way? We could tentatively say that kind people – in the most disparate and desperate situations – tend to include *more* of our dimensions and do not restrict themselves to sharing a bare minimum. Our ordinary geniuses seem capable of being kind, and of doing just that. If one is an ordinary genius one can talk in terms of his own intuition of the value of kindness, rather than just conform with the cultural inertia of rudeness and benumbment. But of course kindness makes us seriously vulnerable. Vulnerability is the acceptance of more and more elements to process. If we do not want to process them we just do not perceive them and exclusion becomes automatic – as if forclusion were established as a rule. Psychoanalytic authors depict in different degrees of closeness what happens in us when things go wrong. One of the points of emphasis is that our basic internalising capacity can become damaged, and when this happens our ability to 'digest,' to process both emotional nutrients and poisons, is injured. In Eigen's view, the ultimate paradox of our psychic vicissitudes is that we can be damaged by bonds that give us life, disabled by connections that help us grow, succoured by processes that hurt us.[44] But then, even if the capacity to include may make us vulnerable, perhaps we have much more to gain from vulnerability than from exclusionary control. 'Sanity' as an ultimately superficial quality is a caricature of mental life. Phillips again: 'For the more deeply sane, whatever else sanity might be, it is a container of madness, not a denier of it.'[45]

Winnicott encourages us to take on, to almost welcome, our own turbulence. It is the capacity to be disturbed by our own feelings and to be nourished by the disturbance that we are promoting. Our pseudo-sanity can be the way we sever connections to the feelings and experiences that matter most to us. The 'sanity' that we seek out as a refuge from fear can also be a way of curtailing ourselves. What was being called madness was, for the 'anti-psychiatrists' of previous decades, simply the return of all the complexities and nuances that so-called sanity wanted to exclude. It is as though there had been a narrowing of the idea of identity and that the approved name for this sort of narrowing should be 'sanity.' As is known, when too much is excluded, it is not sane to be normal – and we turn into McDougall's 'normotic' creatures.[46] What there is to grow out of is something akin to an original madness; what there is to acquire is the creativeness to include this madness. And thus sanity rests on the patience to connect things and to endure the connection. This is the talent for making patience a creative asset.

If it is the genius of the theorist/therapist to take the raw material of the subjective world and try to hold it into a form that opens up new vistas, then the limitations of any theoretical outlook are implicit in that same personal, creative attempt. But then, paradoxically, we could say that a theory is especially successful to the extent that it excludes some of our less visible features. These features, or dimensions, are not thought of as a sequence of ulterior, adjacent spaces. No, we can only think of 'ulterior' dimensions that occupy one and the same personal inner space/time. And again, in James' words: 'Why may not the world be so complex as to consist of many interpenetrating spheres of reality?'[47] There are in fact aspects of any emerging theory that constrain vision and produce rigidity by adhering to reified superstructures. Through such reifications, each theorist's solution to dilemmas and nuclear crises becomes frozen in a static intellectual system that looks like an indisputable vision of 'objective' inner reality. There are too many dangers in connectivity. And yet, if we are to act effectively with our psychic world, some sort of simplified 'map' of the mind, some theory, seems necessary. But theories tend to omit different things, distort and obscure others. And so we cannot do without our ordinary creativeness. We could think of 'ordinary genius' as of a metaphor for our mind's yearning to develop connections rather than separations, to personally savour the unknown rather than asserting whatever knowledge we have. Creativity can expand ubiquitously where there is a shift away from knowledge/control, and towards a propensity for inclusion – even at the cost of becoming vulnerable, of accepting an 'excess' of psychic currents.

In Eigen's view, trauma speaks in dreaming, and dreaming spins webs around trauma in order to digest it at least partially. The fact that dreaming does not stop means that we never really give up on integrating ourselves. And he says: 'Dream-work incessantly signals states of self, often mangled, strangulated threads of being, dangers, obstacles, impossibilities – and refuses to stay still. Dream-work is in constant motion. It does not stop trying to digest the indigestible.'[48] Our interpretations are insistent attempts 'to digest the indigestible.' In certain therapeutic schools there is a tendency to provide very early and very frequent interpretations. But these may force the direction of the dyadic process along specific intellectual lines, thus excluding and leaving unexplored the unique and disquieting lines that are the difference-bearing features of the individual. As if we were sadly shaping the patient's inner world into a Freudian, Kleinian or Lacanian mind. Attention to the 'historic' flow of the sessions has implications for viewing and dealing with the quality of the therapeutic process, its unpredictability and spontaneity. This is a *travail de patience*. Our secret little genius is spirited enough to sprint out of the entire situation and bravely attempt a perspectival gaze. We must have the kindness to be patient as we listen to the 'sleeping beauty' within the analysand or within ourselves, in order to await the emergence of meaning or significance;[49] and only then we reconnect it to the celebrated 'whole personality.' Bion also describes wild thoughts that are the equivalent of Michelangelo's 'prisoners' in the marble, the 'unborn' ones:

> If you can be wide open, then I think there is a chance that you might catch some of those wild thoughts. And if you allow them to lodge in your mind, however ridiculous, ... however fantastic, then there may be a chance of having a look at them. That is a matter of daring to have such thoughts – never mind whether you are supposed to have them or not – and keeping them long enough to be able to formulate what they are.[50]

Patience and kindness, again, as a price for creativity.

We may explicitly formulate theories and consciously use them to guide our behaviour. But, if we entirely adhere to a chosen model, we may ultimately delude ourselves. For in the back of our minds are hidden assumptions and prejudices that determine how we use our models and perceive reality, what facts we include and how we judge their relevance. In Husserl's phenomenology, the 'technique' of bracketing reality is designed to turn our attention from the *objects* of my consciousness to the *consciousness* of those objects, to the way I perceive these elements of reality.[51] Of course there is no risk of discarding the object of experience by placing it within parentheses, as if we were not sure of its existence, or as if we reduced it to our 'idea' of the celebrated 'object of experience.' Rather, the 'phenomenologist' retains her intentional relation to the world but turns her attention to the way in which her own experience is directed to the world – inner and outer – to the objects-just-as-she-experiences-them. At times of great intensity or distress we all become 'phenomenologists.' In a desperate situation we may be impotent; but in a phenomenologic outlook we can somehow become free observers of our condition. In fact the problem of inclusion is central to Husserl's theory of intentionality, in the sense that every experience represents its objects through a specific formation of meaning, without which there cannot be coherent consciousness, but only a kaleidoscopic sequence of sensations and mental states. Phenomenology is some special type of first person reflection on experiences in which we develop descriptions of key forms of consciousness. In this outlook we try to 'bracket' the object that we actually see, and turn our attention instead to the way we experience it. The 'technique' of bracketing may thus aid us to systematically include, rather than exclude, even the more disquieting features of experience; we just let them happen. And so we could enhance our capacity to include even in the absence of exceptionally good theories with which we could elaborate on our experiences. Mitchell remarks that 'It is hard to imagine a time when any one theoretical perspective will demonstrate such compelling reasonableness and truth that proponents of the others will change ranks, and psychoanalysis will once again be whole.'[52] Such victory over competitors might fasten us to theoretical views that may ultimately hinder our creative capacity to include.

6

THE 'I' OF THE PERSONALITY

1. Preliminary remarks

The thesis here is that the recognition of the 'I' of the personality is not an automatic, mechanical process; it is in fact generated and maintained by our daily creativeness. Reflections on this creative capacity derive, of course, from contributions of authors such as Bion, Bollas, Ferro, Fromm, Grotstein, Lear, Meissner, Modell, Rosenfeld, Schaefer, Siegel and Winnicott. I shall thus try to present what amounts to converging notes regarding our increasing appreciation of our inner 'I.'

Perhaps we could initially say that the 'I' of the personality is our primary 'agent' in the attempt to view the internal working of our minds. It enables us to be aware of our mental processes without being swept away by them; it allows us to get ourselves off the ingrained behaviour, the habitual responses, and helps to move us beyond the reactive loops in which we may become fixed. And Siegel incisively remarks: 'Consider the difference between saying "I *am* sad," "I *feel* sad." '[1] The focusing attitude that is part of mindsight makes it possible to see what is inside us, and also try to transform it. If there is no 'I' to observe the variegated vicissitudes of the ego, we might not fully recognise them and thus all too simply we may identify with them; and the ego may ensnare us into homogenising with it again and again. As the clever mediator between unconscious drives and reality, the ego is so tightly organised that it can engulf us without a chance of realising that there is something else in us. This ultimately means that it may take us over, as some kind of false self pretending to be who we really are, and what makes the recognition possible is the increase of consciousness through the 'I' of the personality. We cannot *fight* against the repetitiveness of egoic structures and win; rather than fighting we need the activity of our innermost agency of consciousness.

According to Symington there is in each of us an 'embryo mind' that is capable of developing into a creative source of mental perspicacity: 'It does not grow into an autonomous mind by a natural instinctive progression, but *through cumulative acts of personal insight.*'[2] We each have a sense of our own particular style of self-organisation: a personal 'signature' – according to Spence –;[3] the 'uniquely personal features of the self, the idiom, the "I" – according to Bollas; [4] and Mitchell says: 'This personal sense of self is deeply private and ultimately ineffable, much easier to feel than to describe.'[5] A continuity in action and insight also emerges from the centrality that Schaefer assigns to 'agency' in his 'action language.'[6] As is known, many of our psychic actions are disclaimed, so that we feel that our experience is happening to us, rather than being initiated by us. And perhaps analysis also tends to unmask disclaimed actions, ultimately revealing the person as the agent of experience. The 'I' of the personality is not some fixed entity; it is the innermost part of our personality that can develop from a very basic level onto a higher capacity of insight. If we tentatively think of the 'I' as something comparable to the 'alpha function,' we could say with Bion that 'there is a spectrum of *alpha*-functioning that extends from the most elemental to the most advanced.'[7]

Looking for a term, or for a metaphor, to describe our inner agency of insight, Modell cannot do better than William James' suggestion that one's sense of identity is more than the sum of one's identifications. 'He chose to describe the self not as a psychic structure but as an inner awareness of the ever changing stream of consciousness.'[8] The 'I' of the personality, moreover, is not outside of, or separate from, our inner world. If we try to ask where all of this insight might take place, we find still another enlightening answer offered by James: 'And why, after all, may not the world be so complex as to consist of many interpenetrating spheres?'[9] We often ask: who is it that sees our inner world? Who is it that is aware of the fleetingness of our physical and psychic vicissitudes? It is the 'I' of the personality, the agent that has little to do with calculations, strategies and schemes. Whether we say that the 'I' is more deep, more high or 'more central,' probably depends on the spatial metaphors that we adopt to try to describe our inner world. Whenever we can be aware of our incessant thinking work, our personal source of awareness is not part of it. It is an ulterior function; it is an observing agent that nevertheless occupies the same psychic space/time – the same 'chronotope,' so to speak. The ulterior dimensions are not located somewhere 'above' or 'beyond' our mind. They are co-extensive, they are comparable to James' 'interpenetrating spheres.'

What one thinks in first-person terms cannot be adequately translated into third-person language. A creature with a first-person perspective not only can have thoughts about himself but can also conceive of himself as the author of such thoughts. There cannot be two persons both with the same first-person perspective. In this outlook we could say that our crucial challenge is not so much that of having a mind but, really, of having our own mind. The 'responsibility' of having one's own mind is more innovative and creative than we are prepared to appreciate; it takes genius to bear with oneself and to endure one's own pathology. And also, as we frequently discuss about imitation, acting out, anaesthetising manoeuvres, all this seems to suggest that there must be alternative modes of inner life in which creative action seems to proceed from the innermost part of the personality. Perhaps the repetitive, reactive patterns can only be observed when profiled against the unifying light of personal creativeness.

Freud also seems to indirectly point to the creative 'I' of the personality in his 'Lines of Advance in Psycho-analytic Therapy;' in fact, he insists that 'You can analyze the elements inside a person but the actual job of bringing them together and making something, that's nothing to do with the analyst.'[10] And he refers to this as to 'the synthetic function' *contributed by the patient* – hopefully. This is the analysand's own creative response: elements are not expelled but are repossessed and joined together. And so, 'The psycho-synthesis is achieved during analytic treatment *without* our intervention, automatically and inevitably' – he says even more hopefully.[11] He must have thought that our connective genius is constantly at work in patients. This capacity for psycho-synthesis includes the capacity for coping with our own pathology. It is an operation that connects different parts, aiming to make them into a whole. By contrast, pathology could be described as being strangers to ourselves, detached from a unifying centre.

According to Symington, the analyst's task is to share and illuminate the currents of the inner world, and it is in the light of this exploration that the patient connects the experiences 'through inner mental activity.'[12] But again, the 'I' should be the protagonist of this inner mental activity. Meissner, for instance, speaks of this inner protagonist in terms of 'The self-as-subject, the self functioning as conscious subject of all mental, emotional, and physical actions and experiences.'[13] And in a more clinical approach, he also suggests that,

> The subjective aspect of the self plays a critical role in the analytic process. First of all, there is the question of whether the self-as-subject is sufficiently developed to engage in the analysis. This is the well-known question of analyzability.[14]

Effective analysis must count on the 'I' of the personality, which functions as a perspectival basis, as an instrument for observation, for focusing on whatever is somehow expressed in the transference/countertransference vicissitudes of the dyad. Symington frequently emphasises the essential relevance and function of the 'I.' But the 'I' is not some permanent, absolute psychic entity. And thus he is judiciously concerned that the 'I' of the personality might 'drown,' might be lost to oblivion. In his lively, inimitable language he tells us:

> I hear that a very famous philosopher has come to town ... In an impulse of admiration I donate to him all my good inner resources. I am then left empty, and the famous thinker has pocketed a windfall that does not rightly belong to him ... But things get worse. I open my ears and drink in indiscriminately, so I have my inner domain full of junk, but because it has come from a god, I believe it all to be

good ... I am now victim to every whimsical melody that strikes my ears. *My 'I' has been drowned.*[15]

Nothing less than that. In fact, in our lifetime, we may have attentively absorbed *thousands* of lectures without being able to 'digest' them into something personal; a process comparable to our biological metabolism. One's personal formation cannot be equated to an aggregate of different segments of learning. And thus 'sanity' could be associated with the state of affairs in which there is a responsible source of unifying insight, however minimal, a genius for overseeing our pathology. Even mental illness could be compatible with inner life, with sanity, in the sense that a creative centre, a veritable genius, is there at least to endure, or cope with, a pathology that cannot be resolved.

2. The embracing witness

In Modell's words we could say that

> The very act of introspection means that the self is an object to itself. There is an "I" that is witness to the "Me" as well as to the "Not-me". This "I" exists over time and is equated with a sense of identity that is a witness to the ephemeral "Me".[16]

But the question is why such an ephimeral 'Me' can take over the whole personality to the point of overwhelming the 'I'; this may force us into the blinding delusion that the 'Me,' the egoic apparatus, the periphery with respect to the witnessing 'I,' can constitute who we truly are. And yet, no matter how devastated a personality can be, some inner 'I,' however frail, is capable of a minimal degree of insight. According to Modell, the implication is that the self can be an object of inner perception by the self-as-subject.[17] It is almost as if the 'I's perception of the ego were no different in kind from one's own perception of external reality.

The ego is forever busy with its capacity to calculate, compute, predict, plan and scheme. All of these activities can occupy the whole inner world to the point that we may believe that we actually *are* this complex wiring of egoic activities. The 'I' can be thought of as the loving witness of all of these mental doings. The inner 'I' in fact does know, but its way of knowledge is accepting, listening, embracing – perhaps the indispensable condition for our creativeness. We may not be able to articulate its function as when, for instance, we make decisions instantaneously. This capacity of the 'I' to be an embracing witness can be activated in nanoseconds, so to speak – effortlessly and without elaborate thinking. The egoic functions constitute the unobserved mind that might actually run our entire psychic life when we are not sufficiently present with our embracing witness. In Humphrey's view, the fact is that, whatever may be the logical problems of describing the inner function of the 'I,' 'human beings everywhere openly attempt it.'[18]

Our inner embracing witness not only can perceive the relation between any two inner or outer elements but can also afford an awareness of itself observing them. It is an 'I' that not only sees the ego struggling between instincts and reality, but also perceives our awareness of the struggle. The 'I' enhances a most creative transition from a *duality* to a *triad*. This is somehow analogous to the development of a therapeutic relation. Among others, Ogden reminds us that the analytic process reflects the interplay of three, rather than two, subjectivities and that a triadic involvement is necessary. The process in fact involves

> the subjectivity of the analyst, of the analysand and of the analytic third. The analytic third is the creation of both analyst and analysand, *and at the same time* the analyst and the analysand (*qua* analyst and analysand) are created by the analytic third. (There is no analyst, no analysand, no analysis in the absence of the third.)[19]

In a complementary perspective Bion seems to especially applaud the function of a witnessing 'I.' Grotstein (Bion's analysand) reports him reiterating: 'Don't try to understand *me*! Pay attention to *your* emotional response to me!'[20] It takes an inner 'I' to do just that. In fact, if we *just understand* the analyst we can reproduce his interpretive skills and insights, like truly 'brilliant' analysands or candidates can often do. As if the general policy were that of duplicating the clever egoic structures of the emissaries of a psychoanalytic super-knowledge. By paying attention to *our* emotional responses, and being brave enough to accept them, we can definitely enhance our more creative 'I' and innovative policies. In his work on the 'Jungian' transcendent function, Miller even entitles one of his chapters 'The Third as a *Universal* Psychologic Construct' and insists that 'this construct is broader, deeper and more transformational than any of the concepts to which Jung compares it.'[21] In this same outlook Bion suggests that: 'If alpha is destroyed, thought becomes impossible and the personality ceases to exist.' Nothing less than that. And he goes on:

> The schizophrenic's fear of annihilation may be associated with an experiencing of his non-existence as a personality ... There can be no personality if there is ... no self consciousness. There may be persons, but not personality unless there is the function of self consciousness.[22]

This is the witnessing embrace performed by the 'I'; and it is significantly creative because it is the source of psychic life. 'Self consciousness is the function *sine qua non* of personality. To say someone has personality is to mean that he is aware of himself, not sporadically but permanently.'[23] The ego that Freud 'scientifically' defines as an 'apparatus' is constantly at work, forever intent upon calculating, assessing, comparing, exploring, negotiating, analysing, predicting, accounting, scheming, theorising, etc. It functions so relentlessly that it can even make us ill, thought-obsessed. At a given point we may seek a way of escape in any direction. Just being able to view from a minimal perspectival distance such a permanently over-heated apparatus, we can regain some creative living. In analysis we also intensely seek a supportive witness to sustain our tenuous capacity for embracing our inner life. What we mostly need is the internalisation of an observer of the self. According to Lear, 'It is one of the ironies and paradoxes of human existence that the self comes into being by the internalization of a self observer.'[24] It is somehow comparable to the Oedipal third, which emerges out of a dual symbiosis.

Nobody 'chooses' dysfunction, conflict, insanity. They seem to be associated with an insufficient 'presence' in us; they seem to happen because there is not enough presence to transform our view of ourselves or of others. The problem is that we are not fully here. In the meantime the robotic, unobservable mind may be running our entire life. The ego-identified state – in the absence of an embracing witness – can be severely dysfunctional. The real danger is that if the 'I' does not view our egoic functions, then the ego may overwhelm the 'I,' which becomes asphyxiated *ex non usu*. In Symington's view, when the 'I' is devitalised, never entirely but largely, this source of psychic action is only faintly operative within the personality:

> It seems that once the discordant source is glimpsed and owned, it in itself ceases to be discordant but, rather, becomes part of the creative core. The very action of recognition, of owning – the only way I can put it is owning as opposed to disowning – itself changes reality.[25]

But the moment the thinker re-owns it, a more creative consciousness springs to life.

In the words of Siegel, we could say that beneath all our self-states (or above, or at the centre of), there is a core of self that has receptivity at its heart.[26] Of course 'beneath,' 'above' or 'at the centre' are all spatial, geometric metaphors that we use to explore our psychic world which, strictly speaking, occupies no space – although being necessarily embodied; for many of us the receptive self, the embracing witness, is hard to imagine, much less to feel. But it is the essential 'you'; it rests beneath each of the many self states that are activated in our day-to-day lives. It is ready to receive whatever arrives at the door, inviting all aspects of ourselves into the shelter of its embracing witness. The 'I' of the personality is the one who can both accept and monitor the discordant parts of our ego.[27] We cannot force anyone, or any part, to accept a split off part. The problem is that – without a welcoming witness of the mind as a whole – each different part can be sincere while expressing itself – while the person may be always lying.

Starting from the 'I' we can gradually enter a compassionate state of connection with ourselves and others. This source of focused attention permits us to use awareness to create choice and change. This is the domain of creative integration. Rosenfeld recommended that at certain, very intense or painful moments we should clearly remind the patient that he is the knowing, the knower, not the condition that is known; at the appropriate times we should directly tell the analysand something like this: you are not the same as what you are talking about; the real 'you' is *now* talking to me clearly and confidently, and that is who you are; you are not the madness that you share with me, you are the one who dares to do the showing and the sharing.[28]

In popular 'philosophy' of olden times we read Marcus Aurelius instructing us in this way:

> Wipe out thy imagination by often saying to thyself: now it is in my power to let no badness be in this soul, nor desire, nor any perturbation at all; but looking at all things I see what is their nature, and I use each according to its value. Remember this *power* which thou hast from nature.[29]

Centuries apart, Modell reminds us of a little girl who certainly had this 'power.'[30] He tells us of a young girl who was subjected to the outbursts of a manic-depressive mother and who remained composed amid the mother's attack, and also thrived both scholastically and interpersonally. She was asked to represent, or draw, what it felt like to live with her difficult mother. She drew a castle, which she described as the little space that she had arranged for herself in the household and into which she could retreat when things got rough. And of course a 'castle' is the ideal place from which we can observe things getting rough without the immediate risk of being swept away.

3. The insightful 'I' – beyond the ego

In an attempt to explore the creativity of the 'I' – as distinct from the work of our ego – we could perhaps invoke a remark of Erich Fromm: 'Only the fully developed individual self can drop the ego.'[31] We could think of the ego as a 'success machine;' and we could think of success as a routine sort of business. For the sake of example, if one talks the appropriate jargon and attends the appropriate meetings, some kind of success just simply follows. It is not so with the insightful creativity of our daily lives. Here we need the development of that deeper 'I' that just does not play for any referee or spectator, of the 'I' that 'drops the ego' for the sake of its own development. Bion reiterates that there can be a person but not a personality, unless there is a function of self-consciousness.[32] In Heidegger's view, the celebrated idea of alienation 'is the result of man's falling into the "They" and losing his individuality.'[33]

The 'I' of the personality, as the agent overseeing egoic mechanisms, is constantly at work. According to Eissler, the quest for success and the quest for creativity do not mix well: the former is mainly concerned with the response of the community – Heidegger's 'They' – and is often prone to pass over an emerging truth that may incur disfavour with those who decide upon success.[34] The highest chances of creativity are only given when a person has made his own conscience the principal arbiter of his mental actions. In such a case, questions of rivalry, prestige, appreciation of peers fade into the background: once having lost their power to distract, they are no longer obstacles on the way to personal creativity. According to Kristeva, a spectacular reduction of personal psychic life seems to transpire from our culture; and she asks, 'These days who still has a soul?'[35] Confronting a renewed expansion in the market of low-cost 'enlightening wisdom' – just look in bookshops – she wonders if this interest stems from a legitimate quest or from psychic poverty; almost as if hoping that the so-called 'new age' culture offer 'transcendence,' and give us a super soul capable of replacing an underdeveloped subjectivity.[36] Perhaps people today believe that they can dispense with insight into our personal life. Analysis can be of help in our attempts to insightful creativity and we can develop a capacity to be alone and capable of personal insight: 'For it is in states of solitude [not loneliness] that we extend the domain of the personal over the impersonal. When alone, we are free to experience what is idiosyncratic in us' – says Modell.[37]

Fromm believes that one of the most disastrous mistakes in individual and social life consists of being caught in stereotyped ways of thinking: 'There are always other and new possibilities which become apparent only when one has liberated oneself from the deathly grip of clichés.'[38] And perhaps one of the worst clichés could be this one: for me to be happy the world must radically change; there is nothing for me to do other than hope and wait for a revolutionary change. Observing this outlook we could almost say that 'revolution' has become the 'opium of the people.' Dogmas, whether political or scientific, arise out of the erroneous belief that our thinking apparatus can encapsulate reality and truth. Dogmas seem to function as collective conceptual prisons and, paradoxically, our awakening is waking up from the dream of thought.

Our focus on the 'I' of the personality permits us to use awareness to create choice and change. This is the domain of the integration of consciousness. In Bion's view, 'The attempt to escape [frustration] involves the restoration of alpha which has been destroyed by splitting and projective identification; the fragments have to be recovered and re-united.'[39] However tenuous and incipient, the 'I' is capable of sufficient insight to enhance the recovery and integration of parts. We could shift our perspective and say that, however prone to lose inner coherence, we constantly face the problem of somehow generating action and uniting ourselves into some kind of insightful subject. According to Symington, 'The problem of securing some unifying inner force is so acute that no price is too high for the "promise" of a unified view of the self.'[40] These 'promises' are even perversely paid by entrusting to external agencies the full responsibility of our inner coherence. Just join a particular party, faction or world-view – and everything will become meaningful, enlightened. Not that we should no longer identify with specific cultural orientations or traditions; but to seek something through them that they cannot give – such as a psychic identity or a sense of fulfilment – is perhaps futile. External elements from which we seek identity can be quite disappointing. The whole advertising industry – trying to sell goods, theories, status, connections – might decline if people were more insightful and sane, if they no longer sought identity through external supports. The more we seek happiness through egoic success, the more it will elude us. External supports can at the most give some 'supportive' comfort but no creativity or maturity.

Complying with compulsive thinking may become a collective disease. Pressured thinking tells us that we cannot get to a glorified 'there' from our abjected 'here' unless we find, get, catch 'something' that is absolutely needed for the move. There is some elusive, essential something that we seem to need before we can live creatively. We believe we cannot be creative because of who we are at this point because we are not yet equipped or good enough, and thus we must systematically find means to an end and of course we may be caught into doing so indefinitely. And so we often cling to our little or great egos and see others as existing to fit our plans. We perhaps need to have our ego-lenses shattered before we can be in touch with anyone. What is quite frequent is stumbling into tangles of mutual conflict because we only function through the egos we believe we are, and which we will not surrender. In one of his monumental contributions Eissler reminds us that in Goethe's life, which is so richly documented, one discovers an instructive process of melting down of ego structure. Whether or not such a process could be called a psychosis, is of no relevance here. 'Suffice it to say that a deficit of ego structure in the adult is not necessarily caused by a slowing down or inhibition of structurization during childhood or the latency period, but may be caused by later processes.'[41] Caused by 'later processes'? What does it mean? Perhaps creating a space for the 'I' of the personality that can induce a lessening, an eclipse of our formidable ego structure. In Goethe's case, one can observe with some reliability how his poetical talents, already considerable, suddenly gained in originality. After the ego dissolving crisis they became capable of generating the new style of poetry characteristic of his genius. 'I conclude,' says Eissler, 'that this melting down of structure was a turning point that released the activation of functions previously inhibited.'[42]

Such is our human condition: lost in thoughts. Many of us spend our lives imprisoned within the confines of our own thoughts. Some rarely go beyond their narrow ego-made managing agency which can only perpetuate its own style. A blink of insight breaks the spell occasionally. Paradoxically, things may get worse and better at the same time. Our stream of thinking has such an enormous momentum that can easily drag us along with it. It is easy for people to become trapped in pathological prisons. Rosenfeld again: the one who articulates the uneasiness of being caught in repetitive difficulties is not quite entirely caught; he can share the thick imprisoning tangle with a witnessing, accepting other and by doing so he does not coincide with the sickly tangle.[43]

Anyone can see that the development of human beings in the last few thousand years of history is truly amazing. We have perfected our reason to a point whereby we are solving the riddles of nature and are emancipating ourselves from the blind powers of natural forces. But at the very moment of 'triumph,' at the threshold of a 'new' world, we may succumb to the power of the mental functions that have allowed for our historic development; identified with these functions we do not manage self-awareness very well; ordinary geniuses are the ones that manage to escape. The creative, insightful 'I' is capable of eschewing triumphal traps. The traps are constituted by ego functions that pretend to be all there is in us, and which even claim that we should conform to them.

7

CREATIVE SERVICE

1. Am I my brother's keeper?

'Am I my brother's keeper? No I am not, of course, but sometimes I really wish I could be.' Perhaps we would often like to be caring persons but do not easily succeed. We cannot deny the desire to be nurturing individuals, even though this desire only comes out as a 'minor' voice; a voice that is frequently silenced by the ruling inner organisation. And thus our propensity for care and nurture is not so easily expressed. At times we almost feel it should not exist; as if it should be regarded as a self-diminishing attitude and the concern of a 'lesser' minority. But it does exist, and it can even happen that for a 'fraction of votes' it may temporarily exercise some governance and redirect our psychic gaze. The inclination to nurture and care is not some ephemeral, wishful, idyllic – ultimately irrelevant – part of the self. When this aspiration is deadened, it can be as frustrating as being coerced into the mortification of sexual life. If we think of Eros as a most comprehensive term, the desire to nurture can certainly be thought of as one of its many faces – and an intense, significant one. The inclination to be caring and responsible may be as powerful as other drives, even though we customarily ignore its frequent suffocation. We have no remorse about stifling our inclination to care. The forclusion of our desire for nurturing can be as devastating as the taboos of sexuality in our pre-Freudian culture. In fact, when the functions of sexuality are excluded, we feel that there has been a fraud; we cannot be content with food, shelter and 'glory;' we want to share in our human sexual Eros. But we cannot be content either without our share of Agape, a further aspect of Eros, animating our desire to care and nurture, of kindness and custody. We rarely think of the diffuse sense of humiliation about not being capable of loving, of being a source of love – however much we can be cared for by others.

Phillips and Taylor ask why the pleasures of care astonish us.[1] Paradoxically, disclosing the joys of nurture and custody almost appears as an obscene revelation, as if it were some sad compensatory strategy. Seeing things from a different perspective, Janet Soskice maintains that only if we can be made capable of loving, if we can be truly 'lovely' creatures, we can fully live the experience of being loved.² The rationale of this whole approach points to the necessity of recovering our frequently silenced desires for being actively protective and responsive. Not only is our propensity for kindness and custody vulnerable to obscurity, but also its exclusion/forclusion is not even regarded as a worthy problem. Our erotic Eros is perhaps not enough; even a satisfying sexual life may not be quite enough. We also need something different. We in fact strive to feel caring and loving, even though this longing is often ignored. Similarly, it would be futile, for instance, to try to appease a heterosexual male adolescent with offers of delicious food. He will be silently raging in his desire for a beautiful girl – or even not so beautiful. Similarly, we may want to really care.

We have learned to manage our interactions with caution, and to distrust anyone who comes too close. Generic hostility has become common sense. Ordinary geniuses, by contrast, are those who can extend our reduced range of desires: from the bondage of craving all the way to the amazement of caring. We actually have a need to be loving and lovely creatures; and yet being needy, even in the arena of intense desires, may look deplorable. 'We are all dependent creatures, right to the core,' insist Phillips and Taylor.³ And they even remark that we should admit that 'care' is becoming the new buzz word, which is everywhere today.⁴ Bion also frequently refers to how dependent on companionship and relationship we all are; Grotstein reports him reiterating that 'Man always will be a dependent creature. Man is a dependent creature no matter how autonomous he becomes.'⁵ And he believes that Bion seems to almost accord 'instinctual status' to this essential need/desire for nurturing others.⁶ Freud's life is a good example of psychic survival and creativity enhanced by unsung, silent geniuses that were companions in his itinerary. Competent biographers have been able to draw different lists of the ordinary geniuses who supported and catalysed his extraordinary creations. And Freud significantly happens to remark: 'A strong egoism is a protection against falling ill, but in the last resort we must begin to love in order not to fall ill, and we are bound to fall ill if, in consequence of frustration, we are unable to love.'⁷ Nothing less than that.

Drawing upon the notion of intentionality, we could say that looking at people as simply 'objects' does not make any sense. People exist as 'subjects' in force of their relation to other people, to themselves and to a network of meaning. Van Deurzen offers a synoptic view of our coexistential condition:

> As human beings we are complex bio-socio-psycho-spiritual organisms, joined to the world around us in everything we are and do. We do not ever really stand in isolation. In order to survive we need to be constantly connected, filled and fuelled.⁸

And so our technocratic era and its psychological corollary of deliberate control is perhaps misfiring, or even backfiring. By contrast, in Eigen's view a therapist ought to be a specialist in letting the other in, feeling the impact of the other, and in staying with the images and thoughts that he induces; a patient not only senses the therapist, but also senses how he affects the therapist.[9] There are unspoken, dramatic questions in every human interaction, such as: is there room for me in another's feeling life? And perhaps we can try to allow for this need of the other both inside and outside of therapeutic settings. And when the same deep-seated problem returns in all sorts of disguises and circumstances, it is perhaps useful to actually 'name' it somehow. It should be the sufferer who finds a name for the monotony of conquering satisfactions and who also finds a name for the surprising desire to be protective, responsive, compassionate. And of course the creative listener should be quick at adopting a new name for whatever working purposes.

The thesis here is that kindly care or caring kindness is an essential feature of our human Eros – to use a most comprehensive term. If you feel that you have been seriously offended and you cannot think that this is absurd, you may begin to think that the other deserves retaliation and that no Eros is at work. The kernel of being my brother's keeper, and the exhilaration of it, is a sharing attitude that may reveal the loveableness in the other and consequently his own potential for being a caring/loving individual. And so, we may tentatively opt for custody rather than elimination. The psychic metabolic circuit must be completed in such vicissitudes so that we can freely set out on new cycles. We must get to the point of being capable of compassionate love before we can engage in ulterior caring cycles. The listening geniuses allow for creating stories that reverse our way of seeing things. These stories can be a frightening and yet consoling presence; they promise us upheaval and yet harmony, they shatter and heal our images. The point is that we are constantly confronting both an intense desire for being caring persons *and* a personal/collective fear of it; as if there were an ongoing oscillation.

Phillips and Taylor also emphasise that, in spite of the merits and 'riches' of compassionate kindness, we have almost become phobic of it. There is a widespread suspicion of kindness in our modern world as if we felt

> that it is either a higher form of selfishness (the kind that is morally triumphant and secretly exploitative), or the lowest form of weakness (kindness is the way the weak control the strong, and the kind are only kind because they haven't got the guts to be anything else). And what, after all, can kindness help us win except moral approval? Or possibly not even that, in a society where respect for personal status has become a leading value.[10]

As is known, we seem to secretly believe that kindness is the attitude of losers. But agreeing to talk about 'winners' and 'losers' involves an essentialist, dogmatic, racist outlook that can only support our avoidance of kindness. 'Caregivers' and 'nurturers' equal 'losers.' In spite of this view the desire to be supportive seems to surface in the most adverse and disparate events, where it tends to involve all those connected with the story. After all, why should the desire to be my brother's keeper be either ignored or repressed? Every kind word claims to illuminate events, on condition that it is properly listened to, or it would not exist as such. In this way it may transform traumatic events, attempting to clarify something that would otherwise increase confusion. This process is filled with hope since memories evolve in time and with telling our stories again and again. An enduring *après coup*. But a story only exists in an atmosphere of listening.[11] We thus depend, once again, on the ordinary talent of people, of those who can exercise the genius of listening. The evolution of trauma always depends on the listening capacity of the person who is confided in. And thus the way in which we speak of a trauma is part of the whole traumatic sequence. It may heal or ulcerate, depending on the quality of listening on which we may count. This is why Cyrulnik reminds us that we have to distinguish between the blow that comes in the real world, and the representation of this blow as elaborated in the inner world.[12] The most damaging blows are not always the most spectacular ones. And the way we construe the blow in our mind can be a co-production of the private story that the injured person tells himself and of the account given by caring, listening others. The walking wounded want creative listeners to hear what happened in order to get hold of their shaken personality once again.[13] But when the listeners happen to be untalented for co-creating stories, they tend to make use of archives, repertories, prejudices, and thus are of very little help.

Phillips and Taylor also remark that kindness can even be perceived as the saboteur of the successful life. In their view we need to know how we have come to believe that the best lives we can lead seem to involve sacrificing the best things about ourselves; and we also need to know how we have come to believe that there are pleasures greater than kindness.[14] They argue that kindness – not sexuality, not violence, not money – has become our forbidden pleasure. 'What is it about our times that makes kindness seem so dangerous?' In one sense, of course, kindness is generally a risk because it is based on our susceptibility to others and on the inclination to identify with their joys and sorrows. 'Putting oneself in someone else's shoes...can be very uncomfortable. But if the pleasures of kindness – like the greatest human pleasures – are inherently perilous, they are nonetheless some of the most satisfying we possess.'[15] And also, it takes creative action to discover both hostile and caring attitudes in others, to try to let them be revealed. When some kindness prevails we can attempt a sequence of *full* cycles, from being loved, through becoming lovely and all the way to being a source of love. This is required for psychic life to go on and flourish. Psychoanalysts are thought to be uncovering knowledge that is screened from consciousness. And this seems to suggest that the knowledge is there; just take away the cover, and it will be revealed. In Symington's view, the situation is quite different. There has to be a kindly approach and some creative action *first*, 'and only then, when there has been a creative act, can you know.'[16] In others words, knowledge is not there until the caring act has occurred; to Symington this means that the whole endeavour that we are engaged in is quite different from what he thought.[17] What one is engaged in is the inter-active/intra-active attempt to bring about creative action, because only then can knowledge and awareness spring to life. Consciousness is ultimately the product of kindly creative action.

We could perhaps include at this point an imaginary 'clinical' vignette from ancient times. It goes something like this:

> Cain was an industrious young man, and quite attentive to his personal success. And although he loved his brother Abel very much, he was always in trouble with him. On a particular occasion he could no longer endure the increasing stress and actually eliminated his brother. Not that Cain was completely wicked, but he simply could not resist his inner turmoil. The next day he somehow encounters his God – as if they had made an appointment. Disguised as a Jewish analyst, the polite, friendly God says something like this, 'Oh hello Cain, how are you today? You used to tell me about your beloved but troublesome brother Abel; how is he doing?' At this point the young man becomes abruptly hostile, irritable, defensive – and retorts, 'How can I possibly know? Am I my brother's keeper?' Cain had hoped that this statement would be the end of the conversation. But, no, they would have to develop this topic in subsequent encounters. There is in fact no end to this sort of story.

2. Contact: risks and gains

According to Lear, it is a striking fact that the outcome of our involvement with others turns into a development of psychic structure.[18] We can imagine a world, almost like ours, in which beings sent out love and took it back in just as we do, but in which the identifications produced no development. For identification to enhance growth, we must be able to appreciate complexity and structure – in those with whom we are in contact – that surpasses our own. As we perceive such a shared reality with another person (while allowing them to just be), and as we actually focus on it as if it were a 'third thing' in the relationship, we can see that some new development can occur. Our investments in contacts are good investments: we seem to be able to take in more than we originally gave out. In Lear's words, in fact: 'What I love and what I take back in exists *for me* at a higher level of complexity.'[19]

In human contacts we can sustain the psychic survival of others to the extent that we allow for them an internal, protected psychic space. It is the sort of content that is not felt as an intrusion. And, paradoxically, it is a modicum of authentic interpersonal contact that allows for the subsequent creation of an inviolable space, for the sort of experience that is claimed as mine alone. Modell suggests that these periods of withdrawal are as necessary and as vital as states of relatedness: 'For individuals who must cope with dreadful environments, private space can be the place in which alternative worlds are created, worlds that guarantee psychic survival.'[20] We could speculate what the life of Oedipus – one who closely escaped murder by his father – would have been like, if he only had a good, lasting friendship. According to Buber one must learn to stand in relation to others, and even to meet and be changed by others who are not one's *alter ego*/own type, but rather 'absolutely not' oneself.[21] He describes this condition very eloquently as 'the tiny strictness and grace of the everyday.' We could call it our ordinary creativeness. Such a problematic condition could perhaps be summarised through Winnicott's belief that where instinctual arousal was, there play should be.[22] Or, to put it in another way, the best form our instinctual life can take is in play; we can play as peers in a great variety of close connections, but we can also play as servants, as those who try to be of service.

There is a tendency to refer to persons suffering from narcissistic, psychosomatic or perverse mental conditions as 'difficult patients.' In McDougall's view, however, it would be more useful to think in terms of 'difficult encounters' between patients and therapists.[23] Unconscious vicissitudes that are simple enough to understand are not at all simple to analyse with a therapeutic aim. Thus we could perhaps think that the psychoanalytic function is best served in terms of a transition from understanding to 'standing by' the patient: standing by in the effort to develop mutual arrangements of affective coexistence. 'Standing by' involves the capacity to develop, share and use the sort of relational knowing that may unblock (unlock) the internal impasse of the suffering person. By contrast, we all know people with whom it is best not to share anything that we have at heart. If we have experienced something enlivening and we reveal it to those people, paradoxically it will seem almost dull. If we have a secret, we will keep it safe from certain persons, safe inside us. That way it will not shrivel up and lose all the richness it has for us. Certain persons are just not talented for creative service. But we might have sufficient inner resources to find a person with whom it is the other way around. If you tell that person something creative, it becomes even more appealing. An embryonic story will develop and become a project; you will find yourself telling it in more detail, finding the richness of all its elements, more than when you thought about it alone; whatever matters to you, you save until you can tell it to this sort of person. Talking to a listening other is like that: it makes your experience expand, while the other can experience the immense pleasure/joy of kindness. Creativeness also implies that we can be that sort of person within ourselves. When a wounded person speaks his sorrow, he affirms himself and takes up his position. As soon as he undertakes the task of telling his story, he breaks the spell of the horrific grip that stupefies him and draws him to near-death annihilation.[24] But there can be no story without a listener.

CREATIVE SERVICE

The listening other blows on the embers of resilience. This can be done in the here and now; that is, at any time and without special stipulations. We are all co-authors of the personal stories of those who have been wounded in their souls. By converse, when we do not listen or silence others, we leave them in the claws of devastation. The ordinary genius can listen openly, even without believing the story; he thus responds to our desire for care; he kindles our potential to become caring.

People do not always make sense, just as life does not always make sense. We will never understand everything, and the illusory belief that we can is the asphyxiating derivative of some self-perpetuating omnipotent logic. If we cannot understand, we can psychically give up; we could make a choice of renunciation rather than letting an incomprehensible situation consume us through the illusion of our cognitive control of it. Relations are never entirely clear or flourishing. In fact it is not plausible to present destructiveness itself as an object of direct knowledge, or even as an object of desire (on the pattern of food or sexual satisfaction). It is necessary to try to show how, by perversions and re-combinations of our natural motives, destructiveness may come to be sought out and even come to be our primary purpose. Personal relations can systematically include a chronic element of ambivalence even while they develop and include more features. Sometimes relations go wrong and we refuse to digest the strangeness and otherness of the other. Anger may then harden into resentment, and gradually turn into a demand for the complete freezing of relatedness. This often originates from a denial – the refusal to accept another's independent existence. And it aims eventually at an absence – the 'cancellation' of the other. Why be my brother's keeper? There is hardly any creative service. But then, we cannot be at peace with ourselves when we are alone, and we will actively seek a relationship to cover up the inner unease. But we can be sure that the unease will then reappear in some other form within the subsequent relationship; not only that, we will probably hold our partner responsible for the situation. Perhaps what is needed is to try to bravely accept these vicissitudes: a compensatory arrangement of contact may easily back-fire in a variety of ways. Some ordinary geniuses are capable of helping others avoiding these repetitive results. As we said, we can only speculate which vicissitudes would occur in the life of Oedipus had he been able to cultivate/enjoy the 'simple' friendship of an unsuspected ordinary genius – no kings, queens, seers; no exceptional riddle-solvers like himself.

Acceptance and surrender do not mean that one allows oneself to be used by narcissistic persons. It is perfectly possible to say 'No' firmly to anyone or to exit from a situation, and still be in a state of conscious surrender to the otherness of the other. When an ordinary genius says 'No' to a situation, the 'No' does not come out from a reaction but from insight; it is a creative action arising from an awareness of what might be life-enhancing at that moment – it has the same force as saying 'Yes.'[25] The ordinary genius can even accurately observe what happens to the other person's self when no longer energised by our psychic *reactions* – as distinct from inner actions. Bearing Oedipus in mind, the thesis is that 'sufficiently' healthy human contacts may sustain the laborious completion of our destiny while averting its default into fate.

Until we manage an acceptance of the other-as-a-whole, unconscious role-playing may constitute a large part of our relations. In surrender, we no longer need defensive roles to protect our (false) self. We may become more simple and more real: embodied creatures indeed. The 'false self' may then say that surrender is dangerous, hurtful because we can become excessively vulnerable; what it does not know is that by allowing ourselves to become 'vulnerable' we might get in touch with the much *less* vulnerable 'I' of the personality.[26] Surrender and vulnerability do not of course transform the other. Surrender and acceptance transform instead the protagonist; and once transformed, the entire context is also relatively transformed. In Phillips's and Taylor's view vulnerability may seem traumatic to people, but then everybody is vulnerable: 'Indeed it would be realistic to say that what we have in common is our vulnerability; it is the medium of contact between us, what we most fundamentally recognize in each other.'[27] But this awareness (and the subsequent forms of kindness that emerge from it) is too easily turned away from. 'This turning away we call "self sufficiency" and when we want to pathologize it, "narcissism".'[28] The paradoxical pleasure of vulnerability is that it connects us with others and allows the development of further new cycles of psychic life. The question is of course if we can creatively 'use' friends, or live up to a friendship; these attempts in fact can also fail or degenerate.

Some very ill subjects do not want any bi-personal field. They only want to inhabit the other in a parasitic, adhesive relation. They want us to fall to their project, and to only realise what is happening when it is too late. When an inner processing apparatus is not sufficiently developed and we are in close contact with an excess of primitive psychic elements, then we are subject to intrusion and damage. The question is, which is the part of us that is willing and capable to upgrade our 'processing apparatus?' The geniuses are those who are capable of developing their psychic potential to deal with retard-release poisons, and to escape the parasitic inhabitation of pathogenic others. Only in this way they may continue in their creative service.

What Berlin says with regard to knowledge, we could say about significant human contacts: we ought to seek those connections that are involved when the relationship 'is described *not* as correct or incorrect, skilful or inept, a success or a failure, but as profound or shallow, perceptive or stupid, alive or dead.'[29] A potentially redeeming friendship is aborted if we succeed in absorbing the other to our own self. Obsessed with a goal, we can only insist on recruiting the other into our own project and defeating the opportunity to gain maturational benefits from the other. Obsession may carry with it the atrophy of whatever interpersonal attitudes are not absorbed into the obsessive occupation. And among these attitudes is the creative capacity to care for others. The obsession seems to say: why do you waste your time with futile, caring occupations? Insofar as others are not associates in the obsession, they are of course ignored. Or, to look at it in another way, a destructive attitude towards others, and towards one's own nature, can be satisfied by submitting to an obsession. Clinically speaking, there are sickness gains in avoiding the challenge of interpersonal contacts or reciprocal care. In the intimate contact of friendship we could learn a new language, a new vocabulary, which is exactly what we need to reach our destiny and avoid default into fate. We think of destiny as a personal, constructive itinerary, whereas fate is an impersonal, irresistible inertia; worse than Ananke and Nemesis. For the sake of renewal we need to see our entrenched vocabulary as a nuisance. If it is a nuisance, it is puzzling why we go along with it. In the language of Phillips:

> You might feel, for example, that there was something that mattered a great deal to you that you couldn't get, or get at, in the vocabulary available; but this old vocabulary would have to exist for you to have this feeling. You would be dependent on the way in which it frustrated you; because this very frustration would be a prompt. The old vocabulary would pester you with what it couldn't do for you, with the roads not taken by that set of words.[30]

And so we could come to appreciate the 'nuisance value' of an entrenched vocabulary. Whether nuisance is an invitation or an opportunity or, more obviously, an annoyance, it is ultimately a challenge. The genius-friend is one who 'provides' a different word by means of which we may stop resisting, and perhaps break the vicious circle. For instance, once I am identified with a story in which I am cast in the role of a victim, I do not want it to end, and do not want an end to the problems that it entails. Why? Because they are part of my identity. And if no one will listen to my sad story, I can always repeat it to myself and so I can safeguard an identity as someone who has been mistreated by life. These stories give definition to our self-image, and that is all that matters to the false self. If we succeed in pulling someone into these sad stories, then the most 'fascinating' of perversions seem to unfold. In certain imitative, uncreative relations there seems to be a tacit agreement – comparable to some of Pirandello's plays – whereby I will play who you want me to be, and you will play who I want you to be. That is the uncreative, uncaring and unconscious agreement. And yet, role-playing can be tiresome work and so certain roles cannot be sustained indefinitely. When these roles collapse we see our raw selves divested of their roles, and we perceive in them a parasitic tangle of convictions.

But we could use difficult situations for purposes of personal growth. If Oedipus had a close friend, he could have perhaps used the vicissitudes of friendship to create a better destiny, rather than remaining entangled in a narcissistic atmosphere and submitting to a tragic fate. In a therapeutic relationship or in the blessing of a real friendship we may attempt to disengage ourselves from pathologic inner tangles and gradually try to reverse a trend. Thus, even from a condition of parasitic benumbment there could emerge renewal. According to Stern, there can be between any two persons 'an emergent property of the moving along process, ... an ideal milieu for the irruption of emergent properties ... These are movements of *kairos* ... They set the stage for a crisis that needs some kind of resolution.'[31] These moments tend to reorganise the intersubjective field so that it becomes more creative, and the two people sense an opening up of the relationship, which permits them to explore *new* options together. These moments do not need to be explicitly articulated to effectuate change. They provide a form of creativeness via another's mind. If inner pain and stupor are real, so is the *jouissement* reached through and beyond pain. Nowhere does the personality grow more through its own demise than in everyday confrontations with those who are our friends. To grow enough to encompass antagonistic pressures makes the idea of going beyond polarities more than some kind of abstraction. The 'work' of friendship – which is certainly not an idyll – can broaden our sense of what healing does. It makes us far more respectful of what we achieve in the way of real living in spite of ourselves – in spite of our fragilities. And thus we struggle through a relationship while remaining in the service of creativity.

3. Caring: here and now

As has been argued, we consider our potential for caring and nurture as a significant component of our libidinal drives, of our human Eros (as contrasted to Thanatos); the pleasure/joy of caring is a relevant aspect of our life instincts. In this perspective, the psychoanalytic insistence on working primarily in the here and now has enlightening implications that invest our whole life. The derivatives of the here-and-now approach in fact contribute the basis of our endeavours to live creatively. Winnicott attributes top priority to living creatively and also significantly stresses that it is an attitude that does not demand prerequisites or cognitive stipulations of any kind.[32] Similarly, our potential for caring can simply be activated in the here and now which is constantly our present moment.

Stress is often caused by being 'here' but wanting to be 'there,' being in the present while wanting to be in the future or in the past; it is a split that tears us apart. Trying to live and create with such an inner cleavage is futile. The fact that we all do it to some extent does not make it any better. All that anyone ever has to deal with in real life – as distinct from external projections – can be done in the here and now. Or else, could we be constantly waiting to start living? It is not so uncommon. Attention here is devoted to the small but meaningful affective happenings that unfold in the 'nanoseconds' that make up our here and now. Kindness, for instance, is a form of care that can unfold in the here and now, and that can start at any moment of life; and, of course, we can be kind to others as well as to our own self. Kindness can be an immediate response that sustains any variety of caring ventures and that can instantly function in virtually all interpersonal circumstances: one can be kind in the job of arresting a person, or rude in sexual relations. Kindness is an immediate response; it is to be caring in the here and now. And yet, in Phillips' and Taylor's view, kindly behaviour is often looked upon with suspicion, or else visible demonstrations of kindness are dismissed as insubstantial and sentimental attitudes: 'Kindness is seen either as a cover story or as a failure of nerve.'[33] And they, paradoxically, wonder whether it is time to give up on being kind, or at least to discard kindness as something of value, and instead just enjoy the fleeting moments of kindness in our lives while acknowledging that, for selfish creatures like ourselves, these moments are the exceptions that prove the rule.[34] In our society kindness is incidentally praised while being silently discouraged. The capacity to kindly bear with the vulnerability of others, and of ourselves, could come to be generally regarded as a sign of shameful weakness. On the one hand we perceive our feelings for others, our capacity to share their sufferings and pleasures, as our most intense and precious experiences – in this outlook to feel for others almost appears as akin to an instinct. On the other hand, many of our profound accounts of ourselves are about a resistance to any experience of care. According to Phillips and Taylor, at the extreme, we have come to believe that feeling too much for others, being too empathic, may either endanger our lives or may be against our natures: 'In our most cynical moments we have come to suspect that the whole notion of kindness is a cover story – indeed our most subtly self-deceiving cover story – for an ingeniously ruthless self-interest.'[35] So much for 'creative service.'

To be capable of psychic care in the here and now we must be creative enough to maintain an atmosphere of kindness. It is nothing ephemeral, frivolous or evanescent. It is very serious, especially in the here and now. Phillips' and Taylor's work shows when and why confidence in kindness evaporated in our culture and what the consequences are: 'In giving up kindness – and especially our acts of kindness – we deprive ourselves of a pleasure that is fundamental to our sense of well-being.'[36] Independence and self-reliance are now our primary social aspirations. Kindness and compassion are feared and ignored, as if they were pervasive taboos of our society. As we very well know, all of the insane political regimes loath kindness.[37] They dismiss it as a 'swinish' attitude, totally incompatible with their world view. In such regimes it takes a veritable genius to continue to value kindness in its immediate availability. Indeed, if we identify with social idols, with ideologies, we need not be concerned about being kind to others.

A caring attitude may function in the here and now with patients, of course, and even with 'simple' interlocutors – any sort of interlocutor. We can be caring the instant we try to share the burden of anybody's psychic life, and especially the burden of hostility to their own inner distress; particularly when it cannot be perceived or accepted. Patients often demand that they be helped to cope with mind-like persecutory idols.[38] But how do we identify or reach them? A creative, caring attitude, which can be expressed in the most unlikely ways, may actually function as a path finder. The burden of hostility against mind-like idols may then no longer weigh on the subject alone. Patients and interlocutors often indirectly demand that they be helped to cope with their own hatred of their mind-like idols. And this can be done in a variety of ways, according to Casement; and so 'We may find ourselves getting to where a patient most needs the analysis to reach, if they are to attain release from what has formerly imprisoned them in their minds.'[39]

'Kairos' is known as the passing moment in which something special happens while time unfolds. It is the coming into being of a new state of things – however minimal – and it often happens in a movement of shared awareness. And yet, we usually live through 'kronos.' We use kairos while we are especially inspired, whereas we relapse into kronos when we are less creative. Roughly, kronos is the time of clocks and calendars, while kairos is the time for creative life, for growth. When we are under the aegis of kairos, events can come together, and the meeting enters awareness in such a way that psychic action must be taken to shape our destiny – be it for the minute or for a lifetime. If no action is taken, one's destiny might be changed anyway, but differently, because one did not act. Creativity is for destiny; apathy is for fate. The ordinary geniuses tend to adhere to kairos rather than only live in kronos, and constantly remind us of the vibrancy, renewal and sense of wonder of the present moment. In our consumers' society we seek to be satisfied planning the acquisition of whatever we believe will make us happy in the future. By converse, the ordinary geniuses that we encounter attract us towards whatever the present moment does actually offer. 'Catch them on the spot,' suggested Rosenfeld as a therapeutic strategy.[40] In fact, we can be fooled and obsessed by the future. There have been millions of casualties for the sake of some glorified future. The ordinary geniuses guide us into staying in the present moment and exercising in the here and now whatever degree of creativity.

In fact we can instantly be kind in the most unlikely ways. Winnicott, for instance, suggests that there are times when the patient, or any one of us, cannot even try to organise his own inner nonsense.[41] Organised nonsense can be a defence, just as willed chaos is a denial of chaos. The therapist, or anyone, who cannot accept the communication of nonsense becomes engaged in futile attempts to find some organisation in the nonsense. As a result, the patient will abandon the nonsense area because of hopelessness about communicating his current inner nonsense. In Ferro's view, an opportunity for rest is thus missed because of the therapist's need to find sense where nonsense is.[42] The patient has been unable to rest because of a failure of caring that undoes one's sense of trust. Without knowing it, the therapist has abandoned his professional role and has done so, paradoxically, by aiming to be a 'clever' analyst, even capable of seeing order in chaos. The suffering interlocutor may hint to a different way of addressing a problem. Anyone can immediately assist in supporting the person intent upon re-directing his own psychic gaze. One of the characteristics of ordinary genius is the capacity to put a temporary stop, that is to find his own present moment in the increasing speed of our egoic processes, as if it were a capacity to click on 'pause.' To enjoy caring it is necessary to make a pause and only start again from within the pause. To be able to do that, we need the ordinary genius who loves the present moment, who can endure the pain of not belonging to any acclaimed course of events implying 'progress' or the career of an acclaimed genius. In many cases life itself does cure some of our pathology; it is in fact life-with-others that can sometimes be intensely therapeutic. As we know, full attention frequently means full acceptance. This indicates that whenever the inner distress temporarily takes over, a caring other will definitely not mistake it for who the person really is. And even if distress attacks the caring other, as it probably will, he will not react to it as if the attacker were the *real* other. He will hold a space for intense attention. Any emotion that you can focus upon and take into attention can quickly begin to metamorphose. As long as the egoic mind (incapable of a witnessing embrace) is running our life, we cannot truly be creative; we cannot be at peace or fulfilled except for occasional intervals when we obtain what we wanted or when a craving has just been satisfied. This creates an endless preoccupation with past and future. The compulsion arises when we cannot stop in the here and now, when we cannot sacrifice 'memory or expectations' – in Bion's language.[43] But the past seems to give us identity and the future holds the promise of salvation. The ego cannot understand this; only the 'I' of the personality can.

The here-and-now perspective of psychoanalysis is thus more enlightening than we think. To complain that we cannot be caring normally coincides with the non-acceptance of what is the case; it invariably carries an unconscious negative charge. When you complain you make yourself into a victim who cannot possibly care. It is a denial of any inner knowledge. By converse, we could be the knowing that recognises our emotional pain and thus become able to avoid the compulsive and automatic outward projection of it. In Bion's terms this could be conceptualised as '-K,' as resistance to knowledge. Some people would always rather be somewhere else; their 'here' is never worth knowing; their 'now' is always too soon or too late. If we accept the knowledge of what is the case, a clear and still space of awareness would come into being; the product of our inner knowing, of the embracing witness, of the caring observer. This awareness does not deny the pain, and yet goes beyond it. In this way we can help in the here and now because we do not blend with negation.

If we assume that the desire to be caring is an essential source of creative fulfilment, of pleasure/joy, we should not be misled into believing that special and complex circumstances are required. There is no necessity for inspiration, training, authority. We can try right away. A profusion of discussions have emanated from Bion's celebrated suggestion that the therapist should approach the analysand without memories or expectations.[44] Whatever clinical attitude this suggestion may indicate, it certainly emphasises that we should not be pulled back into the past or escape into the future. Bion actually provides us with his own clinical example of not being able to care because of illusory 'defective' circumstances deriving from the other person:

> What it was that the object [patient] could not stand became clearer in some sessions where it appeared that in so far as I, the analyst, was insisting on verbal communication as a method of making the patient's problems explicit, I was felt to be directly attacking the patient's methods of communication. From this it became clear that when I was identified with the obstructive force, what I could not stand was the patient's methods of communication. In this phase my employment of verbal communication was felt by the patient to be a mutilating attack to *his* methods of communication.[45]

That is, an attack to the patient's *current, provisional* methods of communication. For instance, the ordinary geniuses who daily cope with the ordinary psychotics of our world of life have developed an intuitive grasp of those interpersonal exchanges, and even in the absence of psychoanalytic theories, genetic epistemology or relational strategies, they do ultimately cope because they do not insist on sufficiently appropriate verbal communication. They clearly know that what the other does is *just* his way of dealing with us, and that is just the way they are and that therefore there is no point either in 'education' or 'retaliation.' Our ordinary geniuses in fact manage to cope with the psychotic personalities composing our normal population. A psychotic man was married to an immigrant woman who did not rely upon, or care for articulation in the local language. As a creative way of surviving in marriage, they let each other be just as they were. Caring can be as simple as permitting the child to be a child – just as Bion's clinical caring could have simply allowed for *non*-verbal expression.

8

MINDING OUR BUSINESS

1. The legitimacy of creativeness

That we should be minding our own business sounds like some generic, self-centred suggestion; the thesis, however, is that this attitude is essential to healthy relations and also that it is the way to creative living. We either mind our own concerns and live a creative life, or else we incline to become dispersed into outer persons or world views into which we project our idealised, or unbearable, inner parts. In this outlook, we claim that one cannot be creative if constantly extroflected into external projections. Ultimately, the capacity to break free from outer objects of worship or hatred constitutes the precondition for creatively pursuing our personal destiny, as contrasted to a collective fate. Whenever we are monopolised by 'stars' or 'monsters,' we cannot mind our own business and thus we pre-emptively delegitimise our own daily creativity.

The idea running through this chapter is that projections onto others of hated or idolised features of our inner world may serve the perverse function of draining our personality of psychic energy and endorsing a general policy of dispersion and benumbment. If we cannot mind our own personal business we cannot be creative. And yet, many of us struggle to forge 'perfect' enemies to detest, and colourful idols to worship. Whether I spend my life hating selected enemies or adoring superstars, I deny the legitimacy of my own self as a source of accountability and productivity; I become increasingly passive and incapable of daily action, as different from reaction.[1] And thus we can only survive through reactions to those we use as idols or demons. We can obtusely waste our lives dying for, or against, someone or something – and dying by the million, in fact. We ultimately become enslaved to the bearers of our projections. Not only that: perhaps when we loath someone or something, what we ultimately abhor is our own enslavement to these emotions. We secretly detest our submission to the outer instruments of relief from our struggles. These 'instruments' in fact deprive us of freedom, spontaneity, creativeness: they perform the quintessence of psychic castration. Becoming fixed into our enslavement to external projections and to the hatred of our enslavement results in the most severe forms of abjection. Once we gain some awareness of these processes we can better appreciate the relevance of 'simply' minding our business. Glued to the clothes of the stars I may fail to wash and iron whatever garments I possess.

The uncovering of the processes that lead to this obliteration of our own concerns is one of the major psychoanalytic tasks. In Symington's view, 'Observing and cataloguing these processes in their intricacy, their subtlety, and their complexity is the scientific activity *within* psychoanalysis.'[2] By withdrawing projections we could become capable of minding our business; this sounds of course like some immemorial, pragmatic selfish suggestion. But if we cannot mind our own concerns, all creative options are forfeited and we only homogenise with the external supports of our idealising projections. These 'external' and yet mind-like idols[3] ultimately seem to acquire a life of their own and to rule us from the outside while we bear the inner burden of enslavement. But then, ultimately, 'I am as little able to think by any mind but my own as to breath with another's lungs.'[4]

A silent conviction of non-creativity can be so firmly entrenched that any attempt to dislodge it may seem futile. Why? Perhaps because it cannot be really detected or monitored. Paradoxically, it is a damaging absence and we cannot see an absence very well. Our ordinary geniuses are those who refuse the belief that there is nothing that they can generate, who abhor the awful finality of it and somehow act as if they could be creative. In fact, if we are not gently tormented by a creative propensity we may put aside the issue and pleasurably slip into paralysing idolatries – either of our own making or already culturally available. In the grand scheme of things we may gradually become irrelevant – only that. And perhaps the more we are passive, the more we are psychically dead. Minding our business is a prerequisite for the eradication of parasitic elements sustaining a false, passive self. But, paradoxically, a false, lifeless self may even extroflect itself in manifold guises of proudly exhibiting our enslavement. Once we are alienated into, and enslaved by, the more popular and prestigious projections, we even boast of our subservience to them. We 'rejoice' in being 'normal,' to the point of becoming normotic. According to Bollas, we all often join in an endless 'celebration of commonality.'[5]

There is something that we would like to know: in Winnicott's parlance, what happens to a good-enough person in a good-enough society? For it is in these situations that we clearly see the creativity of the human being and of the society the individual is born in. Freud, of course, began from pathology, from the failure of the environment or of the individual to be good enough. According to Lear, psychoanalysis in that sense is a wisdom won from illness.[6] But if we are to understand ordinary creativeness we must work towards a psychoanalytic understanding of its conscious legitimacy; its plain legitimacy is essential. But then, even acclaimed, official genius is necessary for psychic life; we need it to validate whatever is exceptional within our ordinary lives. In succinct terms, Oliver thus synthesises the question: 'Psychic life depends on a sense of validation and legitimization of the possibility of creativity and greatness *for all of us*.'[7]

When we cannot succeed in minding our own business we find it convenient to do so by proxy and thus we become omnipotent through ideologies, charismatic leaders and the like. We ultimately become omnipotent/impotent in a socially approved and culturally glorified fashion. And thus there is no legitimacy for our creativity or initiative. This situation can be exacerbated by our telematic culture in which we know about everything while there is virtually nothing that we can do about it. Grotstein reports that in the course of his analysis with Bion, his associations revealed that he had unwittingly become grandiose. And Bion interpreted: 'You were *reduced* to becoming omnipotent because you felt you couldn't handle the danger implicit in that circumstance otherwise.'[8] And this is perhaps due to a psychic illegitimacy of creativeness and to the 'danger' of creative actions; a dreadful affliction that we cannot easily monitor – the affliction of passivity. In Symington's view, how I appear to others is unfortunately what motivates me to action;[9] therefore in this state of affairs I am in the other's pocket. The other's approval is essential and therefore I must blend with the other; I am in the power of the other, controlled by the other. I cannot be creative because I cannot mind my own business. But, again, do I have the psychic right to mind my own affairs? We become projected into external 'realities' because we are dependent upon external figures for the redemption of our abjected selves. And so we struggle to be erotised by whatever idealised entities: a perverse cycle.[10] But I also have to control these others so that they continue to 'sustain' me. We may live to obtain a 'loving' touch from any of our kaisers or pharaohs, or even be pulled and dispersed into their orbit.

Of course it is essential to psychic integration that we can perform whatever is required of us in any particular situation – without it becoming a role that we identify with. Otherwise we risk becoming unconscious players in games that may look very important but are ultimately devoid of any *personal* meaning. In a world of role-playing personalities, the few people who do not impersonate an ego-produced image but function from the deeper core of their being are our veritable geniuses. When you do not play a role it means that there is no false self in what you do. As a result, our actions are not automatic reactions and carry a far greater force. Our dependence on projections may become the basis for all further interpretations, or rather misinterpretations of reality, interactions and relationships. Our life becomes a lifeless reflection of our previous projections. By contrast, in the seeing of who you are not, the reality of who you are seems to spontaneously emerge.

Fear seems to have many causes but certainly one of them is the (false) self fear of annihilation. To a false self derived from identification with our projections, death is always around the corner. In such a projective state, in fact, fear of disruption affects every aspect of our life. For example, even such a seemingly trivial and 'normal' thing as the compulsive need to be right in an argument and make the other person 'wrong' – defending the mental position with which you have identified – is due to the fear of annihilation of our enslaved self.[11] If you identify with a mental allegiance and are 'proved' wrong, your projection-based sense of self is seriously threatened with annihilation. And so, we cannot afford to be 'wrong' – or evolve. To be 'wrong' is to die: wars have been fought over this, and countless relationships have been damaged. We cannot bear to be wrong; the genius is able to bear just that. Once an individual has disidentified from her 'convictions' (paranoias?), whether she is right or wrong makes no difference to her sense of self and so the compulsive and unconscious need to be right, which is also a form of violence, will no longer oppress us. We can clearly say how we feel or what we think but there will be no need for aggressiveness or defensiveness about it; we can thus resume creative thinking. Creativity becomes legitimate to the extent to which we become disenchanted with outer stars and unbreakable allegiances.

But how is someone able to efface the worth of one's own self so effectively? By placing omnipotence in outer idols and thus annulling one's own spontaneity and personal accountability. This outlook implies the immediate conclusion that personal creativeness is illegitimate and delusional. Nothing less than that. In order to restore damaged faculties, psychoanalysis has the task of 'observing' and integrating omnipotence so that it does not act destructively, so that creativeness remains legitimate. We often feel that we have understood this mechanism but we do not quite understand it, all at the same time; indeed a major problem. But if the analyst understands this condition, this awareness will probably direct her mind towards describing the mind of the sufferer. And the patient will probably experience this co-description as an adequate psychic way of containing his own abjection – that is, an inclination to not do what he can do. By contrast, once responsibility is sacrificed in favour of some anaesthetised imitation, the opportunities for psychic life seem to close like a valve, impeding any creative inversion of currents. And also, displacement into external objects is somehow cognate to relegating our psychic life to either our 'past' or to our 'future.' Both of these ways of alienation are self-damaging perversions. We can easily forfeit the legitimacy to be creative in the present moment. Unease, anxiety, restlessness are caused by too much future – and not enough present. Similarly, guilt, regret, resentment are induced by too much past devouring the present moment. But is it legitimate to creatively live in the present moment? This is the crucial question.

A clinical example? We crave those magazines full of celebrities, and we can hardly wait to start turning their glossy pages. The covers promise articles on the lives and activities of big stars: a Dalai Lama or an elegant queen, Beckham or Obama ... perhaps a scoop into secret chambers. This often makes for 'interesting' reading because we frequently thirst for connection with superstars: the bearers of our idealisations/idolisations. Being so forcefully pulled in the direction of our idols we are ultimately left with no time to cultivate our own current potentials. As we are irresistibly pulled into the orbit of stars, we tend to become dark planets – forever depending on outer lights. It is like pronouncing perverse vows of creative chastity and enslavement. And perhaps this is not just imaginative, metaphoric language. The millions of casualties resulting from historical conflicts were perhaps not simply due to coerced persons, homogenised into a mad ideology; many of us just very actively seek and follow acclaimed leaders, whoever they are.

2. The affliction of parasitic projections

The excessive dependence on external projections determines an inner life oppressed by parasitic, mind-like elements. We shall thus try to explore the damaging role of mind-like idols as well as our attempts to escape from them.[12] When we cannot utilise good-enough parts of our mind or when we cannot tolerate its bad parts we automatically project them and then become dependent to the point of harbouring them as parasitic components of the self. Unless we become free of these parasitic currents we cannot mind our personal interests and cannot be free for creativity. There is no clear strategy for this exploration but we must nonetheless try, feel our way around and persist. And thus this subchapter amounts to no more than 'notes,' which seem to somehow converge on our present concern: an affliction by mind-like parasites deriving from the implosion of expulsive projections. To illustrate this outlook we use the expression of 'mind-like object' or 'mind-like idol.' The question is whether the paralysing outlooks relied upon in the worst conditions of life continue to poison our development even when growth, would be possible. The subject may be oppressed by what 'saved' him even though he recognises that it is time to move on, if he only could. It is a sort of psychic tangle that seems to claim a life of its own.[13] As time goes on, such a cluster of damaging identifications seems less geared to the survival of the subject than to its own permanence. In Eigen's imagery, this 'tangle' grips the self like a dying hand clutches the flesh of the living. States of mind that may have served well at one point can be hindrances at another. The identificatory steel will that could see us through, can keep us coiled and stop us from opening. This 'tangle' may have played a role in enabling survival, but then it may even put life on hold.[14] Too often it becomes an empty will, feeding its own subsistence without giving the individual much in the way of support. But Eigen incisively asks:

> What of the life that undergoes successive contractions, until what is left is not much more than a strangulated knot? – a will that tightens around itself like a fist that cannot open ... and keeps tightening,

trapped by its own density, becoming like a black hole, denser and darker as time goes on.[15]

Jung can be credited with advocating a comparable outlook when he refers to the function of 'complexes.' In fact, when we endeavour to accomplish something in our daily creativeness and we feel impeded in the enterprise in spite of our best intentions,

> We are really forced to speak of the tendency of complexes to act as if they were characterised by a certain amount of will-power. When you speak of will-power, you naturally ask about the ego. Where then is the ego that belongs to the will-power of the complexes?[16]

Jung even calls them 'little devils.' Also,

> The so-called unity of consciousness is an illusion. It really is a wish dream. We like to think that we are one; but we are not, most decidedly not. We are not really masters in our house ... Complexes have a tendency to move by themselves, to live their own life apart from our intentions.[17]

We are not masters in our own house not only because we are sustained and propelled by immense instinctual forces, but also because we may have passively introjected 'external' projections that may coalesce in the form of mind-like agents acting on their own. The poorly internalised containers of our projections may in turn become figures, or 'characters.' In McDougall's language, 'Whether we will it or not, our inner characters are constantly seeking a stage on which to play out their tragedies and comedies.'[18] And also, language may inform us that the script writer is called 'I.' But then, the 'protagonist' is ruled by these mind-like agents forever craving to reign in the inner stage. In her view, it is only when we try to recreate scenes upon the psychoanalytic stage that we often discover to our dismay that we are in full performance, yet totally ignorant of who the real characters are or what the story is about.[19]

The ordinary geniuses are those who can cope imaginatively with projective identifications once they are established. In fact a parasitic, oracular voice has its own primitive 'intelligence,' not unlike a cunning 'animal,' and its 'logic' is directed primarily at its own survival, not at that of its harbouring mind. Almost like all life-forms it periodically needs to feed on energies compatible with its own. That is why it thrives on drama and destructiveness. This addiction especially craves to force the individual to convert to itself and remain intoxicated. And even innate qualities of intelligence go to the service of this alienating form of 'thinking.' This sort of uncreativeness stands out all the more clearly because the individual still has its native resources of intelligence and also a whole range of virtues such as courage, resolution, enterprise, loyalty. This is as true of 'fallen angels' as it is true of those who embrace the most insane of ideologies.[20]

An oracle may function like any of the tables of a Rorschach test; that is, it functions as a 'revered' instrument of projection. It is said that at the oracular sites there were natural sounds, echoes, leaves moved by the wind, special ways of dreaming and the like. And moreover when an oracular voice proclaims that a child will kill his father and wed his mother there seems to be the awful suggestion that this is all that the subject is capable of. In Symington's view the submission of Oedipus to the fateful voice of the oracle was what generated the subsequent terrible events; he suggests that the inner malign power that gripped the heart of Oedipus is worse than the catastrophic events that follow.[21] And why does Oedipus fulfil all that was pronounced by the oracle? Why does he do it so violently? The voice says 'You will kill your father and marry your mother' and with a benumbed passive mind the consultant says 'Ok, I will.'[22] Our ability to stay present enough, alert enough, may enable us to notice the heavy influx of 'oracular' voices when they become active. When an oracular voice is recognised and identified, it can no longer pretend to be me and to renew itself through me. The 'prophecy' in most cases does not dissolve immediately, but once you have severed the link between it and your thinking, the malign projection begins to lose power. Messages derived from oracles can be extremely dramatic. But why buy into the drama? Do we have to take it so seriously? To avoid the pain of detachment from oracular projections, from parasitic idols, we even produce social philosophies that will safeguard the oracular voices and perpetuate our condition of benumbment. This we have repeatedly observed in not so ancient historical periods. Symington suggests that 'Embodiment of the thoughts of a god has been substituted for thinking.'[23] As is known, dynasties, feuds and schisms (also within our psychoanalytic culture) can be seen as indicators of this pervasive human weakness: submission to idols. People fail to be themselves because it is easier to be somebody else. They can more easily imitate someone else's success than risk their own failure or, paradoxically, risk their own success; in fact, risk can be unbearable. People are in a hurry to magnify themselves by copying what is revered, and are too paralysed or benumbed for coping with their own thoughts. In the academies we even call this 'disciplinary integrity.'

Symington writes that he has actually observed this malign force that had so inexorable a grip on Oedipus:

> I have seen it in myself, I have seen it in friends, I have seen it in patients. It is something that is worse by far than the more sensational manifestations of human depravity. You might say that you cannot get worse than parricide combined with incest, and yet I can state

confidently that these are the epiphenomena of a malignancy that is far worse. In fact the killing of the father is the pseudo-attempt to break free.[24]

Once we have dissolved ourselves into some persecutory idol, we do not want to let go and on a deeply unconscious level we do not want creative change. It would threaten our identity as 'heroic' battered persons. We will then ignore, deny or sabotage the creativeness of our daily life. This is a common phenomenon, but it is also insane.

3. Addictive thinking

The most far removed from our capacity to think creatively is perhaps our compulsive, repetitive addictive way of 'thinking.' What characterises this quasi-obsessive mental behaviour is that we no longer feel we have the choice to stop. Thus we remain in the grip of 'past' and 'future' – confined into a phantasmal sort of time. And yet some ordinary geniuses manage to break free, resume creativeness and even opt for genuine affective investments occupying our here and now. To the self possessed by addictive thinking the present moment hardly exists. Only past and future exist, perhaps for the unconscious purpose of maintaining some lifeless status quo. This persistent travesty of mental life perhaps accounts for the fact that in this enslaved mode our mind is so dysfunctional. It basically says, 'One day when this, that or the other happens, I will be happy, peaceful and creative.' We come to actually think that we need a total 'revolution' to somehow manage our lives; in this sense, then, 'revolutions' might ultimately be used as the celebrated opium of the people.

The egoic mind enslaved to oracular voices is not a condition of *acute* pain but of an almost continuous low level of discontent and boredom – a sort of background static noise that deadens the mind. We may not realise this because it is so much part of 'normal' living, just as we become unaware of a continuous, low background disturbance. And yet, should it suddenly stop, there is an enlivening sense of relief. Humans frequently use alcohol, sex, food, fights as anaesthetics in an unconscious attempt to remove some basic unease. When this happens, an activity that might be enlivening in an inner atmosphere of freedom and spontaneity becomes imbued with an addictive, compulsive quality. The same is true with our repetitive, unremitting thoughts. Thinking is no longer adaptive or productive (let alone 'creative') when it is reduced to an addiction. Theory, likewise, is no longer theoretical – and inclines to ideology – when it loses sight of its conditional nature and constantly circulates as a form of epistemic inquisition. Ordinary geniuses manage not to be dominated by this oppressive use of thinking and rethinking oracular voices. Every addiction arises from an unconscious refusal to face and move through our pain, however 'moderate' it may be. We become incapable of inner actions and constantly 'opt' for outer actions such as killing Laius, ingesting something or even falling in the grip of unstoppable thinking. Drug-like substances, world views or mental habits do not actually cause the pain, they bring out the pain and unhappiness that is already in us. All addictions probably do that. If we slightly shift our point of observation we could even say that addictive thinking is one of the derivatives of the oracular voices that we have passively absorbed to relieve distress, voices that are imploded into us in the form of mind-like scripts on which we constantly elaborate.

If we are pulled into unconscious identification with oracular voices through lack of personal wakeful presence, the voices become who we are and even tend to metamorphose into our ways of thinking. Ordinary geniuses disguised as simple friends are often effective in drastically waking us. And yet, often a vicious circle builds up between our thinking and our mind-like idols – and they ultimately feed on each other. By dwelling mentally on idolised messages our own thinking confers energy to the oracular voice, which in turn energises our addictive thinking and patterns and so on. In fact, the striving for endless growth is a dysfunction and a disease; it is the virulence of the parasitic mind-like idols whose only goal is to increase themselves, unaware that they are bringing about, eventually, our/their destruction by destroying the organism of which they have become part. But in this blind outlook there is no accountability or care for life. To look at it in a slightly different way, we could say that our incessant mental noise prevents us from finding that realm of inner stillness that is inseparable from creative thinking. It is not so much that you use your cluster of identifications wrongly. You probably do not use it at all, because it uses you. This is our diseased, addictive thinking. You may believe that you use your identificatory functions but this is a delusion because the instrument has taken you over.

And thus, trying to present convergent notes on the elusive topic of uncreative thinking, we should remark with Silverman that it is possible that some sensitive individuals become incapable of perceiving the addictive ideological thinking by which they have been defined. They somehow fall into the reflecting mirror of their projective identifications.[25] They then erroneously imagine that they really are what they are insanely defined as being. For instance, 'You simply are one who can only murder a father and wed a mother,' and so on indefinitely. The consultant's mind becomes the unstoppable continuation of the oracle. Perhaps we could ask if our minds are as incessantly active as those of severely disturbed persons; they think out loud while we mostly think silently in our head. Perhaps differences are in degree only. Sometimes, for a moment, a genius friend is capable of making us stand back from our own mind and see it in a different perspective. There is a brief shift from compulsive thinking to peaceful awareness. At the moment of detachment from addictive thinking we could perhaps smile compassionately to ourselves, and only in these moments can creativeness can once again become legitimate.

Creativeness means rising above addictive thinking. You can use your thought processes as they are needed, but in a much more focused and effective way. Isolated, addictive thinking, no longer connected with the vaster realm of creativity and strong relations, may quickly become barren, insane, destructive. Liberation from parasitic thinking is the joy of good functioning that the individual can only experience when she partially 'gets out of her head,' so to speak. Health must be felt and not just thought: we learn water by drinking. Rosenfeld repeatedly emphasised the immense joy of good mental functioning;[26] he insisted that it is psychically 'tangible' and treasured.

In our outlook of converging notes, we could also consider that our addictive thinking may re-awaken from occasional states of dormancy – when it gets 'hungry,' when it is time to replenish itself. Under these circumstances, a creative thought is indigestible for addictive thinking, and it must first be degraded into something sufficiently abjecting. The oracular voices sustaining addictive thinking will soon be telling sad, angry stories about everything: forever blaming, devaluing, complaining. As we identify totally with these voices we believe all their distorted thoughts. In turn, this becomes a confirmation of addiction.

We are largely responsible for the production of idolisable ideals to which we relinquish our souls. And even though it is the subject that has turned something into a domineering idol, he often falls prostrate before it, in thrall to its bewitching lustre. What is ironic is that there is a magnetic attraction towards aspects of our personality once they are dislodged into something external. Yet ordinary geniuses manage to escape these enslavements. Silverman suggests that certain cultural objects or ideological conglomerations are so widely represented as being worthy of idealisation that they become the most sought-after containers of our idolic projections; they even soar to the status of normative standards.[27] These are ideal containers for idolic parts of our mind. And yet, no matter how often it is reiterated, an 'ideal figure' remains a bloodless abstraction until it has been psychically affirmed by our subservience. When we push mind-like idols into significant others in the environment, individuals become tranquilly forced into their mental subservience. The attachment to the person or group who harbours an expelled mental element has the quality of adhesive fixity, and the person who has made the projection derives her thinking from the displaced idol to whom she is bound. Creative thinking becomes smothered in addictive thoughts. The problem, then, is not the presence of mind-like idols per se, but our blindness, our unwillingness to confront and recognise them. Clinical experience also seems to suggest that a mental attitude of acceptance – rather than unconscious hatred – might actually reduce darkness. One may creatively wonder what use Oedipus might have made of the oracular voices in his soul and how a lively relationship might have transformed and redirected his personality. The atrophy of creative thinking leading to self-destruction follows the benumbment of an addicted mind. As the most thorough form of destruction, death may come to be desired for oneself or others. The horror attending to the whole issue may, moreover, cause a great deal of repression, forcing us to deny it all, and to be left merely wondering why life seems so absurd.[28] The ordinary geniuses are those who secretly, silently resist this common folly. As Damasio pointed out, in the totalitarian regimes of the twentieth century, ideologies easily prevailed upon a presumably normal apparatus of reason with devastating consequences.[29] Adherence to addictive thinking could involve detrimental outcomes for which we hardly have a vocabulary, such as the inconspicuous and deadening pathology of indifference and benumbment. The everyday geniuses are those unsung heroes who are capable of resisting the hypnotic power of ideologies.

4. Escape from projections and ransom of the self

The thesis here is that the capacity of withdrawing projections is the way to ransom our more vital self. Parts of our psyche are frequently expelled and embodied into outer objects to which we become enslaved through either worship or hatred. The retrieval of our own selves and the escape from 'alienation' could be regarded as one of the most creative human ventures. We project into oracular sites in order to gain some super-knowledge or strategic forecasts; we project into 'stars' in order to quickly win some super-identity; we project into appropriate villains in order to get free of unbearable elements. Paradoxically, it is our knack for expediency that is psychically damaging.

Theories are of course useful to reflect on ourselves and especially on our capacity for dealing with psychic, interpersonal, intangible reality. And yet the ubiquitous phenomenon of projective identification is not some sophisticated invention of psychoanalysts; but rather a typical behaviour of our species. In this sense our psychic ways of life seem somehow pre-existent to our ways of naming or conceptualising them. And perhaps geniuses are those who have become capable of transformation as an alternative to evacuations and acquisitions. A biological organism can get rid of toxic, non-metabolised substances quite independently of others. But when it comes to psychic life and mental states, we absolutely need *others* to absorb and embody toxic elements. This is a central problem in our human condition. As is known, there can be inner currents that are too explosive with respect to any processing apparatus; we dislodge them for the purpose of 'tranquil' hatred. All we can do is help and be helped to contain and process negative emotions. We can often help the other to transform murderous attitudes into narratives that can be deconcretised and rewoven. Ordinary geniuses are especially great at supporting the psychic metabolism of others. For Grotstein, projective identifications are the enzymes of every transference whether it concerns past or present states of mind.[30] Probably many more dynamics than we currently know and recognise actually unfold between one mind and the other.

Owning bad motives can indeed lead to fatalism, as if any move whatsoever could only make the situation worse; but disowning them can conceal their presence in us. We then tend to project them and attribute them to others. Geniuses secretly resist oppressive micro- or macro-ideologies. In fact the image of the passive victim of any '... ism' is as suspect as the picture of the entirely active instigator who imposes his insane strategies. In Midgley's view, influential psychopaths derive their power not from inventiveness but from a perception of just what unacknowledged motives lie waiting to be exploited.[31] There is, therefore, a significant sense in which our demagogues are themselves the tools of their followers. As is known, 'dictators' are not wholly active, nor their subjects entirely passive; a perverse synergy is at work. Perhaps what makes projections hard to discern is that same pervasive diffusion which sustains their power. Perhaps the apparently innocuous hostility towards the *other* group, whether ethnic or scientific, is barely noticeable. And a very significant characteristic of some diffuse hostility is its great versatility, namely the nimbleness with which it can be shifted from one antagonist to another.[32] Anyone who has read history books for even just a few years will easily observe that alliances are changed far more easily than one might expect and that hostility is even more easily redirected. There are strong components of fantasy in our hostility to 'alien' groups; an hostility induces common paranoiac accusations sustaining the hunt of witches, heretics, counter-revolutionaries. The idea that a tyrant may have imposed a paranoiac conviction on a passive mob of supporters is not quite plausible. Probably the leaders can only take people where they are willing to go. No movement consists solely of followers.

To different degrees of intensity we are unconsciously at work recruiting persons to enact with us, or for us, scenes and scripts deriving from our inner world. If we get our scripts endorsed by any oracular sites or services, everything becomes more expedient. The tragedy of our laborious struggles in our inclination to seek pre-emptive authorisation by whatever oracular voices are available in the environment. The seekers of endorsement may even *force* some appropriate person – a therapist, for instance – to function as an oracular source of guidance. The source of tragedy may actually reside in the propensity to consult oracles; a 'consultation' that simply endorses our projections. The essential element of disaster is the endorsement by whatever oracular agent, the ratification from whatever source of 'superior' approval. What actually happens is that both in therapy and ordinary life we subject others to the most intense pressure intended to make them feel just as our unconscious wishes want them to. We then feel justly authorised by them. No less than that. As a hypothetical clinical vignette we could think of something that we are often tempted to do: when we intend to discredit someone – to 'destroy' someone – we force a 'prestigious' interlocutor to 'share' our disparaging remarks. When we believe that the interlocutor has sufficiently endorsed our view, we can then expediently use 'his' views to produce 'our' destructiveness.

It can be painful at times to suddenly wake up and realise that the collective world view we have identified with and worked for is insane. A collective ego is perhaps more unconsciously tenacious than the individuals that make it up. Some human beings, however, are natural geniuses, so to speak, in coping (maybe, just secretly laughing) with this widespread human condition. A great deal of psychoanalytic acumen seems focused on the exploration of repression, denial, forclosure; that is, inclinations to make trouble unconscious, egoically declaring it non-existent and relegating it to an unconscious domain. It is equally creative to explore our inclination to use others in our attempt to 'deliver' ourselves from whatever the problem is. Something as essential and creative as the elaboration of projective identifications is not of course limited to that infinitesimal part of humankind who has access to high-quality psychoanalytic treatment. Some gifted individuals can encourage it in the most disparate circumstances; our ordinary geniuses do not merely react to projections and in their responses to them remain capable of action proper – indeed a therapeutic action. One of the most highly regarded psychoanalysts in my city 'confessed' that every Sunday he went for afternoon tea in a beautiful hotel where a waiter/friend was capable of somehow 'clarifying' his most profound thoughts, especially in the way of demolishing convictions that seemed to oppress him. This sort of superlative waiting-on function can perhaps be performed by innumerable individuals.[33]

Submission to oracular figures is a way of deadening vital parts of our own self. If we manage to withdraw alienating projections by means of creative actions (as contrasted with automatic reactions) we can be on the way to reclaiming our more creative aspects. In Symington's view, 'false gods' are parts of the personality that are embodied in external figures. Through their expulsion we remain in a sort of gelatinous condition:

> The god I have been trying to describe I call a "false god" in that it deceives the believer into trusting its dictates ... The presence of this god precludes the possibility of thinking. It is intrinsically antagonistic to thinking ... There is no option other than to capitulate in total submission. The god and the gelatinous substance are two parts of an interlocking system ... and what is said does not represent the thought of a person. It is a pretend person, something standing for a person that could be there but is not.[34]

If we can break free from such deadening idolatries we can reclaim our true creative selves. False gods can make us grandiose, omnipotent and also basically gelatinous. We ultimately become incapable of minding our own affairs. Being 'reduced' to omnipotence paradoxically evokes the inertia of a gelatinous substance. Symington suggests that 'It is in the free act that we come to see our madness ... the waste of our lives ... the shocking damage we do to ourselves.' And also: *'The* creative act is that one whereby I gather all the disparate parts of myself into a new personal synthesis.'[35] Gathering into a synthesis? The fundamental question cannot be merely internal unity, coherence, seamless logicality, but whether we can make our souls our own.

NOTES

1 INTRODUCTORY REMARKS

1 Michael Parsons, *The Dove that Returns – The Dove that Vanishes: Paradox and Creativity in Psychoanalysis*, London, Routledge, 2000, The New Library of Psychoanalysis, p. 24. In connection with Parson's 'new light,' we could quote one of Wittgenstein's remarks: 'The important fine shades of behaviour are not predictable.' Ludwig Wittgenstein, *Last Writings in the Philosophy of Psychology*, Vol. II, 'The Inner and the Outer' 1949–1951, Oxford, Blackwell Publishers, 1992, paragraph 65 e. In the *Encyclopaedia of Psychology* Howe suggests that geniuses are admired and valued for a number of reasons, not least because their achievements touch the lives of the human community. We are interested here in the ordinary geniuses whose interactive achievements have also touched, actually shaped, the lives of millions of creatures, and yet are unsung, unrecorded, anonymous. Michael Howe, 'Genius,' in *Encyclopaedia of Psychology*, Vol. 3, Alan E. Kazdin (ed.), Oxford: Oxford University Press, 2000, p. 467.
2 Sigmund Freud, 'Psychopathology of Everyday Life,' Vol. 6, *The Standard Edition*, 1991.
3 Adam Phillips and Barbara Taylor, *On Kindness*, London: Hamish Hamilton, Penguin Books, 2009, p. 119. If there is no accepted term for our daily creativity, we may even come to think that this potential does not exist. This can easily be appreciated in a reversed logic: if there is a consensual term for 'something' in our vocabulary, we are inclined to believe in its 'verifiable' existence. A significant remark by John Stuart Mill can be reported here: 'The tendency has always been strong to believe that whatever received a name must be an entity or being, having an independent existence of its own. And if no real entity answering to that name could be found, men did not for that reason suppose that none existed, but imagined that it was something particularly abstruse and mysterious.' Quoted in S.J. Gould, *The Mismeasure of Man*, New York, W.W. Norton, 1981, p. 185; subsequently quoted in Steven Mitchell, *Hope and Dread in Psychoanalysis*, New York, Basic Books, 1993, p. 100.
4 A. Phillips and B. Taylor, p. 120.
5 In Bion's view, science is 'appropriate only for inanimate objects. The science that is apposite for psychoanalysis is a… science of emotions that are infinite and consequently complex and non-linear in nature.' James Grotstein, *A Beam of Intense Darkness: Wilfred Bion's Legacy to Psychoanalysis*, London, Karnac, 2007, p. 328. Infinite and non-linear emotions have been theorised in the monumental contributions of Ignacio Matte Blanco, *The Unconscious as Infinite Sets: An Essay in Bi-Logic*, London, Karnac, 1975; *Thinking, Feeling and Being: Clinical Reflections on the Fundamental Antinomy of the Human Being and World*, London, Routledge, 1988.

NOTES

6 J. Grotstein, *A Beam of Intense Darkness*, pp. 18–19.
7 This topic has been previously developed in Gemma Corradi Fiumara, *Spontaneity: A Psychoanalytic Inquiry*, chapter 9, 'Empathy and Sympathy,' London, Routledge, 2009, pp. 92–112.
8 Galileo Galilei, *Dialogue on the Great World Systems*, the Salisbury translation, revised, annotated and with an introduction by G. De Santillana, Chicago, University of Chicago Press, 1953, pp. 116–17.
9 Marcus Aurelius, *The Meditations of Marcus Aurelius: Spiritual Teachings and Reflections*. George Long (trans.), introduction by Alan Jacobs, London, Watkins Publishing, 2008, book 6, paragraph 19, p. 91.
10 Immanuel Kant, *Anthropology from a Pragmatic Point of View*, R.B. Louden trans. and ed., Cambridge, Cambridge University Press, 2006, p. 122. We could note in this connection that using the word 'genius' to designate an exceptional kind of individual was largely unknown until the eighteenth century; our modern meaning derives as much from the Latin word *ingenium*, indicating technical inventiveness, as from the Latin term *genius*, in the sense of muse, protective 'spirit' of a family or place – the celebrated *genius loci*.
11 Salimbene de Adam of Parma, 'Chronicon Parmense: Avvenimenti tra il 1167 ed il 1287', in *La letteratura italiana: Storia e testi: Le origini*, Antonio Viscardi *et al.* (eds), Milan-Naples, Ricciardi Editore, 1946, p. 979.
12 Aristotle, *Poetics*, *The Complete Works of Aristotle*, Vol. II, Bollingen Series LXXX 1. 2., revised Oxford Translation, ed. Jonathan Barnes (ed.), Princeton NJ, Princeton University Press, 1985, paragraph 22, 1457b, 6–9, p. 2235.
13 Aristotle, *Poetics*, paragraph 22, 1459a, 5–8, p. 2234.
14 Aristotle, *Poetics*, 10–15, p. 2239.
15 Aristotle, *Rhetoric*, *The Works of Aristotle*, Vol. II, 11, 1354–1420 W.R. Roberts trans., ed. W.D. Ross (ed.), Oxford, Clarendon Press, 1924.
16 Donald Winnicott, *Playing and Reality*, London, Tavistock Publications, 1971, p. 100.
17 Ibid., p. 67.
18 Ibid., p. 68.
19 See Christopher Bollas, *The Shadow of the Object: Psychoanalysis of the Unthought Known*, London, Free Association Books, 1987, p. 19. On this same topic see Arnold Modell, *The Private Self*, Cambridge MA and London, Harvard University Press, 1993, p. 75.
20 Eugenio Gaddini, 'On Imitation,' *The International Journal of Psychoanalysis*, 1969, 50: 475–84. In this connection we should invoke a remark that Freud made about Leonardo da Vinci: 'Even if the historical material at our disposal were very abundant and if the psychical mechanisms could be dealt with the greatest assurance, there are ... important points at which a psycho-analytic inquiry would not be able to make us understand how inevitable it was that the person concerned should have turned out in the way he did and in no other way ... *We must recognize here a degree of freedom which cannot be resolved any further by psycho-analytic means.*' Sigmund Freud, 'Leonardo da Vinci and a Memory of His Childhood,' in *Five Lectures on Psycho-Analysis, Leonardo da Vinci and Other Works*, Vol. 11, *The Standard Edition*, 1910, p. 135. (Emphasis added.)
21 This issue is explored in Gemma Corradi Fiumara, *The Other Side of Language: A Philosophy of Listening*, chapter 4 'The Power of Discourse and the Strength of Listening,' London, Routledge, 1990, pp. 28–51.
22 D. Winnicott, *Playing and Reality*, p. 54.
23 Ibid., p. 54.
24 Wilfred R. Bion, *Bion's Brazilian Lectures*, Vol. 2, Jayme Salomao (ed.), Rio de Janeiro, Imago Editora, 1975, p. 203.

NOTES

25 D. Winnicott, *Playing and Reality*, p. 69.
26 Herbert Rosenfeld reiterated elaborately this point in the course of his regular clinical seminars conducted at the Rome Institute of Psychoanalysis (*Centro Psicoanalitico di Roma*) between 1975 and 1985.
27 D. Winnicott, *Playing and Reality*, p. 69.
28 Ibid., p. 98.
29 Margaret Boden, *The Creative Mind: Myths and Mechanisms*, London, Routledge, 2004, p. 1.
30 Julia Kristeva, *New Maladies of the Soul*, R. Guberman (trans.) New York, Columbia University Press, 1995; also see *The Sense and Non-Sense of Revolt*, New York, Columbia University Press, 2000.
31 D. Winnicott, *Playing and Reality*, p. 65.
32 Ibid., p. 69.
33 Neville Symington, *The Blind Man Sees: Freud's Awakening and Other Essays*, London, Karnac, 2004, p. 179.
34 Ibid., p. 179.
35 Kelly Oliver, *The Colonization of Psychic Space: A Psychoanalytic Social Theory of Oppression*, Minneapolis, MN–London, University of Minnesota Press, 2004, p. 159.
36 Antonino Ferro, 'Book Review Essay: *A Beam of Intense Darkness: Wilfred Bion's Legacy to Psychoanalysis* by James Grotstein, London, Karnac, 2007, *The International Journal of Psychoanalysis*, 2008, 89(4), pp. 867–84.
37 Jonathan Lear, *Love and Its Place in Nature: A Philosophical Interpretation of Freudian Psychoanalysis*, New Haven–London, Yale University Press, 1990, p. 205. It is widely considered that someone who has made dazzling contributions is regarded as a person of genius. Consequently, despite appearances, calling someone a genius is more a matter of bestowing an accolade, rather than providing a description of that person. We are impressed and proclaim them 'stars', superhuman. In this way we become rather blind, for we insist on looking without actually seeing – a paradoxical form of blindness.
38 Adam Phillips, *Going Sane*, London, Penguin Books, 2005, p. 119.
39 Ibid., p. 119.
40 This issue is discussed in George Steiner, *Nostalgia for the Absolute*, Toronto, House of Anansi Press, 2004, p. 13.
41 George Steiner, *Grammars of Creation: Originating in the Gifford Lectures for 1990*, London, Faber and Faber, 2002, p. 24.
42 Prestigious institutions incessantly emphasise their educational focus on logocentric, logocratic power, probably in order to attract individuals potentially aspiring to extraordinary, official geniushood.
43 This is discussed in Christopher Bollas, *The Forces of Destiny: Psychoanalysis and Human Idiom*, London, Free Association Books, 1991. The notion of an 'I' of the personality is also presented in A. Modell, *The Private Self*, p. 34; the comparable notion of a 'subjective self' is developed by William Meissner, 'The Genesis of the Self: IV. The Implications for the Analytic Relation and Process Part 1. The Self as Integral Subject,' *Psychoanalytic Review*, 2009, 96(2), pp. 297–336.
44 Neville Symington, *A Pattern of Madness*, London, Karnac, 2002, p. 33.
45 A. Modell, *The Private Self*, p. 75.
46 Naomi Scheman, *Engenderings: Constructions of Knowledge, Authority and Privilege*, London, Routledge, 1993, p. 247.
47 Giambattista Vico, *The New Science of Giambattista Vico*, E. Bergin and M.H. Fisch (trans.), Ithaca NY, Cornell University Press, 1968, p. 60.
48 This issue is developed in G. Corradi Fiumara, *The Other Side of Language*, pp. 28–51.

49 Immanuel Kant, 'An Answer to the Question "What is Enlightenment?"' in *Political Writings*, trans. H.B. Nisbet, (ed.) H. Reiss, Cambridge, Cambridge University Press, 1987, p. 54.
50 J. Lear, *Love and Its Place in Nature*, p. 205.
51 D. Winnicott, *Playing and Reality*, pp. 67–8.
52 George Eliot, *Middlemarch*, 'Prelude', London, Wordsworth Editions, 2000, p. 4.
53 Isahia Berlin, *Against the Current: Essays in the History of Ideas*, Oxford, Oxford University Press, 1979; quoted in Neville Symington, *The Spirit of Sanity*, London, Karnac, 2001, p. 69.
54 D. Winnicott, *Playing and Reality*, p. 65.
55 The expression 'Blowing on the embers' is of course derived from Boris Cyrulnik, *The Whispering of Ghosts: Trauma and Resilience*, Susan Fairfield (trans.), New York, Other Press, 2003; a chapter of his book is in fact entitled 'Blowing on an Ember of Resilience May Give It New Life.' pp. 21–23. The expression is used a few times in the book; for instance, 'He blows on the ember of resilience, the part of himself that is still alive,' p. 38.
56 See, for instance, Joyce McDougall, *Plaidoyer pour une Certaine Anormalité*, Paris, Editions Gallimard, 1990, and also *The Many Faces of Eros: A Psychoanalytic Exploration of Human Sexuality*, London, Free Association Books, 1995.
57 B. Cyrulnik, *The Whispering of Ghosts*, p. 2. We could also wonder what happens if children's desire for care and affection results in neglect, rejection or even abuse; when the therapist behaves in a kind way, this can reactivate the patients' desire for care and affection; but of course these feelings are associated with memories of great fear, so that compassion can be tricky for people. On this issue see Paul Gilbert, *The Compassionate Mind: A New Approach to Life's Challenges*, London, Constable, 2009, p. xxi.
58 B. Cyrulnik, *The Whispering of Ghosts*, p. 2.
59 Neville Symington, *Narcissism: A New Theory*, London, Karnac, 1993, p. 108.
60 Susan Bers, a review of S. Houser *et al.*, *Out of the Woods: Tales of Resilient Teens*, Cambridge MA, Harvard University Press, 2006, *The International Journal of Psychoanalysis*, 2008, 89(1): pp. 204–9.
61 Ibid., pp. 204–9.
62 Ibid., p. 206.
63 Stuart T. Hauser, Joseph P. Allen and Eve Golden, *Out of the Woods: Tales of Resilient Teens*, 2006, Cambridge MA, Harvard University Press, p. 13.
64 B. Cyrulnik, *The Whispering of Ghosts*, p. 29.
65 Ibid., p. 148.
66 A. Phillips and B. Taylor, *On Kindness*, p. 62.
67 Ibid., p. 62. Phillips and Taylor also write: 'We are profoundly ambivalent about kindness. We love it and we fear it; we feel its absence very acutely – it is the misery of everyday life – and we resist our own kind impulses ... It is not merely that we are not as kindly as we ought to be, but that it seems peculiarly difficult for us to hold on to the fact that we get powerful pleasure from our own acts of kindness.' Ibid., p. 8.
68 Ibid., p. 70.
69 B. Cyrulnik, *The Whispering of Ghosts*, p. 140.
70 Erich Fromm, *The Fear of Freedom*, London, Routledge, 2005, p. 221.

2 UNSUNG HEROES

1 Donald Winnicott, *Playing and Reality*, London, Tavistock Publications, 1971, p. 69.
2 George Eliot, 'Prelude' *Middlemarch*, London, Wordsworth Editions, 2000, p. 3.

NOTES

3 Antonino Ferro, 'Book Review Essay': *A Beam of Intense Darkness: Wilfred Bion's Legacy to Psychoanalysis* by James S. Grotstein, London, Karnac, 2007, *The International Journal of Psychoanalysis*, 2008, 89(4), p. 876.
4 Adam Phillips, *Going Sane*, London, Penguin Books, 2005, p. 19.
5 They are tried and tested to the extent to which they are real, personal, evolving. In Scheman's view, we need to explore the appalling extent to which any person (culture, or part of the self) has been reduced to the 'dreams' of any reigning coalition of theorists; and yet, any marginalised person, or part of the self, can hold on to his deeply felt, though perhaps unaccountable, untheorisable conviction that he is something *other* than the product of those 'dreams' and theories. Naomi Scheman, *Engenderings: Constructions of Knowledge, Authority and Privilege*, London, Routledge, 1993, p. 69.
6 D. Winnicott, *Playing and Reality*, p. 54.
7 Perhaps we could initially say that the 'I' of the personality is our primary means to begin viewing the internal working of our minds. It enables us to be aware of our mental processes without being swept away by them. Reflections on this creative capacity derive from contributions of authors such as Bion, Bollas, Ferro, Fromm, Grotstein, Lear, Meissner, Modell, Rosenfeld, Schaefer, Siegel and Winnicott. This topic will be discussed in chapter 6.
8 George Steiner, *Grammars of Creation originating in the Gifford Lectures for 1990*, London, Faber and Faber, 2002, p. 279.
9 Ibid., p. 279.
10 Kurt Eissler, *Talent and Genius: The Fictitious Case of Tausk Contra Freud*, New York, Quadrangle Books, 1974, p. 278.
11 On this issue see D.R. Hofstadter, *Fluid Concepts and Creative Analogies: Computer Models of the Fundamental Mechanisms of Thought*, New York, Basic Books, 1995.
12 This thesis has already been presented in Gemma Corradi Fiumara, *Spontaneity: A Psychoanalytic Inquiry*, London, Routledge, 2009, pp. 45–53.
13 D. Winnicott, *Playing and Reality*, p. 70.
14 G. Eliot, *Middlemarch*, p. 688.
15 D. Winnicott, *Playing and Reality*, p. 106.
16 Ibid., p. 107.
17 Ibid., p. 98.
18 Janet Martin Soskice, *The Kindness of God: Metaphor, Gender, and Religious Language*, Oxford, Oxford University Press, 2007. See especially chapter 9 'Being Lovely: Eschatological Anthropology,' pp. 181–188. Martin Soskice also quotes from a popular hymn that includes the verse 'Love to the loveless shown, that they might lovely be.'
19 Daniel Stern, *The Present Moment: In Psychotherapy and Everyday Life*, New York–London, W.W. Norton and Company, 2004, p. 157.
20 Ibid., p. 157.
21 Adam Phillips and Barbara Taylor, *On Kindness*, London, Hamish Hamilton, Penguin Books, 2009, p. 54.
22 Ibid., p. 54.
23 Immanuel Kant, *Anthropology from a Pragmatic Point of View*, R.B. Louden trans. and ed., Cambridge, Cambridge University Press, 2006, p. 124.
24 Michael Eigen, *Damaged Bonds*, London, Karnac, 2001, p. 126.
25 C. Kahn, 'The Analyst's Creativity During the Treatment Process,' *The Psychoanalytic Review*, 2009, 96(1): 22.
26 Z. Bauman, *Liquid Times: Living in an Age of Uncertainty*, Cambridge, Polity Press, 2007, pp. 1–4.
27 Ibid., p. 4.

28 Kelly Oliver, *The Colonization of Psychic Space: A Psychoanalytic Social Theory of Oppression*, Minneapolis MN–London, University of Minnesota Press, 2004, p. 162.
29 Neville Symington, *The Blind Man Sees: Freud's Awakening and Other Essays*, London, Karnac, 2004, pp. 170–1.
30 Ibid., p. 169.
31 D. Winnicott, *Playing and Reality*, p. 68.
32 J. Epstein, *Envy: The Seven Deadly Sins*, Oxford, Oxford University Press, 2003, pp. xvi–xvii.
33 N. Symington, *The Blind Man Sees*, p. 168.
34 Ibid., p. 167.
35 A. Phillips, *Side Effects*, London, Penguin Books, 2008, p. 162.
36 Adam Phillips, *Going Sane*, 2005, p. 111.
37 D. Winnicott, *Playing and Reality*, p. 68.
38 G. Steiner, *Grammars of Creation*, p. 270.

3 EGO DEVELOPMENT AND DE-CREATION OF OUR EGOS

1 Antonino Ferro, 'Book Review Essay: *A Beam of Intense Darkness: Wilfred Bion's Legacy to Psychoanalysis* by James Grotstein,' London, Karnac, *The International Journal of Psychoanalysis*, 2008, p. 867.
2 A. Ferro, 'Book Review Essay,' p. 867.
3 This issue is discussed in Gemma Corradi Fiumara, *Spontaneity: A Psychoanalytic Inquiry*, chapter 10, 'Self-Formation and Self-Decreation,' London, Routledge, 2009, pp. 113–20.
4 See Robert Nozick, *Philosophical Explanations*, Oxford, Clarendon Press, 1981, p. 4.
5 Neville Symington, *The Spirit of Sanity*, London, Karnac, 2001, p. 106.
6 This issue is extensively discussed in Gemma Corradi Fiumara, *The Mind's Affective Life: A Psychoanalytic and Philosophical Inquiry*, chapter 2, 'From Philosophy to Epistemophily', London, Routledge, 2001, pp. 20–8.
7 This notion will be discussed in chapter 6, 'The 'I' of the Personality.' pp. 79–88.
8 James Grotstein, *A Beam of Intense Darkness*: Wilfred Bion's Legacy to Psychoanalysis, London, Karnac, 2007, p. 328.
9 On this issue also see Gemma Fiumara Corradi, *Philosophy and Coexistence*, Leyden, Sijthoff, 1976.
10 George Steiner, *Grammars of Creation*, Oxford, Oxford University Press, 2002, p. 12.
11 Neville Symington, *The Blind Man Sees: Freud's Awakening and Other Essays*, London, Karnac, 2004, p. 167.
12 Ibid., p. 167.
13 Ibid., pp. 118–19.
14 Sigmund Freud, 'Some Character-Types Met with in Psycho-Analytic Work,' Section I, 'The Exceptions,' Vol. 14, *The Standard Edition*, 1916, p. 312.
15 Ibid., p. 313.
16 Kurt Eissler, *Talent and Genius: The Fictitious Case of Tausk Contra Freud*, New York, Quadrangle Books, 1974, p. 251.
17 G. Steiner, *Grammars of Creation*, p. 217.

4 GENIUS: ORDINARY AND EXTRAORDINARY

1 These issues are explored in a generic cognitive perspective in Margaret Boden, *The Creative Mind: Myths and Mechanisms*, London, Routledge, 2004.
2 Wilfred R. Bion, *Learning from Experience*, London, William Heinemann, 1962, pp. 3–4.

NOTES

3 Kelly Oliver, *The Colonization of Psychic Space: A Psychoanalytic Social Theory of Oppression*, Minneapolis MN–London, University of Minnesota Press, 2004, p. 161.
4 Michael Howe, *Genius Explained*, Cambridge, Cambridge University Press, 1999, p. 205.
5 Immanuel Kant, *Anthropology from a Pragmatic Point of View*; R.B. Louden trans. and ed., Cambridge, Cambridge University Press, 2006, p. 120.
6 Kurt Eissler, *Talent and Genius: The Fictitious Case of Tausk Contra Freud*, New York, Quadrangle Books, 1974, p. 251.
7 M. Boden, *The Creative Mind*, p. 275.
8 Kurt Eissler, *Leonardo da Vinci: Notes on the Enigma*, New York, International Universities Press, 1961, p. 28. (Emphasis added.)
9 Eissler provides us with monumental contributions on the topics of art, creativity and genius; his research is all conducted in a psychoanalytic perspective. Among his main contributions we should list: 'Notes on the Environment of a Genius,' *The Psychoanalytic Study of the Child*, 1959, 4:267–313; *Leonardo da Vinci: Notes on the Enigma*, New York, International Universities Press, 1961; *Goethe: A Psychoanalytic Study*, Detroit, Wayne State University Press, 1963; 'Psychopathology and Creativity,' American Imago, 1967, 24:35–81; *Discourse on Hamlet and HAMLET: A Psychoanalytic Inquiry*, New York, International Universities Press, 1971; *Talent and Genius: The Fictitious Case of Tausk Contra Freud*, New York, Quadrangle Books, 1974.
10 Sigmund Freud, 'Leonardo da Vinci and a Memory of His Childhood,' *Five Lectures on Psycho-Analysis, Leonardo da Vinci and Other Works*, Vol. 11, *The Standard Edition*, pp. 59–137.
11 K. Eissler, *Leonardo da Vinci*, p. 13.
12 Ibid., p. 82.
13 Ibid., p. 13.
14 M. Shapiro, 'Leonardo and Freud: An Art-Historical Study,' *Journal of the History of Ideas*, 1956, 17: 147–78, p. 152. Quoted in K. Eissler, *Leonardo da Vinci*, p. 15.
15 I. Kant, *Anthropology from a Pragmatic Point of View*, p. 121.
16 S. Freud, 'An Autobiographical Study,' Vol. 20, *The Standard Edition*, 1925, pp.7–74. *Standard Edition*. Quoted in K. Eissler, *Talent and Genius*, p. 255.
17 Ibid., p. 253.
18 Ibid., p. 248.
19 Ibid., p. 778.
20 Ibid., p. 282.
21 K. Eissler, *Discourse on Hamlet and HAMLET*, p. 356.
22 K. Eissler, *Leonardo da Vinci*, p. 285.
23 Ibid., p. 131.
24 Arthur Koestler, *The Act of Creation*, London, Picador, 1975, p. 240.
25 M. Boden, *The Creative Mind*, p. 270.
26 Ibid., p. 270.
27 George Steiner, *My Unwritten Books*, London, Weidenfeld and Nicholson, 2008, p. 49.
28 Ibid., p. 47.
29 Ibid., p. 47.
30 See K. Eissler, *Talent and Genius*, p. 252.
31 S. Freud, 'Leonardo da Vinci and a Memory of His Childhood,' p. 75.
32 Ibid., p. 75.
33 M. Boden, *The Creative Mind*, p. 259.
34 Ibid., p. 322.
35 Ibid., p. 322.
36 Donald Winnicott, *Playing and Reality*, London, Tavistock Publications, 1971, p. 65.

NOTES

37 S. Freud, S. (1910), 'Leonardo da Vinci and a Memory of his Childhood', p. 77.
38 Kaja Silverman, *The Threshold of the Visible World*, London, Routledge, 1996, pp. 31–7.
39 C. Kahn, and G. Piorkowski, 'Conditions Promoting Creativity in Group Rearing of Children,' *The Psychoanalytic Study of the Child*, 1974, 29: 231–55.
40 K. Eissler, *Goethe: A Psychoanalytic Study*, p. 1353.
41 I. Kant, *Anthropology from a Pragmatic Point of View*, p. 120.
42 Melanie Klein 'Der Familienroman in *Statu Nascendi*', was first published in 1920 in the *Internationale Zeitschrift für Psychoanalyse*, VI.6. It is the first publication of Melanie Klein, at that time aged thirty-eight, and the child she talks about in the paper is her son Eric. In a subsequent paper entitled 'The Development of a Child' published in 1921 in the journal *Imago*, VI.7, are inserted parts of her first paper. But perhaps in order to comply with the objection of using clinical material regarding her own child, the name of the little boy is changed to 'Fritz.' The work has been translated from German into Italian by my late colleague Rosario Merendino, an outstanding psychoanalyst and scholar who lived in Germany for 20 years. The paper was published in the *Rivista di Psicoanalisi*, Organo della Società Psicoanalitica Italiana, No. 2, April–June 1983, pp. 125–31, in a volume entirely dedicated to Melanie Klein. Some British colleagues suggested that 'The Family Romance in *Statu Nascendi*' was never published with that title in English; but they are also fairly certain, that it was included in some form in 'The Development of a Child' and in 'Love, Guilt and Reparation' in Klein's *Contributions to Psycho-Analysis 1921–1945*, London, Hogarth Press and the Institute of Psychoanalysis, 1973. The work of Melanie Klein from which I am quoting has only been read in Italian because I was unable to find an English translation and because I am not sufficiently familiar with German. As I have no ambition to academic 'perfection,' I try to be content with the translation of the original paper from German into Italian. In my effort to write in English I have of course tried to translate as literally as I possibly can. Of course it would have been better if I had the original German paper carefully translated into English, or if I had found the parts of it that are translated in English, and if I had worked on that material. May I also add that the volume dedicated to Melanie Klein includes a beautiful picture of the elderly Klein – exuding charm, intelligence, status.
43 Melanie Klein, 'Il Romanzo di una Famiglia *in Statu Nascendi*', Rosario Merendino, Italian trans *Rivista di Psicoanalisi* Organo della Società Psicoanalitica Italiana, No. 2, April–June 1983, pp. 125–31, p. 125.
44 Ibid., p. 130.
45 Gemma Corradi Fiumara, 'Riflessioni Sul Saggio di Melanie Klein "Il Romanzo di una Famiglia in *statu Nascendi*",' *Rivista di Psicoanalisi*, No. 1, January–March 1984, pp. 133–42.
46 M. Klein, 'Il Romanzo di una Famiglia in *statu Nascendi*,' p. 126.
47 Ibid., p. 126.
48 Ibid., p. 126.
49 Ibid., p. 126.
50 Ibid., p. 127.
51 Ibid., p. 126.
52 Ibid., p. 126.
53 Ibid., p. 126.
54 Ibid., p. 127.
55 Ibid., p. 128.
56 Ibid., p. 129.
57 Ibid., p. 129.
58 Ibid., p. 129.

59 Ibid., p. 130.
60 Ibid., p. 125.
61 Ibid., p. 130.
62 Ibid., p. 130.
63 Ibid., p. 130.
64 Ibid., p. 131.
65 Ibid., p. 131.
66 Marcus Aurelius, *The Meditations of Marcus Aurelius: Spiritual Teachings and Reflection* George Long (trans.), introduction by Alan Jacobs, London, Watkins Publishing, 2008, Book 1, paragraph 11, p. 11.

5 THE CONNECTIVE FUNCTION

1 See Donald Winnicott, *Playing and Reality*, London, Tavistock Publications, 1971.
2 Sigmund Freud, 'Lines of Advance in Psycho-Analytic Therapy,' Vol. 17, *The Standard Edition*, 1919, p. 161.
3 Ibid., p. 161.
4 Ibid., p. 161.
5 Boris Cyrulnik, *The Whispering of Ghosts: Trauma and Resilience*, Susan Fairfield (trans.), New York, Other Press, 2003, p. 32.
6 Neville Symington, *The Blind Man Sees: Freud's Awakening and Other Essays*, London, Karnac, 2004, p. 64.
7 Ibid., p. 70.
8 Ibid., p. 177.
9 Kurt Eissler, *Talent and Genius: The Fictitious Case of Tausk Contra Freud*, New York, Quadrangle Books, 1974, p. 278.
10 Carol Gilligan, *In a Different Voice: Psychological Theory and Women's Development*, Cambridge MA, Harvard University Press, 1982.
11 N. Symington, *The Blind Man Sees*, p. 65.
12 In a very popular saga, the antagonist of our Harry Potter actually splits his soul into seven different parts in order to gain immortality and permanently control everything.
13 Robert Louis Stevenson, *The Strange Case of Dr Jekyll and Mr Hyde*, London, Nelson, 1954.
14 Mary Midgley, *Wickedness: A Philosophical Essay*, London, Routledge, 1984, p. 122.
15 Ibid., p. 123.
16 Ibid., p. 126.
17 Ibid., p. 127.
18 Ibid., p. 196.
19 Neville Symington, *A Pattern of Madness*, London, Karnac, 2002, p. 47.
20 James Grotstein, *Who is the Dreamer Who Dreams the Dream? A Study of Psychic Presences*, Hillsdale NJ, Analytic Press, 2000, p. 11.
21 Daniel Stern, *The Present Moment: In Psychotherapy and Everyday Life*, New York–London, W.W. Norton and Company, 2004, p. 28.
22 Ibid., p. 28.
23 Ibid., p. 209.
24 Ibid., p. 224.
25 C. Kahn, 'The Analyst's Creativity During the Treatment Process,' *The Psychoanalytic Review*, 2009, 96(1): 32.
26 Howard Gardner, *Frames of Mind: The Theory of Multiple Intelligences*, London, Fontana Press, 1993, p. 138.

NOTES

27 Adam Phillips and Barbara Taylor, *On Kindness*, London, Hamish Hamilton, Penguin Books, 2009.
28 This issue has been extensively discussed in Gemma Corradi Fiumara, *Spontaneity: A Psychoanalytic Inquiry*, chapter 9 'Empathy and Sympathy,' London, Routledge, 2009, pp. 92–112.
29 A. Phillips and B. Taylor, *On Kindness*, p. 50.
30 N. Schwartz-Salant, *The Mystery of Human Relationships: Alchemy and the Transformation of Self*, London, Routledge, 1998, p. 11.
31 A. Phillips and B. Taylor, *On Kindness*, p. 61.
32 Ibid., p. 12.
33 On this issue, see Janet Martin Soskice, *The Kindness of God: Metaphor, Gender, and Religious Language*, Oxford, Oxford University Press, 2007. A line of a liturgical hymn – 'Love to the loveless shown, that they might lovely be' – is also quoted in her work at p. 81.
34 A. Phillips and B. Taylor, *On Kindness*, p. 12.
35 Carl Gustav Jung, *The Collected Works of C.G. Jung*, Vol. 6, R.F.C. Hull (trans.), *'Psychological Types,'* Princeton NJ, Princeton University Press, 1971, p. 253.
36 J. C. Miller, *The Transcendent Function: Jung's Model of Psychological Growth Through Dialogue with the Unconscious*, Albany, State University of New York, 2004, p. 112.
37 D. Stern, *The Present Moment*, p. 214.
38 Ibid., p. 214.
39 J.G. Miller, *The Transcendent Function*, p. 141.
40 Antonino Ferro, Seminar conducted at the Rome Institute of Group Analysis – Società Gruppo-Analitica Italiana, 1910.
41 James Grotstein, *A Beam of Intense Darkness: Wilfred Bion's Legacy to Psychoanalysis*, London, Karnac, 2007, p. 296.
42 Adam Phillips, *Going Sane*, London, Penguin Books, 2005, p. 92.
43 Ibid., p. 92.
44 Michael Eigen, *Damaged Bonds*, London, Karnac, 2001, p. 1.
45 A. Phillips, *Going Sane*, p. 121.
46 Joyce McDougall, *Plaidoyer pour une Certaine Anormalité*, Paris, Editions Gallimard, 1990.
47 William James, The Varieties of Religious Experience, New York, Mentor, 1958, p. 107.
48 M. Eigen, *Damaged Bonds*, p. 76.
49 J. Grotstein, *A Beam of Intense Darkness*, p. 76.
50 Wilfred R. Bion, *The Italian Seminars*, London, Karnac, 2005, p. 44.
51 Among Edmund Husserl's monumental contributions, the ones more relevant to this issue could be: *Ideas Pertaining to a Pure Phenomenology and to a Phenomenological Philosophy. First Book: General Introduction to a Pure Phenomenology*, F. Kersten, The Hague, Nijhoff, 1982; *Ideas Pertaining to a Pure Phenomenology and to a Phenomenological Philosophy. Second Book: Studies in the Phenomenology of Constitution*; R. Rojcewicz and A. Schuwer (trans.), Dordrecht, Kluwer, 1989; and *On the Phenomenology of Consciousness of Internal Time*; J.B. Brough (trans.), Dordrecht, Kluwer, 1990.
52 Steven Mitchell, *Hope and Dread in Psychoanalysis*, New York, Basic Books, 1993, p. 45.

6 THE 'I' OF THE PERSONALITY

1 D. Siegel, *Mindsight*: Oxford: Oneworld Publications, 2010, p. xi.
2 Neville Symington, *The Blind Man Sees: Freud's Awakening and Other Essays*, London, Karnac, 2004, p. 59.

NOTES

3 See Donald Spence, 'Turning Happenings into Meanings: The Central Role of the Self,' in P. Young-Eisendrath and J. Hall (eds), *The Book of the Self: Person, Pretext and Process*, 1987. Also see D. Spence, 'Rain Forest or Mud Field?', Guest Editorial, *The International Journal of Psychoanalysis*, 1998, 79: 643–8.
4 Christopher Bollas, *The Shadow of the Object: Psychoanalysis of the Unthought Known*, London, Free Association Books, 1987, p. 19.
5 Steven Mitchell, *Hope and Dread in Psychoanalysis*, New York, Basic Books, 1993, p. 109.
6 Roy Schaefer, *A New Language for Psychoanalysis*, New Haven CT, Archon Press, 1978.
7 James Grotstein, *A Beam of Intense Darkness: Wilfred Bion's Legacy to Psychoanalysis*, London, Karnac, 2007, p. 271.
8 Arnold Modell, *The Private Self*, Cambridge MA–London, Harvard University Press, 1993, p. 4.
9 William James, The Varieties of Religious Experience, New York, Mentor, 1958, p. 107.
10 Sigmund Freud, 'Lines of Advance in Psycho-Analytic Therapy', *Standard Edition*, 1919, p. 161.
11 Ibid., p. 161.
12 Neville Symington, *Narcissism: A New Theory*, London, Karnac, 1993, pp. 109–10.
13 William Meissner, 'The Genesis of the Self: IV. The Implications for the Analytic Relation and Process. Part 1, The Self as Integral Subject', *Psychoanalytic Review*, 2009, 96(2), p. 298.
14 Ibid., p. 323.
15 N. Symington, *The Blind Man Sees*, p. 182.
16 A. Modell, *The Private Self*, p. 34.
17 Ibid., p. 26.
18 N. Humphrey, *Consciousness Regained*, Oxford, Oxford University Press, 1984, p. 5.
19 T. Ogden, *Subjects of Analysis*, Northvale NJ, Jason Aronson, 1994, p. 93.
20 J. Grotstein, *A Beam of Intense Darkness*, pp. 7–8.
21 J.C. Miller, *The Transcendent Function: Jung's Model of Psychological Growth Through Dialogue with the Unconscious*, Albany, State University of New York, 2004, p. 97.
22 Wilfred R. Bion, *Cogitations Pensieri*, Estate of Wilfred R. Bion by arrangement with Mark Peterson and Francesca Bion; P. Bion Talamo and S. Merciai (Italian trans.), *Cogitations: Pensieri*, Rome, Armando Editore, 1992, pp. 76–7.
23 Ibid., pp. 76–7.
24 Jonathan Lear, *Love and Its Place in Nature: A Philosophical Interpretation of Freudian Psychoanalysis*, New Haven–London, Yale University Press, 1990, p. 2.
25 N. Symington, *The Blind Man Sees*, pp. 92–3.
26 D. Siegel, *Mindsight*, p. 208.
27 Ibid., p. 204.
28 This is all derived from the clinical seminars conducted by Herbert Rosenfeld at the Centro Psicoanalitico di Roma, from 1975–85.
29 Marcus Aurelius, *The Meditations of Marcus Aurelius: Spiritual Teachings and Reflections*. George Long (trans.); introduction by Alan Jacobs, London: Watkins Publishing, 2008, book 8, paragraph 29, p. 137.
30 A. Modell, *The Private Self*, p. 92.
31 Erich Fromm, *Beyond the Chains of Illusion: My Encounter with Marx and Freud*, New York–London, Continuum Press, 1962, p. 136.
32 W.R. Bion, *Cogitations*, pp. 76–7.
33 Martin Heidegger, *Being and Time*, John Macquarrie and Edward Robinson, New York, Harper and Row, 1962, p. 178 and p. 223.

34 Kurt Eissler, *Talent and Genius: The Fictitious Case of Tausk Contra Freud*, New York, Quadrangle Books, 1974, p. 296.
35 Julia Kristeva, *New Maladies of the Soul*, R. Guberman (trans.), New York, Columbia University Press, 1995, p. 7.
36 Ibid., p. 7.
37 A. Modell, *The Private Self*, p. 122.
38 E. Fromm, *Beyond the Chains of Illusion*, p. 138.
39 W.R. Bion, *Cogitations*, p. 95.
40 N. Symington, *Narcissism*, p. 53.
41 Kurt Eissler, *Leonardo da Vinci: Notes on the Enigma*, New York, International Universities Press, 1961, pp. 214–15.
42 Ibid., p. 215.
43 Elaborated by Herbert Rosenfeld in his Rome seminars.

7 CREATIVE SERVICE

1 Adam Phillips and Barbara Taylor, *On Kindness*, London: Hamish Hamilton, Penguin Books, 2009, pp. 1–2.
2 This thesis runs through the book of Janet Martin Soskice, *The Kindness of God: Metaphor, Gender and Religious Language*, Oxford: Oxford University Press, 2007.
3 A. Phillips and B. Taylor, *On Kindness*, p. 98. In this connection we could recall that Karol Wojtyla had a life-long friendship with his compatriot Cardinal Andrej Deskur. In a meeting of 1994 – as Pope John Paul II – he is reported saying to a friend of Andrej Deskur: 'Reverend father, I want it to be known that I am who I am because father Andrej is as he is.' Quoted in A. Socci, *I segreti di Karol Wojtyla*, Milan, Rizzoli, 2009, p. 31.
4 Ibid., p. 98.
5 James Grotstein, *A Beam of Intense Darkness: Wilfred Bion's Legacy to Psychoanalysis*, London, Karnac, 2007, p. 31.
6 Ibid., p. 31.
7 Sigmund Freud, 'On Narcissism: An Introduction,' *The Standard Edition*, 1914, p. 85.
8 E. van Deurzen, *Everyday Mysteries: A Handbook of Existential Psychotheraphy*, London, Routledge, 2009, p. 131.
9 Michael Eigen, *Damaged Bonds*, London, Karnac, 2001, p. 5.
10 A. Phillips and B. Taylor, *On Kindness*, p. 7.
11 The topic of listening is extensively discussed in Gemma Corradi Fiumara, *The Other Side of Language: A Philosophy of Listening*, London, Routledge, 1990. In everyday relationships, the listening experiences that shape our life usually occur in a moment that is felt as key, not only after it has happened, but also while it is happening. 'Now' is when we directly live our lives. The only time of raw subjective reality is the present moment – the moment for genius.
12 Boris Cyrulnik, *The Whispering of Ghosts: Trauma and Resilience*, Susan Fairfield (trans.) New York, Other Press, 2003, p. 168.
13 Ibid., p. 168. By telling one's story to a responsive, expressive listener, some form of therapy can be initiated: 'It is precisely through words that an analysis comes to life, has power and becomes a talking cure.' Language thus assumes the 'importance of major and powerful action.' W. Poland, 'The Analyst's Words: Their Context and Their Formation', *The Psychoanalytic Quarterly*, 1986, No. 55, pp. 244. Also see C. Schwartz, 'Language as Artistry in the Treatment of a Borderline Psychotic Patient', *Psychoanalytic Review*, 2009, N. 96 (1), pp. 1–20.

NOTES

14 A. Phillips and B. Taylor, *On Kindness*, p. 3.
15 Ibid., p. 3. To be truly nurturing, in the sense of being responsible and accountable, we should be able to keep promises; in this connection we could quote Nietzsche: 'To breed an animal *with the right to make promises* – is not this the paradoxical task which nature has set itself in the case of man?... This animal which needs to be forgetful, in which forgetfulness represents a force, a form of *robust* health, has bred in itself an opposing faculty ... with the aid of which forgetfulness is abrogated in certain cases – namely in those case where promises are made.' Friedrich Nietzsche, *On the Genealogy of Morals*, W. Kaufman and R.J. Hollingdate (trans.) New York, Vintage Books, 1969, pp. 57–8.
16 Neville Symington, *The Blind Man Sees: Freud's Awakening and Other Essays*, London, Karnac, 2004, p. 87.
17 Ibid., p. 87.
18 Jonathan Lear, *Love and Its Place in Nature: A Philosophical Interpretation of Freudian Psychoanalysis*, New Haven–London, Yale University Press, 1990, p. 165.
19 Ibid., p. 166.
20 Arnold Modell, *The Private Self*, Cambridge MA–London, Harvard University Press, 1993, p. 95.
21 Martin Buber, *Between Man and Man*, Ronald G. Smith, London, Kegan Paul, 1947, p. 36.
22 This issue is extensively explored in Donald Winnicott, *Playing and Reality*, London, Tavistock Publications, 1971. See especially chapter 3 'Playing: A Theoretical Statement,' pp. 38–52 and chapter 4 'Playing: Creative Activity and the Search for the Self,' pp. 53–64.
23 Joyce McDougall, *The Many Faces of Eros: A Psychoanalytic Exploration of Human Sexuality*, London, Free Association Books, 1995, p. 238.
24 B. Cyrulnik, *The Whispering of Ghosts*, p. 38.
25 Hornsby reports the case of a magistrate recommending the acquittal of a man accused of rape, and quotes Judge David Wild saying: 'Women who say No, do not always mean 'No.' It is not just a question of No.' In this example, lucidly analysed by Hornsby, it is the case of a person not believed to perform a specific illocutionary act by saying No. But then we could use this instance to take better notice of those innumerable occasions in which individuals cannot properly succeed in saying 'Yes.' If we transformed into the affirmative the statement of judge Wild – 'Women who say Yes do not always mean Yes. It is just not a question of saying Yes' – would imply a massive devaluational attitude; it would tend to cast doubt on statements such as 'Yes, I will pay,' 'Yes I can do that' and 'Yes I understand.' If it is so difficult to say 'No' successfully under adverse circumstances, it is perhaps even more difficult to say 'Yes' in comparable situations. In the face of these difficulties it becomes even clearer that it takes great maturity and creativeness to communicate successfully. J. Hornsby, 'Speech Acts and Pornography,' *Women's Philosophy Review*, 1993, 10: 38–45.
26 See chapter 6, 'The 'I' of the Personality'.
27 A. Phillips and B. Taylor, *On Kindness*, p. 10.
28 Ibid., p. 10.
29 Isahia Berlin, in I. Berlin and H. Hardy (eds), *Against the Current: Essays in the History of Ideas*, Oxford, Oxford University Press, 1979; quoted in N. Symington, *The Spirit of Sanity*, London, Karnac, 2001, p. 69.
30 Adam Phillips, *Side Effects*, London, Penguin Books, 2008, pp. 183–4.
31 Daniel Stern, *The Present Moment: In Psychotherapy and Everyday Life*, New York–London, Norton, 2004, p. 220. The linear time of calendars and chronometers is basically different from kairos, which is the time for creative service. It could be

an hour but it feels like a split of a second. When we are intensely listening or speaking, the course of time is only a now, it is the present moment. Resorting to Stern's words we could say: 'How can we pry open chronos to create a present long enough to accommodate kairos?,' Ibid., p. 26.

32 D. Winnicott, *Playing and Reality*, pp. 38–85.
33 A. Phillips and B. Taylor, *On Kindness*, p. 6.
34 Ibid., p. 6.
35 Ibid., p. 51.
36 Ibid., p. 4.
37 In concentration camps the supervisors consistently described feelings of compassion, and empathy as 'swinish,' or 'pig-like.' See Viktor Frankl, *Man's Search for Meaning: An Introduction to Logotherapy*, Boston, Beacon Press, 1963.
38 This issue is extensively discussed in Gemma Corradi Fiumara, *Spontaneity: A Psychoanalytic Inquiry*, London, Routledge, 2009, pp. 11–23.
39 P. Casement, *Learning from Our Mistakes: Beyond Dogma in Psychoanalyses and Psychotherapy*, London, Brunner-Routledge, 2002, p. xv.
40 This suggestion was repeatedly given by Herbert Ronsenfeld in the course of his regular seminars conducted at the *Centro Psicoanalitico di Roma* between 1975 and 1985.
41 D. Winnicott, *Playing and Reality*, p. 56.
42 Antonino Ferro, 'Book Review Essay: *A Beam of Intense Darkness: Wilfred Bion's Legacy to Psychoanalysis* by James Grotstein, London, Karnac, 2007, *The International Journal of Psychoanalysis*, 2008, 89(4): 867–84.
43 'The analyst has to *become infinite* by the suspension of memory, desire, understanding.' Bion, W.R. (2004), *Attention and Interpretation: A Scientific Approach to Insight in Psycho-Analysis and Groups*, London: Karnac, 2004, p. 46. And also: 'Psychoanalytic "observation" is concerned neither with what has happened or with what is going to happen, but with what is happening.' W.R. Bion, *Cogitations*, p. 380.
44 W.R. Bion, *Attention and Interpretation*, p. 46 and *Cogitations*, p. 380.
45 Wilfred R. Bion, 'On Arrogance', in *Second and Thoughts: Selected Papers on Psychoanalysis*, London, Heinemann, 1957, pp. 86–97.

8 MINDING OUR BUSINESS

1 The issue has been explored in Gemma Corradi Fiumara, *Spontaneity: A Psychoanalytic Inquiry*, London, Routledge, 2009, pp. 68–74.
2 Neville Symington, *The Blind Man Sees: Freud's Awakening and Other Essays*, London, Karnac, 2004, p. 76.
3 I have used the expression 'mind-like idols' in *Spontaneity: A Psychoanalytic Inquiry*, pp. 20–3.
4 Henry Newman, *An Essay in Aid of a Grammar of Assent*, London, Longmans, Green and Co, 1888, p. 389. Quoted in N. Symington, *The Blind Man Sees*, p. 43.
5 This topic has been extensively discussed in Christopher Bollas, *Cracking Up: The Work of Unconscious Experience*, London, Routledge, 1997, p. 100.
6 See Jonathan Lear, *Love and Its Place in Nature: A Philosophical Interpretation of Freudian Psychoanalysis*, New Haven–London, Yale University Press, 1990, p. 157.
7 Kelly Oliver, *The Colonization of Psychic Space: A Psychoanalytic Social Theory of Oppression*, Minneapolis MN–London, University of Minnesota Press, 2004, p. 161.
8 James Grotstein, *A Beam of Intense Darkness*, p. 33.
9 N. Symington, *The Blind Man Sees: Wilfred Bion's Legacy to Psychoanalysis*, London, Karnac, 2007, p. 155.

NOTES

10 Ibid., p. 156.
11 The 'necessity of being right in arguments' has already been explored in Gemma Corradi Fiumara, *The Mind's Affective Life: A Psychoanalytic and Philosophical Inquiry*, London, Brunner Routledge, 2001, p. 8. On this same topic see Robert Nozick, *Philosophical Explanations*, Oxford, Clarendon Press, 1981, pp. 4–6.
12 The idea of 'mind-like idols' has been developed in the fourth paragraph of chapter 2 'Rethinking Internalization' in G. Corradi Fiumara, *Spontaneity*, pp. 20–3. The expression 'mind-like idols' is used in the general background of projective mechanisms and especially of projective identification. On this issue especially see Thomas Ogden, *Projective Identification and Psychotherapeutic Technique*, Northvale NJ–London, Jason Aronson, 1991; T. Ogden, *Subjects of Analysis*, Northvale NJ, Jason Aronson, 1994; T. Ogden, *Rediscovering Psychoanalysis: Thinking and Dreaming, Learning and Forgetting*, London, Routledge, 2008.
13 In this connection, see Carl Gustav Jung, 'The Tavistock Lectures – Lecture III', in *The Collective Works of C.G. Jung, The Symbolic Life*, Vol. 18, London, Routledge and Kegan Paul, 1977, pp. 72–3.
14 Michael Eigen, *Damaged Bonds*, London, Karnac, 2001, p. 9.
15 Ibid., p. 10.
16 C.G. Jung, *The Symbolic Life*, pp. 72–3.
17 Ibid., p. 73.
18 Joyce McDougall, *Theatres of the Mind: Illusion and Truth on the Psychoanalytic Stage*, London, Free Association Books, 1986, p. 4.
19 Ibid., p. 4.
20 Mary Midgley, *Wickedness: A Philosophical Essay*, London: Routledge, 1984, p. 137.
21 N. Symington, *The Blind Man Sees*, p. 170.
22 Ibid., p. 171.
23 Ibid., p. 15.
24 Ibid., p. 169.
25 Kaja Silverman, *The Threshold of the Visible World*, London, Routledge, 1996, p. 31.
26 Herbert Rosenfeld repeatedly highlights the incomparable pleasure/joy of being able to function well. He frequently elaborated on this issue in the course of the regular seminars he conducted at the Centro Psicoanalitico di Roma between 1975 and 1985.
27 K. Silverman, *The Threshold of the Visible World*, p. 40.
28 M. Midgley, *Wickedness*, p. 182.
29 Antonio Damasio, *Descartes' Error: Emotion, Reason and the Human Brain*, London, Papermac – MacMillan General Books, 1996, p. 52.
30 J. Grotstein, *A Beam of Intense Darkness*, pp. 184–5. Reported in A. Ferro, Book Review Essay: *A Beam of Intense Darkness: Wilfred Bion's Legacy to Psychoanalysis* by James Grotstein, *The International Journal of Psychoanalysis*, 2008, 89(4): 878.
31 M. Midgley, *Wickedness*, p. 132.
32 Ibid., p. 128.
33 A colleague visiting a beautiful hotel for the purpose of organising an international congress mentioned, with surprise, that he had met this prestigious training analyst quietly having tea there. Of course I was not surprised because he had confided to me this very laudable habit. As this revered analyst is no longer with us, I cannot have permission to introduce more enlightening details.
34 N. Symington, *The Blind Man Sees*, pp. 115–6.
35 Ibid., p. 176.

BIBLIOGRAPHY

Altieri, C. (1994) *Subjective Agency: A Theory of First-Person Expressivity and Its Social Implications*, Oxford UK–Cambridge MA: Blackwell Publishers.
Amati Mehler, J. (2007) 'Identificazione Proiettiva: Fondamenti Teorici', *Psicoanalisi*, January–June 2007, pp. 48–83.
Ancelin Schützenberger, A. (2007) *La Sindrome Degli Antenati. Psicoterapia Transgenerazionale e i Legami Nascosti Genealogico*, Roma: De Renzo Editore.
Annas, J. (2011) *Intelligent Virtue*, Oxford: Oxford University Press.
Anthony, J. and Cohler, B. (1987) *The Invulnerable Child*, New York: Guilford Press.
Anzieu, D. (1974) *Psychanalyse du Génie Créateur*, Paris: Dunod.
Arbib, M. and Hesse, M.B. (1986) *The Construction of Reality*, Cambridge: Cambridge University Press.
Argentieri, S. (2008) *L'ambiguità*, Torino: Einaudi.
Ariely, D. (2008) *Predictability Irrational. The Hidden Forces that Shape Our Decisions*, London: Harper Collins.
Aristotle (1985) *Poetics, The Complete Works of Aristotle*, revised Oxford translation, Jonathan Barnes (ed.), Princeton NJ: Princeton University Press, pp. 2234–5.
Aristotle (1924) *Rhetoric, The Works of Aristotle*, Vol. 2, 11, 1354–1420, W.R. Roberts (trans.), W.D. Ross (ed.), Oxford: Clarendon Press.
Austin, J. L. (1975) *How to Do Things with Words*, William James Lectures delivered at Harvard University in 1955, J.O. Urmson and M. Sbisà (eds), Oxford: Clarendon Press.
Baker, L. (2007) *The Metaphysics of Everyday Life*, Cambridge: Cambridge University Press.
Baron-Cohen, S. (1995) *Mindblindness: An Essay on Autism and Theory of Mind*, Cambridge MA–London: MIT Press.
Bauman, Z. (2007) *Liquid Times: Living in an Age of Uncertainty*, Cambridge: Polity Press.
Benjamin, J. (1988) *The Bonds of Love: Psychoanalysis, Feminism and the Problem of Domination*, New York: Pantheon.
Berge, A. (1968) 'L'art et la Psychanalyse,' in *Entretiens sur l'art et la Psychanalyse*, A. Berge et al. (eds), Décades du Centre Culturel International de Cérisy-la-Salle, Nouvelle Série 6, Paris: Mouton.
Berlin, I. (1991) *The Crooked Timber of Humanity: Chapters in the History of Ideas*, New York: Knopf.

BIBLIOGRAPHY

Berlin, I. and Hardy, H. (eds) (1979) *Against the Current: Essays in the History of Ideas*, Oxford: Oxford University Press.
Bernstein, P. (1996) *Against the Gods: The Remarkable Story of Risk*, New York: John Wiley and Sons.
Bernstein, R. (1983) *Beyond Objectivism and Relativism: Science, Hermeneutics and Praxis*, Philadelphia PA: University of Pennsylvania Press.
Bers, S.A. (2008) Book Review: *Out of the Woods: Tales of Resilient Teens* by Stuart T. Hauser, Joseph P. Alten, Eve Golden, *The International Journal of Psychoanalysis*, 89(1): 204–9.
Besdine, M. (1968) 'The Jocasta Complex, Mothering and Genius,' Part 1, *The Psychoanalytic Review*, 55: 259–77.
Besdine, M. (1968) 'The Jocasta Complex, Mothering and Genius,' Part 2, *The Psychoanalytic Review*, 55: 574–600.
Bion, W.R. (1957) 'On Arrogance!,' in *Second Thoughts: Selected Papers on Psychoanalysis*, pp. 86–92, London: Heinemann, pp. 86–92.
Bion, W.R. (1959) 'Attacks on Linking,' *The International Journal of Psycho-Analysis*, 40: 308–15.
Bion, W.R. (1962) *Learning from Experience*, London: William Heinemann. pp. 3–4
Bion, W.R. (1975) *Bion's Brazilian Lectures*, Vol. 2, Jayme Salomao (ed.), Rio de Janeiro: Imago Editora.
Bion, W.R. (1977) *Seven Servants: Four Works by Wilfred Bion*, New York: Jason Aronson.
Bion, W.R. (1982) *The Long Week-End, Vol. 1: 1897–1919. Part of a Life*, Abingdon: Fleetwood Press.
Bion, W.R. (1985) *The Long Week-End, Vol.2: All My Sins Remembered (Another Part of Life). The Other Side of Genius* (Family Letters), Abingdon: Fleetwood Press.
Bion, W.R.(1992) *Cogitations: Pensieri*, Estate of Wilfred R. Bion, by arrangement with Mark Paterson and Francesca Bion. Partenope Bion Talamo and Silvio Merciai (trans.), Rome: Armando Editore.
Bion, W.R. (1992) *Cogitations*, Francesca Bion (ed.), London: Karnac.
Bion, W.R. (1994) *Cogitations: New Extended Edition*, London: Karnac.
Bion, W.R. (2004) *Attention and Interpretation: A Scientific Approach to Insight in Psycho-Analysis and Groups*, Francesca Bion (ed.), London: Karnac.
Bion, W.R. (2005) *The Italian Seminars*, London: Karnac.
Bocca, G. (1958) *The Adventurous Life of Winston Churchill*, New York: Julian Messner.
Boden, M.A. (2004) *The Creative Mind: Myths and Mechanisms*, London: Routledge.
Bollas, C. (1987) *The Shadow of the Object: Psychoanalysis of the Unthought Known*, London: Free Association Books.
Bollas, C. (1991) *The Forces of Destiny: Psychoanalysis and Human Idiom*, London: Free Association Books.
Bollas, C. (1997) *Cracking Up: The Work of Unconscious Experience*, London: Routledge.
Bollas, C. (2008) *The Infinite Question*, London: Routledge.
Boszormenyi-Nagy, I. (1988) *Lealtà Invisibili: La Reciprocità Nella Terapia Famigliare Intergenerazionale*, Rome: Astrolabio.
Boszormenyi-Nagy, I. and Framo, L.P. (1997) *La Psicoterapia Intensiva Della Famiglia*, Torino: Boringhieri.
Brakel, L. (2010) *Unconscious Knowing and Other Essays in Psycho-Philosophical Analysis*, Oxford: Oxford University Press.
Buber, M. (1947) *Between Man and Man*, Ronald G. Smith (trans.), London: Kegan Paul.

Caper, R. (2008) *Building Out into the Dark: Theory and Observation in Science and Psychoanalysis*, London: Routledge.
Cartwright, D. (2009) *Containing States of Mind: Exploring Bion's 'Container Model' in Psychoanalytic Psychotherapy*, London: Routledge.
Casement, P. (1991) *Learning from the Patient*, New York: Guilford.
Casement, P. (2002) *Learning from Our Mistakes: Beyond Dogma in Psychoanalysis and Psychotherapy*, London: Brunner-Routledge.
Cassam, Q. (ed.) (2004) *Self-Knowledge*, Oxford: Oxford University Press.
Chaudhuri, H. (1987) *The Philosophy of Love*, London: Routledge and Kegan Paul.
Chesterton, G.K. (1910) *What's Wrong with the World*, London, New York, Toronto, Melbourne: Cassell.
Chorfas, D.N. (1994) *The Chaos Theory in the Financial Markets*, Chicago: Probus.
Corradi Fiumara, G. (1976) *Philosophy and Coexistence*, Leyden: Sijthoff.
Corradi Fiumara, G. (1984) 'Riflessioni Sul Saggio di Melanie Klein "Il Romanzo di una Famiglia in *statu nascendi*",' *Rivista di Psicoanalisi*, Organo della Società Psicoanalitica Italiana, No. 1, January–March, pp. 133–42.
Corradi Fiumara, G. (1990) *The Other Side of Language: A Philosophy of Listening*, London–New York: Routledge.
Corradi Fiumara, G. (1992) *The Symbolic Function: Psychoanalysis and the Philosophy of Language*, Oxford, UK–Cambridge MA: Blackwell Publishers.
Corradi Fiumara, G. (1995) *The Metaphoric Process: Connections between Language and Life*, London–New York: Routledge.
Corradi Fiumara, G. (2001) *The Mind's Affective Life: A Psychoanalytic and Philosophical Inquiry*, London–New York: Brunner-Routledge.
Corradi Fiumara, G. (2009) *Spontaneity: A Psychoanalytic Inquiry*, London–New York: Routledge.
Csikszentmihalyi, M. (1997) *Creativity: Flow and the Psychology of Discovery and Invention*, New York: Harper Perennial.
Cyrulnik, B. (2003) *The Whispering of Ghosts: Trauma and Resilience*, Susan Fairfield (trans.), New York: Other Press.
Damasio, A. (1996) *Descartes' Error: Emotion, Reason and the Human Brain*, London: Papermac – Macmillan General Books.
Dartuall, T. (ed.) (2002) *Creativity, Cognition and Knowledge: An Interaction*, London: Praeger.
de Adam of Parma Salimbene (1946) 'Chronicon parmense. Avvenimenti tra il 1167 ed il 1287', in *La letteratura italiana: Storia e Testi: Le Origini*, Antonio Viscardi et al. (eds), Milan–Naples: Ricciardi Editore.
de Certeau, M. (1984) *The Practice of Everyday Life*, Steven Rendall (trans.), Berkeley CA: University of California Press.
Ehrenberg, D. (1920) *The Intimate Edge*, New York: W.W. Norton.
Ehrenwald, J. (1984) *Anatomy of Genius*, New York: Human Sciences Press.
Eigen, M. (1999) *Toxic Nourishment*, London: Karnac.
Eigen, M. (2001) *Damaged Bonds*, London: Karnac.
Eissler, K.R. (1959) 'Notes on the Environment of a Genius', 1, *Psychoanalytic Study of the Child*, 14(1): 267–313.
Eissler, K.R. (1961) *Leonardo da Vinci: Notes on the Enigma*, New York: International Universities Press.

Eissler, K.R. (1963) *Goethe: A Psychoanalytic Study*, Detroit: Wayne State University Press.

Eissler, K.R. (1967) 'Psychopathology and Creativity,' *American Imago*, 24: 35–81.

Eissler, K.R. (1971) *Discourse on Hamlet and HAMLET: A Psychoanalytic Inquiry*, New York: International Universities Press.

Eissler, K.R. (1974) *Talent and Genius: The Fictitious Case of Tausk Contra Freud*, New York: Quadrangle Books.

Eliot, G. (2000) *Middlemarch*, London: Wordsworth Editions.

Epstein, J. (2003) *Envy: The Seven Deadly Sins*, Oxford: Oxford University Press.

Esposito, R. (2007) *Terza Persona: Politica della vita e Filosofia dell'impersonale*, Torino: Einaudi.

Eysenck, H.J. (1995) *Genius: The Natural History of Creativity*, Cambridge: Cambridge University Press.

Fairbairn, W.R.D. (1976) *Psychoanalytic Studies of the Personality*, London–Boston: Routledge and Kegan Paul.

Federn, P. (1952) *Ego Psychology and the Psychoses*, New York: Basic Books.

Ferro, A. (2008) Book Review Essay Review of James G. Grotstein (2007) *A Beam of Intense Darkness. Wilfred Bion's Legacy to Psychoanalysis*, London: Karnac. Vol. 89, No. 4 August (2008), *The International Journal of Psychoanalysis*, by James Grotstein, 89(4): 867–84.

Ferro, A. (2004) *Seeds of Illness, Seeds of Recovery: The Genesis of Suffering and the Role of Psychoanalysis*, London: Routledge.

Fonagy, P. and Target, M. (2003) 'A Homage to the Contributions of a Child-Analytic Genius,' *The Psychoanalytic Study of the Child*, 58: 307–21.

Frank, J.D. and Frank, J.B. (1991) *Persuasion and Healing: A Contemporary Study of Psychotherapy*, Baltimore MD: Johns Hopkins University Press.

Frankl, V. (1963) *Man's Search for Meaning: An Introduction to Logotherapy*, Boston: Beacon Press.

Freud, S. (1901) *Psychopathology of Everyday Life*, Standard Edition, Vol. 6. *The Standard Edition of the Complete Psychological Works of Sigmund Freud*, James Strachey in collaboration with Anna Freud (trans. and eds), London: Hogarth Press and the Institute of Psycho-Analysis (1996–1974).

Freud, S. (1910) 'Leonardo da Vinci and a memory of his childhood', *Five Lectures on Psycho-Analysis, Leonardo da Vinci and Other Works*, Vol. 11. *The Standard Edition of the Complete Psychological Works of Sigmund Freud*, James Strachey in collaboration with Anna Freud (trans. and eds), London: the Hogarth Press and the Institute of Psycho-Analysis, 1966.

Freud, S. (1914) 'On Narcissism: An Introduction', Vol. 14. *The Standard Edition of the Complete Psychological Works of Sigmund Freud*, James Strachey in collaboration with Anna Freud (trans. and eds), London: Hogarth Press and the Institute of Psycho-Analysis (1996–1974).

Freud, S. (1916) 'Some Character-Types Met with in Psycho-Analytic Work', Section I,'The exceptions,' Vol. 14. *The Standard Edition of the Complete Psychological Works of Sigmund Freud*, James Strachey in collaboration with Anna Freud (trans. and eds), London: Hogarth Press and the Institute of Psycho-Analysis (1996–1974).

Freud, S. (1919) 'Lines of advance in psycho-analytic therapy,' *Standard Edition*, Vol. 17.
Freud, S. (1925) 'An Autobiographical Study,' Vol. 20. *The Standard Edition of the Complete Psychological Works of Sigmund Freud*, James Strachey in collaboration with Anna Freud (trans. and eds), London: Hogarth Press and the Institute of Psycho-Analysis (1996–1974).
Fromm, E. (1962) *Beyond the Chains of Illusion: My Encounter with Marx and Freud*, New York–London: Continuum Press.
Fromm, E. (2005) *The Fear of Freedom*, London–New York: Routledge.
Gaddini, E. (1969) 'On imitation,' *International Journal of Psycho-Analysis*, 50: 475–84.
Galilei, G. (1953) *Dialogue on the Great World Systems*, the Salisbury translation, revised, annotated and with an introduction by G. de Santillana, Chicago: University of Chicago Press.
Gardner, H. (1993) *Creating Minds: An Anatomy of Creativity Seen Through the Lives of Freud, Einstein, Picasso, Stravinsky, Eliot, Graham and Gandhi*, New York: Basic Books.
Gardner, H. (1993) *Frames of Mind: The Theory of Multiple Intelligences*, London: Fontana Press.
Gardner, H. (1997) *Extraordinary Minds: Portraits of Four Exceptional Individuals and an Examination of our Own Extraordinariness*, New York: Basic Books.
Gedo, J.E. (1972) 'On the Psychology of Genius,' *The International Journal of Psycho-Analysis*, 53: 199–203.
Gedo, J.E. (1979) 'The Psychology of Genius Revisited,' *The Annual of Psychoanalysis*, 7: 269–83.
Gedo, J.E. (1980) 'Nietzsche and the Psychology of Genius,' *Psychoanalytic Quarterly*, 49: 79–91.
Gilbert, P. (2009) *The Compassionate Mind: A New Approach to Life's Challenges*, London: Constable.
Gillespie, W.H. (1960) *The Edge of Objectivity: An Essay in the History of Scientific Ideas*, Princeton NJ: Princeton University Press.
Gilligan, C. (1982) *In a Different Voice: Psychological Theory and Women's Development*, Cambridge MA: Harvard University Press.
Gould, S.J. (1981) *The Mismeasure of Man*, New York: W.W. Norton.
Grand, S. (2009) *The Hero in the Mirror: From Fear to Fortitude*, London: Routledge.
Grossman, W. (1982) 'The Self as Fantasy: Fantasy as Theory,' *Journal of the American Psychoanalytic Association*, 30: 919–38.
Grotstein, J. (1990) 'Nothingness, Meaninglessness, and the "Black Hole",' I, *Contemporary Psychoanalysis*, 26: 257–90.
Grotstein, J. (1990) 'Nothingness, Meaninglessness, and the "Black Hole",' II, *Contemporary Psychoanalysis*, 26: 277–407.
Grotstein, J. (2000) *Who Is the Dreamer Who Dreams the Dream? A Study of Psychic Presences*, Hillsdale NJ: Analytic Press.
Grotstein, J. (2007) *A Beam of Intense Darkness: Wilfred Bion's Legacy to Psychoanalysis*, London: Karnac.
Hadot, P. (2008) *La Filosofia Come Modo di Vivere*, Torino: Einaudi.
Hartmann, H. (1958) *Ego Psychology and the Problem of Adaptation*, London: Imago.
Hayes, S.C. and Follette, V.M. (eds) (2011) *Mindfulness and Acceptance: Expanding the Cognitive-Behavioural Tradition*, London: Routledge.

BIBLIOGRAPHY

Heidegger, M. (1962) *Being and Time*. John Macquarrie and Edward Robinson (trans.), New York: Harper and Row.

Hobson, P. (2002) *The Cradle of Thought*, London: Macmillan.

Hofstadter, D.R. (1995) *Fluid Concepts and Creative Analogies: Computer Models of the Fundamental Mechanisms of Thought*, New York: Basic Books.

Honderich, T. (2005) *On Determinism and Freedom*, Edinburgh: Edinburgh University Press.

Hornsby, J. (1993) 'Speech Acts and Pornography,' *Women's Philosophy Review*, 10: 38–45.

Houser, S.T., Allen, J.P. and Golden, E. (2006) *Out of the Woods: Tales of Resilient Teens*, Cambridge MA: Harvard University Press.

Howe, M. (1999) *Genius Explained*, Cambridge: Cambridge University Press.

Howe, M. (2000) 'Genius,' *Encyclopedia of Psychology*, Vol. 3, Alan E. Kazdin, American Psychological Association, Oxford: Oxford University Press.

Hume, D. (2000) *A Treatise of Human Nature*, David Fate Norton and Mary J. Norton (eds), Oxford: Oxford University Press.

Humphrey, N. (1984) *Consciousness Regained*, Oxford: Oxford University Press.

Humphrey, N. (1986) *The Inner Eye*, London: Faber and Faber.

Husserl, E. (1960) *Cartesian Meditations: An Introduction to Phenomenology*. Dorton Cairns (trans.), The Hague: Martinus Nijhoff.

Husserl, E. (1982) *Ideas Pertaining to a Pure Phenomenology and to a Phenomenological Philosophy*. First Book: *General Introduction to a Pure Phenomenology*, F. Kersten (trans.), The Hague: Nijhoff.

Husserl, E. (1989) *Ideas Pertaining to a Pure Phenomenology and to a Phenomenological Philosophy*. Second Book: *Studies in the Phenomenology of Constitution*, R. Rojcewicz and A. Schuwer (trans.), Dordrecht: Kluwer.

Husserl, E. (1990) *On the Phenomenology of the Consciousness of Internal Time*, J.B. Brough (trans.), Dordrecht: Kluwer.

Jaegwon, K. (1993) *Supervenience and Mind: Selected Philosophical Essays*, Cambridge: Cambridge University Press.

Jahoda, M. (1977) *Freud and the Dilemmas of Psychology*, London: Hogarth Press.

James, W. (1890) *The Principles of Psychology*, Vol. 1, New York: Dover Publications.

James, W. (1956) *The Will to Believe and Other Essays in Popular Philosophy*, New York, Dover Publications; also Cambridge MA, Harvard University Press, 1979.

James, W. (1958) *The Varieties of Religious Experience*, New York: Mentor.

Jardine, A.A. (1985) *Gynesis: Configurations of Woman and Modernity*, Ithaca NY–London: Cornell University Press.

Jaspers, K. (1969) *Philosophy*, three volumes, E.B. Ashton (trans.), Chicago IL: University of Chicago Press.

Jones, E. (1956) 'The Nature of Genius', *Sigmund Freud: Four Centenary Addresses*, New York: Basic Books, pp. 3–34.

Jung, C.G. (1933) *Modern Man in Search of a Soul*, New York: Harvest.

Jung, C.G. (1971) *Psychological Types: The Collected Works of C.G. Jung*, Vol. 6, R.F.C. Hull (trans.), Princeton NJ: Princeton University.

Jung, C.G. (1977) 'The Tavistock Lectures: Lecture III,' in *The Collected Works of C.G. Jung: The Symbolic Life*, Vol. 18, R.F.C. Hull, H. Read, M. Fordham, and G. Adler (trans.), London: Routledge and Kegan Paul.

Kahn, C. (2009) 'The Analyst's Creativity During the Treatment Process,' *The Psychoanalytic Review*, 96(1): 21–34.

Kahn, C. and Piorkowski, G. (1974) 'Conditions Promoting Creativity in Group Rearing of Children,' *Psychoanalytic Study of the Child*, 29: 231–55.

Kant, I. (1987) 'An Answer to the Question "What is Enlightenment?",' in *Political Writings*, H.B. Nisbet (trans.), H. Reiss (ed.), Cambridge: Cambridge University Press.

Kant, I. (2006) *Anthropology from a Pragmatic Point of View*, translated and edited by R.B.Louden, Cambridge: Cambridge University Press.

Kazdin, A.E. (editor in chief), (2000) *Encyclopedia of Psychology – 'Genius,'* Vol. 3, Michael Howe, American Psychological Association: Oxford University Press.

Keeny, B. (2008) *The Creative Therapist: The Art of Awakening a Session*, London: Routledge.

Klein, M. (1920) 'Der Familienroman in *Statu Nascendi*', first published in the *Internationale Zeitschrift für Psychoanalyse*, VI. 6.

Klein, M. (1983) 'Il Romanzo di una Famiglia in *Statu Nascendi*'. Rosario Merendino (trans.), *Rivista di Psicoanalisi*, Organo della Società Psicoanalitica Italiana, No. 2, April–June, pp. 125–31.

Koestler, A. (1975) *The Act of Creation*, London: Picador.

Kretschmer, E. (1931) *The Psychology of Men of Genius: The International Library of Psychology, Philosophy and Scientific Method*, London: Kegan Paul.

Kris, E. (1952) *Psychoanalytic Explorations in Art*, New York: International Universities Press.

Kristeva, J. (1995) *New Maladies of the Soul*, R. Guberman (trans.), New York: Columbia University Press.

Kristeva, J. (2000) *The Sense and Non-Sense of Revolt*, New York: Columbia University Press.

Kristeva, J. and Roudiez, L.S. (1982) *Powers of Horror: An Essay on Abjection*, New York: Columbia University Press.

Kuhn, T.S. (1970) *The Structure of Scientific Revolutions*, Chicago and London: University of Chicago Press.

Lear, J. (1990) *Love and Its Place in Nature: A Philosophical Interpretation of Freudian Psychoanalysis*, New Haven–London: Yale University Press.

Lear, J. (2007) 'Working Through the End of Civilization', *International Journal of Psychoanalysis*, 88: 291–308.

Lefebvre, H. (1991) *The Critique of Everyday Life*, Vol. 1, John Moore (trans.), London: Verso.

Leibniz, G.W. (1968) *Nuovi Saggi Sull'intelletto Umano*, Torino: UTET.

Loewald, H. (1988) *Sublimation*, New Haven CT: Yale University Press.

Lonergan, B. (1957) *Insight*, London: Darton, Longman and Todd.

MacCurdy, E. (ed.) (1956) *The Notebooks of Leonardo da Vinci*, New York: George Braziller.

McDougall, J. (1986) *Theatres of the Mind: Illusion and Truth on the Psychoanalytic Stage*, London: Free Association Books.

McDougall, J. (1990) *Plaidoyer pour une Certaine Anormalité*, Paris: Editions Gallimard.

McDougall, J. (1995) *The Many Faces of Eros: A Psychoanalytic Exploration of Human Sexuality*, London: Free Association Books.

Makridakis, S., Hogarth, R. and Gaba, A. (2009) *Dance with Change. Making Luck Work for You*, Oxford: Oneworld.

BIBLIOGRAPHY

Malpas, J.E. (1992) *Donald Davidson and the Mirror of Meaning: Holism, Truth, Interpretation*, Cambridge: Cambridge University Press.

Masson, J.M. (1976) Review of D. Anzien et al. *Psychanalyse du génie créateur, Psychoanalytic Quarterly*, 45: 642–5.

Matte Blanco, I. (1975) *The Unconscious as Infinite Sets: An Essay in Bi-Logic*, London: Karnac.

Matte Blanco, I. (1988) *Thinking, Feeling and Being: Clinical Reflections on the Fundamental Antinomy of the Human Being and World*, London–New York: Routledge.

Matussek, P. (1974) *Kreativität als Chance. Der Schöpferische Mensch in Psychodynamischer Sicht (The creative Person in a Psychodynamic Perspective)*. München: Piper.

Meissner, W.W. (2009) 'The Genesis of the Self: The implications for the Analytic Relation and process. Part 1 The self as integral subject' *Psychoanalytic Review*, 96(2): 297–336.

Midgley, M. (1984) *Wickedness: A Philosophical Essay*, London–New York: Routledge.

Miller, A. (2005) *Il Dramma del Bambino Dotato e la Ricerca del Vero Sé*, Bollati Boringhieri.

Miller, J.C. (2004) *The Transcendent Function: Jung's Model of Psychological Growth Through Dialogue with the Unconscious*, Albany: State University of New York.

Mitchell, S.A. (1993) *Hope and Dread in Psychoanalysis*, New York: Basic Books.

Modell, A.H. (1993) *The Private Self*, Cambridge, MA–London: Harvard University Press.

Morgan, E. (1995) *The Descent of the Child: Human Evolution from a New Perspective*, Oxford: Oxford University Press.

Murdoch, I. (2001) *The Sovereignty of Good*, London: Routledge Classics.

Murray, P. (ed.) (1989) *Genius: The History of the Idea*, Oxford: Basil Blackwell.

Newman, J.H. (1888) *An Essay in Aid of a Grammar of Assent*, London: Longmans, Green and Co.

Nietzsche, F. (1969) *On the Genealogy of Morals*, W. Kaufmann and R.J. Hollingdale (trans.), New York: Vintage Books.

Nozick, R. (1981) *Philosophical Explanations*, Oxford: Clarendon Press.

Nunberg, H. (1961) *Curiosity* (Freud Anniversary Lecture Series, The New York Psychoanalytic Institute), New York: International Universities Press.

Nussbaum, M.C. (2011) *Creating Capabilities: The Human Development Approach*, Cambridge MA–London: The Belknap Press of Harvard University Press.

Ogden, T.H. (1991) *Projective Identification and Psychotherapeutic Technique*, Northvale NJ–London, Jason Aronson.

Ogden, T.H. (1994) *L'Identificazione Proiettiva e la Tecnica Psicoterapeutica*. Dianella Marani (trans.), Roma: Astrolabio.

Ogden, T.H. (1994) *Subjects of Analysis*, Northvale NJ: Jason Aronson.

Ogden, T.H. (2008) *Rediscovering Psychoanalysis. Thinking and Dreaming, Learning and Forgetting*, London: Routledge.

Oliver, K. (2004) *The Colonization of Psychic Space: A Psychoanalytic Social Theory of Oppression*, Minneapolis MN–London: University of Minnesota Press.

Parsons, M. (2000) *The Dove that Returns – The Dove that Vanishes: Paradox and Creativity in Psychoanalysis*, London: The New Library of Psychoanalysis, Routledge.

Perkins, D.M. (1981) *The Mind's Best Work*, Cambridge MA: Harvard University Press.

Phillips, A. (2005) *Going Sane*, London: Penguin Books.
Phillips, A. (2008) *Side Effects*, London: Penguin Books.
Phillips, A. (2010) *On Balance*, London: Penguin Books–Hamish Hamilton.
Phillips, A. and Taylor, B. (2009) *On Kindness*, London: Hamish Hamilton, Penguin Books.
Poland, W. (1986) 'The Analyst's Words: Their Content and Their Formation', *Psychoanalytic Quarterly*, 55: 244–72.
Porter, R. and Tomaselli, S. (1989) *The Dialectics of Friendship*, London–New York: Routledge.
Quinodoz, D. (2009) *Growing Old: A Journey of Self-Discovery*, London: Routledge.
Rorty, R. (1989) *Contingency, Irony and Solidarity,* Cambridge: Cambridge University Press.
Roth, N. (1985) 'Review of Jan Ehrenwold, *Anatomy of Genius.*' *The Journal of the American Academy of Psychoanalysis and Dynamic Psychiatry*, 13: 280–1.
Rothemberg, A. (1988) *The Creative Process of Psychotherapy*, New York: Norton.
Rudder Baker, L. (2007) *The Metaphysics of Everyday Life: An Essay in Practical Realism*, Cambridge: Cambridge University Press.
Salzman, L. (1974) 'Review of K. R. Eissler, *Talent and genius*, *The Journal of the American Academy of Psychoanalysis and Dynamic Psychiatry*, 2: 75–6.
Sarton, G. (1948) *Life of Science*, New York: Schumann.
Schaefer, R. (1978) *A New Language for Psychoanalysis*, New Haven CT: Archon Press.
Scheman, N. (1993) *Engenderings: Constructions of Knowledge, Authority and Privilege*, London: Routledge.
Schwartz, B. (2004) *The Paradox of Choice: Why More is Less,* New York: Harper Collins.
Schwartz, C. (2009) 'Language as Artistry in the Treatment of a Borderline Psychotic Patient,' *Psychoanalytic Review*, 96(1): 1–20.
Schwartz-Salant, N. (1998) *The Mystery of Human Relationships: Alchemy and the Transformation of Self,* London–New York: Routledge.
Sen, A. and Nussbaum, M. (eds) (1993) *The Quality of Life,* Oxford: Oxford University Press.
Shapiro, M. (1956) 'Leonardo and Freud: An Art-Historical Study', *Journal of the History of Ideas*, 17: 147–78.
Shoshani Rosenbaum, M. (2009) *Dare to be Human: A Contemporary Psychoanalytic Journey,* London: Routledge.
Siegel, D. (2010) *Mindsight: Transform Your Brain with the New Science of Kindness*, Oxford: Oneworld Publications.
Silverman, K. (1996) *The Threshold of the Visible World,* London–New York: Routledge.
Simmel, G. (1918) *Goethe*, Leipzig: Klinkhardt und Biemann.
Simonton, D.K. (1994) *Greatness: Who Makes History and Why*, New York: Guilford.
Simpson, K.E. (2009) 'Beautiful Minds: A Seminar Course on the Psychology of genius,' *Teaching of Psychology*, 36: 46–50.
Singer, P. (1997) *How Are We to Live?*, Oxford: Oxford University Press.
Socci, A. (2009) *I segreti di Karol Wojtyla*, Milan: Rizzoli.
Solmi, E. (1908) *Leonardo da Vinci*, German trans. E. Hirschberd, Berlin: Ernst Hoffmann.

Soskice Martin, J. (2007) *The Kindness of God: Metaphor, Gender and Religious Language*, Oxford: Oxford University Press.
Spearman, C. (1931) *The Creative Mind*, New York: D. Appleton and Co.
Spence, D.P. (1987) 'Turning Happenings into Meanings: The Central Role of the Self,' in *The Book of the Self: Person, Pretext and Process*, New York: New York University Press.
Spence, D.P. (1987) *La Voce Retorica della Psicoanalisi*, Rome: Fioriti Editore.
Spence, D.P. (1998) 'Rain Forest or Mud Field?,' Guest Editorial, *The International Journal of Psychoanalysis*, 78: 643–8.
Steiner, G. (2002) *Grammars of Creation: Originating in the Gifford Lectures for 1990*, London: Faber and Faber.
Steiner, G. (2004) *Nostalgia for the Absolute*, Toronto: House of Anansi Press.
Steiner, G. (2008) *My Unwritten Books*, London: Weidenfeld and Nicholson.
Steiner, J. (1993) *Psychic Retreats: Pathological Organizations in Psychotic, Neurotic and Borderline Patients*, London: Routledge.
Stern, D.N. (2004) *The Present Moment: In Psychotherapy and Everyday Life*, New York–London: W.W. Norton and Company.
Stern, D.N. (2010) *Forms of Vitality: Exploring Dynamic Experience in Psychology, the Arts, Psychotherapy and Development*, Oxford: Oxford University Press.
Stevens Sullivan, B. (2009) *Weavings From Jung and Bion*, London: Routledge.
Stevenson, R.L. (1956) *The Strange Case of Dr Jekyll and Mr Hyde*, London: Nelson.
Streznewski, M.K. (1999) *Gifted Grownups: The Mixed Blessings of Extraordinary Potential*, New York: Wiley.
Symington, N. (1993) *Narcissism: A New Theory*, London: Karnac.
Symington, N. (2001) *The Spirit of Sanity*, London: Karnac.
Symington, N. (2002) *A Pattern of Madness*, London: Karnac.
Symington, N. (2004) *The Blind Man Sees: Freud's Awakening and Other Essays*, London: Karnac.
Symington, N. (2006) *A Healing Conversation: How Healing Happens*, London: Karnac.
Symington, N. (2007) 'A Technique for Facilitating the Creation of Mind', *International Journal of Psychoanalysis*, 88: 1409–22.
Taylor, C. (1989) *Sources of the Self: The Making of the Modern Identity*, Cambridge: Cambridge University Press.
Taylor, C. (2007) *A Secular Age*, Cambridge MA: Harvard University Press.
van Deurzen, E. (2009) *Everyday Mysteries: A Handbook of Existential Psychotherapy*, London: Routledge.
Vico, Giambattista (1928) translation of Giambattista Vico, *Scienza Nuova*, based on the text of the third edition (Naples 1744) as edited by Fausto Nicolini in volume 112 and in the first 166 pages of volume 113 of the *Scrittori d'Italia*, Bari: Laterza.
Vico, Giambattista (1968) *The New Science of Giambattista Vico*, revised edition of the third edition of 1744, G. Bergin and M.H. Fisch (trans.), Ithaca NY: Cornell University Press.
Vico, Giambattista (1968) unabridged translation of the third edition (1744), with the addition of 'Practice of the New Science,' Thomas Goddard Bergin and Max Harold Fish (trans. and eds), Ithaca NY and London: Cornell University Press.
Vico, Giambattista (2007) *The First New Science*, Leon Pompa (trans. and ed.), Cambridge: Cambridge University Press.
Wallas, G. (1926) *The Art of Thought*, New York: Harcourt Brace.

BIBLIOGRAPHY

Weisberg, R.W. (1993) *Creativity: Beyond the Myth of Genius*, New York: Freeman.

Winnicott, D.W. (1965) *The Maturational Process and the Facilitating Environment*, New York: International Universities Press.

Winnicott, D.W. (1971) *Playing and Reality*, London: Tavistock Publications.

Winnicott, D.W. (1974) *Between Reality and Phantasy: Transitional Objects and Phenomena*, S.A. Grolnick and L. Boskin, in collaboration with W. Muensterberger (eds), New York: Aronson.

Winnicott, D.W. (1987) *The Spontaneous Gesture: Selected Letters of D.W. Winnicott*, F.R. Rodman (ed.), Cambridge MA: Harvard University Press.

Winnicott, D.W. (1989) *Psychoanalytic Explorations*, (eds) C.Winnicott, R.Shephard and M. Davis (eds), Cambridge MA: Harvard University Press.

Wittgenstein, L. (1992) *Last Writings on the Philosophy of Psychology: The Inner and the Outer, 1949–1951*, Vol. 2, C.G. Luckardt and M. Ana (trans.) G.H. von Wright and H. Nyman (eds), Oxford: Blackwell Publishers.

Woodruff Smith, D. (2007) *Husserl*, London: Routledge.

Woolley, L. (1963) *The Beginnings of Civilization*, New York: Mentor Books.

Wright, K. (2009) *Mirroring and Attunement: Self-Realization in Psychoanalysis and Art*, London: Routledge.

Zižek, S. (1997) *The Plague of Fantasies*, London: Verso.

INDEX

absolute creativity 28, 49
acceptance: and attention 101; in interpersonal relations 25, 43, 94–6; of unconscious conflict 32, 33, 34, 112
achievements, human 88
action: creative 19; generating 86–7; language 80
activity 103, 104, 105, 114; cycles 46
Adam and Eve story 35, 66
addictive thinking 110–13
adulthood 34–5. *see also* maturity/immaturity
adversarial egoic structures 33, 38–40, 43. *see also* anger/aggression
advertising industry 87
affect. *see* emotion
Agape 89
agency 26, 69, 79, 80
aggression/anger 23, 95. *see also* hostility
alchemical metaphors 71, 72
alienation 65, 69, 86, 114, 115
alpha function 74, 80, 83, 86
altruism 30
always being right 38–40, 43, 44, 106
ambivalence 66, 67, 95
analytic third 83. *see also* psychoanalysis
anger/aggression 23, 95. *see also* hostility
annihilation, fear of 105–6
Anthropology (Kant) 5, 31, 50
apathy 100
archetypes, dark angel 36
arguments, egoic 38–40, 43, 44, 106
Aristotle 5–7, 74
artistic creativity 48
artistic genius. *see* extraordinary genius
associations, terminological 47–8
assurances, benevolent 69

attachment 72; to identifications 112
attention: and acceptance 101; focused 85
Aurelius, Marcus 5, 64, 85
authenticity 25, 29, 37, 85, 115
authoritative agents of knowledge 15–16, 58–9
autoeroticism 39, 43, 55, 90
autonomous mind 68, 79

balanced relations 32
banality: routine 25; of sanity 26
bandaging symbolism 66
Bauman, Z. 31, 32
beam of darkness 12
behaviour, expressive 74
being oneself (authenticity) 25, 29, 37, 85, 115
being right 38–40, 43, 44, 106
beliefs, children's 59–60
benevolent assurances 69
Berlin, I. 18, 96
Bers, Susan 21
Bible stories 50–1
Bion, W. R. 9, 42, 47, 77, 80, 83, 85, 90, 101–2, 105
blindness: of extraordinary genius 58, 64; to ordinary genius 11–16
blowing on the embers 19, 20, 23
Boden, M. A. 10, 48, 52
Bollas, C. 13, 80, 104
bracketing technique 77–8
breathing, enjoyment of 10, 25
brown devil 59
Buber, M. 94

Cain and Abel story 93
canonic creativity 54

INDEX

capacity to include 74–8
caregivers 91
caring, creative 90, 91, 97, 98–102
Casement, P. 100
caste system of creativity 14–15
castle metaphor 85
catalysts 71
catastrophe 46
change. *see* integration; psychic growth; transformation
chaos 55
charismatic leaders 53, 105
child rearing 30
children: analysis 57, 58, 59–60, 61, 63–4; memories 50; trauma 21, 85; verbal abuse of 21, 22–3
choice, and creativity 71
chosen ones 54. *see also* innate genius
chronotope 80
Cicero 50
Civilization and Its Discontents (Freud) 42
clichés 86
clinging to the past 46
coexistential condition 90
coherence: inner 86–7; narrative 21–2. *see also* integration
collective: ego 115; fate 103; identifications 39, 69
combative approach, to conflict 33. *see also* adversarial egoic structures
commonality 104
communication: connective function 70; nonverbal 102
compassion 12, 20, 30; fear of 99
compassionate kindness 91, 93
competitiveness 27–8
complaining 44, 101
complexes, Jungian 108
complexity theory 42
compliance 10, 18, 54, 56. *see also* conformity
compulsion: to succeed 54; to be right 38–40, 43, 44, 106
compulsive thinking 87, 101
conflict, unconscious 32–6
conformity 11; psychoanalytic 70. *see also* compliance
connective function: capacity to include 74–8; creative 65–9, 70–4, 97; and health 67; nurturing instinct 90; and relational progressions 70–4;

witnessing 'I' 85. *see also* interpersonal relations
consciousness 9, 73; and compassionate kindness 93; and connective function 70; illusion of unity 108; integration 67, 86; of objects/ experience 77–8; repression 92; stream of 80, 88; transformation 17; and unconscious 79
constraints: compliance 56; dogma 12, 86; egoic structures 37–43, 87–8; theories/models 76, 77, 78
construction/deconstruction 43
contact, interpersonal. *see* connective function; interpersonal relations
containment 74, 75
contradiction 66
control, exclusionary 75–6. *see also* capacity to include
convictions, firmly held 43
co-optosis 15, 27
coping: with madness 45; with projective identification 108
correcting others 38–40, 43, 44, 106
cosmos, re-creation 56–7
courage to surrender 32–6
creative: actions 19; caring 90, 91, 97, 98–102; connections 65–9, 70–4; integration 85; listening 91; living 10, 18, 65, 67, 69, 98; transformation 46, 74, 110
creative service 89–93, 94; caring 98–102; risk/gains 93–8
creativity: absolute 28, 49; artistic 48; caste system 14–15; inner 8; nature of 47, 53, 55, 69; in psychoanalysis 2, 31; and success 86. *see also* everyday creativity
cultural élites 14
cycles, success/failure 46
Cyrulnik, B. 21, 22, 66, 92

da Vinci, Leonardo 49–50, 52, 53, 55
Damasio, A. 113
dark angel archetype 36
death: fear 105–6; instinct/wish 42, 69, 113. *see also* dying
deconstruction/construction 43
defensiveness 9, 10, 76; egoic structures 37–42; and interpersonal relations 96
definitions: genius 56; health 7, 10; phantasy 67

144

deities, ancient 36
demagogues 114. *see also* leaders
denial 28; of envy 34
dependence 90
destiny 49, 97, 98, 100, 103
destructiveness 42, 115; interpersonal relations 95; parasitic projections 108; self-destruction 112–13
detachment 67
determinism 19
detoxification, interpersonal relations 32. *see also* toxicity
development. *see* integration; psychic growth; transformation
'The Development of a Child' (Klein) 57
devil/s: brown 59; little (complexes) 108
dictators 114. *see also* leaders
difficult patients 94
digestion: learning 82; psychic elements 74, 75, 113; trauma 76
dimensions, ulterior 76. *see also* spatial metaphors
disapproval, social 25
discernment 71
discipleships, psychoanalytic 45
disciplinary integrity 109
disconnection 65, 67, 68, 86. *see also* connective function
dis-identification 41, 45
dissolution 46
diversity 1, 27
Doctor Jekyll and Mr Hyde 68–9
dogma, political/scientific 12, 86. *see also* theories/models
drama: of insanity 26, 32; of parasitic projections 108, 109
dread 72
dream-work 76
duality 83
dying, interpersonal relations 18. *see also* death

Easter rabbit 59
Edison, Thomas 52–3
egoic arguments 38–40, 43, 44, 106
egoic structures 9, 16, 87; collective 115; constraints 37–43, 87–8; extraordinary genius 58, 64; identification with 37–41, 58, 79, 87; learning/unlearning 37–43; and integration of personality 65; moving beyond 82, 84, 85–8;

thinking/unthinking/rethinking 43–6
Eigen, M. 75, 76, 90–1, 107–8
Einstein, Albert 13, 54
Eissler, K. R. 27, 46, 48, 49, 50, 51, 52, 56, 67, 86, 87
electricity metaphor 29
Eliot, George 18, 25, 29
Eliot, T. S. 54
embers of resilience 19, 20, 23
embracing witness 82–5
embryo mind 79
emergent properties, friendships 73, 98
emotion: digestion of 75; in psychoanalysis 67–8, 83
empathy 71; fear of 99
empiricism. *see* science
enemies, hatred of 103
energy, psychic 103
enslavement 45, 112, 113; oracular voices 110; projections 103–4, 107
environment that obtains 29, 34
environments, facilitating 71
envy, of parents 34. *see also* Oedipus myth
Epstein, J. 34
equity, in interpersonal relations 32
Eros 66, 89–90, 91, 98. *see also* love
eroticism 39, 43, 55, 90
essential creativity 47, 53, 55, 69
essential genius 6, 49, 50. *see also* innate genius
everyday creativity 1–3, 19; and addictive thinking 111–12; Freud on 51; and healing/health 17, 26, 35, 52; historical perspectives 5; and 'I' of personality 79; insightful 86, 87; and integration of personality 69; and interpersonal relations 17, 29–30, 74, 94; and kindness 77, 99; and madness/sanity 76; minding our own business 103–7; and patience 77; repression of 64; unrecognised 56; Winnicott on 7–11, 17, 28, 34–6, 54. *see also* ordinary genius
evil 67, 68, 69
examined life 25
exceptions, Freud on 45–6
exchange 72
exclusionary control 75–6. *see also* capacity to include
experience: objects of 77–8; personal 31

external: idols 106; projections 105, 108
extraordinary genius 1, 2, 47;
    blindness for ordinary genius 11–16;
    blindness of 58, 64; examples 4–5,
    13, 54, 57–64, 77; nature of 52–4;
    need for unlearning 39–40;
    Winnicott on 9

facilitating environments 71
facing the truth 74. *see also* integration
    of personality
failure, cycles of 46
fallen angels 109
false gods 115
false self 37, 39, 96, 79, 104–6
'The Family Romance in Statu
    Nascendi' (Klein) 57–64
fatalism 114
fate 100; collective 103
fear of annihilation 105–6
Ferenczi, Sándor 63
Ferro, A. 12, 26, 37, 74
First World War 42
first-person perspective 80
flexibility 31
Fliess, Wilhelm 49
flying kites 49–50
fluidity 73
focused attention 85
forgiveness 32
fragmentation 68. *see also* splitting
Frederick II of Sicily 5
freedom 24, 32; and creativity 55;
    inner 11
Freud, Anna 63–4
Freud, Sigmund 9, 23, 31, 77, 84, 104;
    analysis of Anna 63–4; biological
    foundation of psychoanalysis 12; on
    exceptions 45–6; on genius 49–50,
    52, 53, 55; on 'I' of personality 81;
    identification with Biblical Joseph
    50–1; on integration of personality
    65; on nurturing instinct 90;
    personality profile 54; *The
    Psychopathology of Everyday Life* 3,
    16; unlearning 42
Freudian slips 16–17
friendships 24, 71, 96–7, 98. *see also*
    interpersonal relations
Fromm, Erich 85, 86
frustration, of nurturing instinct
    89–90

fulfilment 87
futility 10, 18

Galilei, Galileo 4
Gandhi 54
garden metaphor 66
Gardner, H. 54, 71
gender differences, interpersonal
    relations 68
genius: definitions 56; nature of 6,
    47–52, 55; and talent 52. *see also*
    extraordinary genius; ordinary genius
getting in touch/touching 71
ghosts, unacceptable 20
Gilligan, C. 68
gods: false 115; immortal 36
Goethe, Johann Wolfgang von 53,
    73, 87
gold-making, alchemical metaphors 72
good enough: parents 21, 31; persons/
    society 104
good lives 12
grandiosity 105. *see also* omnipotence
greed 34
Grotstein, J. 3, 37, 70, 74, 83, 90,
    105, 113
ground work, Stern on 73, 75
growth, psychic. *see* psychic growth

happiness 44; and success 87
harmony 67
hatred 23; of enemies 103; innate 22;
    projections 113; unconscious 35, 112
health/healing 11, 14, 23, 60, 101; and
    creativity 17, 26, 35, 52; definitions
    7, 10; and friendship/connection 67,
    98; and ordinary genius 20, 56, 92;
    psychic 60, 65; seeking after 19–20,
    26. *see also* illness; insanity
heart 9; analogy 73; -learning 26
Hegel, Georg Wilhelm Friedrich 1
Heidegger, M. 86
here-and-now approach. *see* present
    moments
hero: identity 45–6; unrecognised.
    see unsung heroes
hierarchisations: creativity 14–15;
    values 2
historic genius. *see* extraordinary
    genius
historical perspectives: creativity 17–18;
    genius 4–5

INDEX

Hofstadter, D. R. 27
Homer 53
homogenisation: mass culture 14; values 55–6
hope 72
hostility 100; generic 90; to otherness 114. *see also* anger/aggression
Houser, S. T. 21
Howe, M. 48
human achievements 88
human condition 115
humanness 3
humility 13
Humphrey, N. 82–3
Husserl, E. 77

'I' of personality 9, 79–82; and egoic structures 37, 42; and extraordinary genius 13; insightful 85–8; and ordinary genius 54, 56; present moments 101; and vulnerability 96; and whole personality 26; witnessing 82–5
idealisations 11, 28, 55
idealism 74
identification: with egoic structures 37–41, 58, 79, 87; Freud's 51; oracular voices 111, 112; with projections 105–6; with roles 105
identity 80, 82, 97; defending 38, 39; hero/victim 45; psychic 87; and sanity 76
idols, external 106; escaping from 115; identification with 112; mind-like 107, 108, 111; submission to 109; worship of 103, 104, 105, 107, 113
illness: and death 69; and disconnection 67; and frustration 90. *see also* health/healing; insanity
illumination, moments of 2
imagination, children's 59–60
imitation 18, 57
immaturity. *see* maturity/immaturity
immortal gods 36
inclusion (capacity to include) 74–8
independence 99
infantile, integration of 67
infants, interpersonal relations 18
inference of unconscious 31, 32
inhibition of aggression 23
inimical function of reality 39

innate genius 49–52, 53, 54. *see also* essential genius; extraordinary genius
innate hatred 22
inner: coherence 86–7; creativity 8; freedom 11; objects 44; reality 12, 76; resources 27; self 18
insanity 110, 111, 115, 116; coping with 45; and hatred 35; and integration 69; and sanity 75–6; theatrical nature 26, 32; and unconscious conflict 33; Winnicott on 75; witnessing 'I' 84, 85. *see also* pathology
insight: egoic structures 42; 'I' of personality 79, 80, 82, 85–8
inspiration 50
instinctual: experience 10, 32, 37; forces 108
integration of personality 65–9, 72–3, 81, 86, 105, 116; capacity to include 74–8; creative 85; omnipotence 106; and self-awareness 88; *see also* connective function; 'I' of personality; psychic growth; whole personality
integrity, disciplinary 109
intellect 9
intentional level 19
intentionality 77, 90
interdependence, psychic attitudes 73
internalisation 8, 21, 75, 84
interpenetrating spheres 80
interpersonal relations 14, 55; children's 23; creativity 17; and egoic structures 42, 87; friendships 24, 71, 96–7, 98; and genius 2; Klein family 57–64; meaning in 19; nurturing instinct 90–1; ordinary genius 18, 57; risks/gains of 93–8; unsung heroes 28–32; women 68. *see also* connective function; therapeutic relation
interpretations, psychoanalytic 70, 76–7
intersubjective field 70, 73, 98. *see also* interpersonal relations
intra-psychic experiences, psychoanalytic 70
invisibility, of sanity 26
isolation 63, 72

James, William 76, 80
Jekyll and Hyde 68–9
jeux de massacre 19, 40

INDEX

Joseph, Biblical 50–1
jouissement 98
Jung, C. G. 73, 83, 108

'-K' 101
Kahn, C. 56, 70
kairos 98, 100. *see also* present moment
Kant, I. 5, 16, 31, 48, 50
kindness 23, 30, 71, 73, 75, 92; caring 91, 92; and creativity 77, 89–90, 99; ordinary 71–2; psychoanalytic settings 70; and relational progressions 74; ways to show 100
kites, flight of 49–50
Klein, Eric ('Fritz') 57, 58, 59–60, 61
Klein, Melanie 57–64, 66–7, 77
knowing our own minds 29
knowledge: authoritative agents of 15–16, 58–9; resistance 101
Koestler, A. 52
Kristeva, J. 10, 48, 86
kronos (time awareness) 100

Lacan, Jacques 77
language: metaphors 5–7; nuisance value 97; written 4–5, 48
leaders: charismatic 53, 105; following 107, 114
leading-strings 31
Lear, J. 12, 17, 93, 104
learning 37–43
legitimacy, creativity 103–7
Leonardo da Vinci 49–50, 52, 53, 55
letting people be themselves 102
liberation 45
licence, and freedom 11
life, psychic 3, 7–8, 11, 96, 104–5, 106
Lines of Advance in Psycho-analytic Therapy (Freud) 81
linguistics. *see* language
liquid modernity 31–2
listening: creative 91; geniuses 22, 91, 92, 94–5
literary figures/literature 18, 25, 26, 27, 29, 54. *see also* story
little devils (complexes) 108
living creatively 10, 18, 65, 67, 69, 98
living in the present. *see* present moments
logos 66
loneliness 63, 72

love/loveliness 23, 29, 30, 61, 62, 72, 89–91. *see also* Eros

madness. *see* insanity; pathology
male autonomy 68
marginalisation 15
Marx, K. 43
mass culture 14
mass pathology 12
mathematical analogy, connective function 71
Matte-Blanco, I. 42
maturity/immaturity 16, 31, 87; acceptance of unconscious 32; and integration of personality 66, 67; and interpersonal relations 32; in Oedipus myth 33, 34–5, 44. *see also* psychic growth
McDougall, J. 19, 76, 108
'Me' egoic structure 82
meaning 12, 13, 19; emergence 77; in interpersonal relations 29; narrative coherence 21–2; original 31; personal 105; and success 27–8; and trauma 21
mediating/medicating/meditating 66, 68
mediocrity 25
Meissner, W. W. 81
memories: childhood 50; painful 46
mental illness. *see* insanity
mentality 9
mentoring, psychoanalytic 45
metamorphosis. *see* integration; psychic growth; transformation
metaphors: alchemical 71, 72; castle 85; electricity 29; garden 66; self 80; spatial 9, 80, 84; use in language 5–7
Michelangelo 77
Midgley, M. 68–9, 114
midwives, creativity 17–18
Miller, J. C. 73
Miller, J. G. 83
mind 9. *see also* consciousness; unconscious
minding our own business: addictive thinking 110–13; escaping from projections 113–16; legitimacy of creativeness 103–7; parasitic projections 107–10
mind-like idols/objects 107, 108, 111
mirroring/reflection 20, 71, 111

148

INDEX

Mitchell, S. A. 78, 80
Modell, A. H. 15, 80, 82, 85, 94
models, constraints of 76, 77, 78. *see also* dogma
modernity, liquid 31–2
moment-by-moment living. *see* present moments
mortality, sorrow of 36
Mozart 13
mythology 35, 36, 50, 66. *see also* Oedipus myth

Napoleon Bonaparte 40
narcissism 18–19, 26, 28, 95–6, 98
narrative coherence 21–2. *see also* story, personal
navigators, creativity 17–18
Neanderthal man 4
near-death psychic experiences 21
need to be right 38–40, 43, 44, 106
negation, of unconscious conflict 33, 34
negotiation, interpersonal relations 29–30
neurotic personality traits 52
new age culture 86
nonsense, inner 100–1
nonverbal communication 102
normalcy/commonality 104
normotic creatures 76
Nozick, R. 38
nuisance value, vocabulary/language 97
numinosity, genius 49
nurturing instinct 89–90, 98, 101. *see also* creative service

'O' 26
objectivity: inner reality 76; truth 59
objects: of consciousness 77–8; inner 44; mind-like 107, 108, 111; people as 90; self 21
observer of the self 84. *see also* witnessing 'I'
obsessive personality traits 52
Oedipal third 84
Oedipus myth 33–5, 44, 94–8, 109–10, 112
Ogden, T. H. 83
Oliver, K. 11, 32, 48, 105
omnipotence 105, 106, 115
openness, to wild thoughts 77
opium of the people 28, 86
oracular voices 109–15

ordinary genius 1–2, 4–5, 47, 54–7; and addictive thinking 111; connective function 73, 76, 77; coping with psychotic patients 102; creative service 90; cultural blindness to 11–16; and health/healing 20, 56, 92; and ideology 113; and interpersonal relations 18, 31, 32, 57, 95, 96; kindness 71–2, 75; metaphor, use 5–7; nature of 54–7; opportunities 16–19; present moments 101; and projections/projective identification 108, 113, 115; resistance of enslavement 45; and of unconscious conflict 33; whole personality 39–41, 66, 67, 88; Winnicott on 7, 9, 11. *see also* everyday creativity
original meaning 31
originality, ordinary genius 57
otherness 29; acceptance 94–5, 96; hostility to 114
outsmarting others 38–40, 44
ownership: soul 116; witnessing 'I' 84

painful memories 46
parasitic: projections 107–10, 112; relations 96, 98, 104
parenting: and psychopathology 21, 22; and resilience 22–3
parents, envy of 34. *see also* Oedipus myth
Parsons, M. 2
passion 7, 16, 22
passive responses to trauma 18–19
passivity 103, 104, 105, 114; cycles 46
past, clinging to 46
pathology: and aggression 23; effects of parenting 21, 22; focus on 3; in interpersonal relations 32; mass 12; narcissistic 96; rage 15. *see also* insanity
pathos 66
patience 76, 77
patients: communication with 102; understanding 94
patricians 64
peer group, acceptance 25
perceptions, internal/external 82
perfectibility of man 12
personal: destiny 49, 97, 98, 100, 103; experience 31; meaning 105;

story 21–2, 25–6, 94–5, 97; sense of self 80
personality 9, 13, 26, 85; profiles 54; and self-awareness 83–4, 85–6; transformational metaphor 72. *see also* 'I' of personality; integration of personality; whole personality
perspectival gaze 77
perspectives: narrative coherence 22; ordinary genius 12, 18, 20
perspicacity 73
phantasy, and reality 66–7
phenomenology 77–8
Phillips, A 12, 23, 26, 30, 35, 71, 72, 75, 89–92, 96, 97, 99
philosophy: and psychoanalysis 17; western 74
physicians, creativity 17–18
Picasso 54
pictograms 4
pilots, creativity 17–18
Piorkowski, C. 56
Plato 43, 74
playful creativity 10, 26, 29, 94
poetry 87
Poincaré, Henri 71
pollution. *see* toxicity
power of self 85
present moments 10, 70; creativity 106; friendships 71; psychoanalysis 98–102
privacy, Eric ('Fritz') Klein 58
projections: alienation 115; compulsive thinking 101; and disconnection 69; enslavement to 103–4, 107; escaping from 113–16; external reality 105; hatred 113; identification with 105–6; narcissistic 28; parasitic 107–10; toxic 19
projective identification 44, 86, 113; coping with 108; creatively dealing with 115; reflecting mirror of 111
proving others wrong 38–40, 43, 44, 106
pseudo-knowledge 37
pseudo-sanity 75–6
psyche 9. *see also* consciousness; unconscious
psychic attitudes 73
psychic elements, digestion 74, 75, 113
psychic energy 103

psychic growth 8, 46; and compliance 56; and integration of personality 74, 75; and interpersonal relations 93, 96, 98; listening genius 22; and success 28. *see also* transformation
psychic health 60, 65
psychic identity 87
psychic integration. *see* integration of personality
psychic life 3, 7–8, 11, 96, 104–5, 106
psychic spaces 19, 93–4
psychic survival 3, 14, 19, 38, 57, 63, 90, 93–4
psychic tangles 107–8
psychic whole. *see* whole personality
psychoanalysis 20, 115; and affect 67–8; creativity in 2, 31; here-and-now approach 98–102; integration of models 78; and integration of personality 65; and omnipotence 106; and patience 77; and philosophy 17; and psychic growth 28; as science 12, 42, 58, 104; triadic nature 83. *see also* psychotherapy; therapeutic relation
psychoanalytic congresses 16
psychodiversity 1, 27
psychopathology. *see* insanity; pathology
The Psychopathology of Everyday Life (Freud) 3, 16
psychopaths 114
psychosis 83, 87, 102
psycho-synthesis.*see* integration of personality
psychotherapy 43, 90–1. *see also* psychoanalysis
Pythagoras 53

quality of genius 48, 49–52, 53. *see also* innate genius

rage 15, 43, 45, 71
ransom of self 113–16
Raphael: *The School of Athens* 74
rationality 67. *see also* objectivity
real self 25, 29, 37, 85, 115
reality: inner 12; interpenetrating spheres 76; and phantasy 66–7
reason 9
reciprocity, interpersonal relations 29–30
recognition, witnessing 'I' 84

re-creation, cosmos 56–7
redirected alliances 114
reflection/mirroring 20, 71, 111
regardless of magnitude 25–8
relational connections. *see* connective function; interpersonal relations
relational progressions 70–4. *see also* therapeutic relation
religious emotion 53
repairs to interpersonal relations 29–30
repetition compulsion 69; addictive thinking 110–13; egoic structures 79; interpersonal relations 95
repression 113; consciousness 92; of creativity 64; and integration of personality 67
reptilian brain 16
resentment 95
resilience 19, 20, 22, 66; effects of parenting 22–3
resistance: clinging to the past 46; to enslavement 45; to knowledge 101
resistors, ordinary geniuses as 12, 15, 45
resources, inner 27
responses to trauma 18–19
responsibility 106; of sense of self/identity 80, 82
rethinking 43–6, 48
revolution 28
rich and poor 13
rigidity, defensive 9, 10, 37–42, 76
Robin Hood 21
role playing/roles: egoic structures 42, 44, 46; and friendships 97; identification with 105; unconscious 96
Rosenfeld, H. 9, 85, 88, 100, 112
routine, banality of 25

Salimbene de Adam of Parma 5
sanity 3; and capacity to include 75; and integration of personality 69; invisibility of 26; and madness 75–6; and sense of self/identity 82
savagery/savages 69, 71
Schaefer, R. 80
Schapiro, M. 50
Scheman, N. 15
schizoid attitude 67
schizophrenia 83, 87, 102

The School of Athens (painting by Raphael) 74
Schwartz-Salant, N. 72
science 73, 74; psychoanalysis as 12, 42, 58, 104
scientific genius. *see* extraordinary genius
secret lives 35–6
security 11
self 11; and creativity 8, 9; and ego 37–40; inner 18; power of 85; ransom of 113–16; sense of 80; subjective 81; true 25, 29, 37, 85, 115; usurping of 15. *see also* personality
self-awareness 67, 83–4, 85–6, 88
self-damaging 67, 68
self-decreation 37, 41
self-destruction. *see* destructiveness
self-identity. *see* identity
self-interest 99
self-objects 21
self-questioning 25
self-reliance/self sufficiency 96, 99
selfishness 72
separation 72
service, creative. *see* creative service
seven deadly sins 34
sex/sexuality 72; explaining to a child 60, 62; and ordinary genius 18; sublimation 51
shadow 65; acknowledging 68–9; and friendships 71
Shakespeare, William 13
Siegel, D. 79, 84
signature, personal 80
significance, creative 17, 77
Silverman, K. 55, 111, 112
slaves, Ancient Greece 6–7
small ways 31
social disapproval 25
sorcerer's apprentice 39–40
sorrow: and mental illness 30; of mortality 36
Soskice, Janet. 29, 72, 89
soul 9, 86; ownership 116
spaces, psychic 19, 93–4
spatial metaphors 9, 80, 84
Spence, D. P. 80
spirit 9
splitting 65, 67, 68, 86. *see also* connective function

spontaneity 13
standing by patients 94
Steiner, G. 13, 27, 36, 43, 46, 53
stereotypy 29, 86
Stern, D. N. 30, 70, 73, 75
story, personal 21–2, 25–6, 94–5, 97
straitjackets. *see* constraints
Stravinsky, Igor 54
stream of consciousness 80, 88
subjective self 81
subjects, people as 90
sublimation, of sexual instinct 51
submission: external projections 103; idols 45, 109; obsession 97; oracular voices 115
submissive acts 45
success 27–8; and creativity 86; cycles 46; and happiness 87; psychotherapy 43; role of ego 85
Sumerians, ancient 4
superficiality 25
superhuman/supernatural genius 49–52. *see also* innate genius
surrender: courage to 32–6; and interpersonal relations 95–6
survival, psychic 3, 14, 19, 38, 57, 63, 90, 93–4
symbolic articulation 74
Symington, N. 11, 21, 34, 39, 44–5, 67–9, 79, 81, 84, 87, 92–3, 104–5, 109–10, 115
sympathy 71
synthesis, personal. *see* integration of personality
synthetic function 81

talent, and genius 52
talking: function of 57; repression of 63
talking cures 33
tangles, psychic 107–8
Taylor, C. 71, 72, 89–92, 96, 99
technique of bracketing 77–8
terminological associations 47–8
theatricality. *see* drama
theories/models, constraints of 76, 77, 78. *see also* dogma
therapeutic relation 83, 98; and connective function 70–4; difficult encounters 94; transference 33, 44, 81
'They' 86

thinking/thought: addictive 110–13; made urgent 27; unthinking/rethinking 43–6, 48; wild 77
third, analytic 83
third, Oedipal 84
third-person perspective 80
third way, transcendence 73
time awareness (kronos) 100
time for joy and a time of sorrow 30
time/space conditions, friendships 71
torment/toil, and innate genius 53, 54
total personality. *see* whole personality
totalitarian regimes 15
touching/getting in touch 71
toxicity: interpersonal relations 32; projections 19; psychic elements 113
transcendence 73, 86; genius 49–52
transcendent function 83
transference 33, 44, 81
transformation 3, 21; acceptance of unconscious 32; consciousness 17; creative 46, 74, 110; relational progressions 70; witnessing 'I' 84. *see also* psychic growth
transformational metaphor 72
trauma 35; dream-work 76; and listening geniuses 92, 94; and narcissism 26; passive response to 18–19; resilience to 20–1
triad/third, analytic 83
true self 25, 29, 37, 85, 115
trust 100
truth 26, 27; facing 74; objective 59
tyrants 114. *see also* leaders

ulterior dimensions 76
Ulysses 36
uncertainty 31–2
unconscious 68, 73; conflict 32–6; and connective function 70; and consciousness 79; Freudian slips 16–17; hatred 112; inference of 31, 32; and integration of personality 67; relational progressions 70; role playing 96; in therapeutic relation 94
un-creativeness 108, 111
understanding patients 94
unicity 49
unified self. *see* whole personality

unity of consciousness, illusion of 108
unlearning 37–43
unrecognised creativity 56
unsung heroes: courage to surrender 32–6; and interpersonal relations 28–32; regardless of magnitude 25–8
unthinking 43–6, 48
Unwritten Books (Steiner) 53

value 27
values 14; hierarchisations 2; homogenisation 55–6
Van Deurzen, E. 90
vanity 68
verbal abuse of children 21, 22–3
verbal communication 102
vicious circles 111
Vico, Giambattista 15, 16
victim/s; of abuse 62; identity 45–6
vision 76
vocabulary 97
vulnerability 75, 96

walking wounded 92
western philosophy 74

whole personality 17, 37, 40, 44, 46, 87; and capacity to include 77; connective function 65; and creativity 26–7; and disconnection 69; psycho-synthesis 81; and psychotherapy 43; and success 28. *see also* 'I' of personality; integration of personality
wild thoughts, openness to 77
Winnicott, D. W. 5, 7–11, 17, 18, 26, 98, 100, 104; capacity to include 75; creativity, everyday 28–9, 34, 35–6, 54; on living creatively 65, 69; on madness 75; on play 94; psychoanalysis and science 42
withdrawal: from interpersonal relations 94; projections 104
witnessing 'I' of personality 82–5
wizardry, strategic 40, 41
women, interpersonal relations 68
work of friendship 98
World War I 42
worship of idols 103, 104, 105, 107, 113
written language 4–5, 48